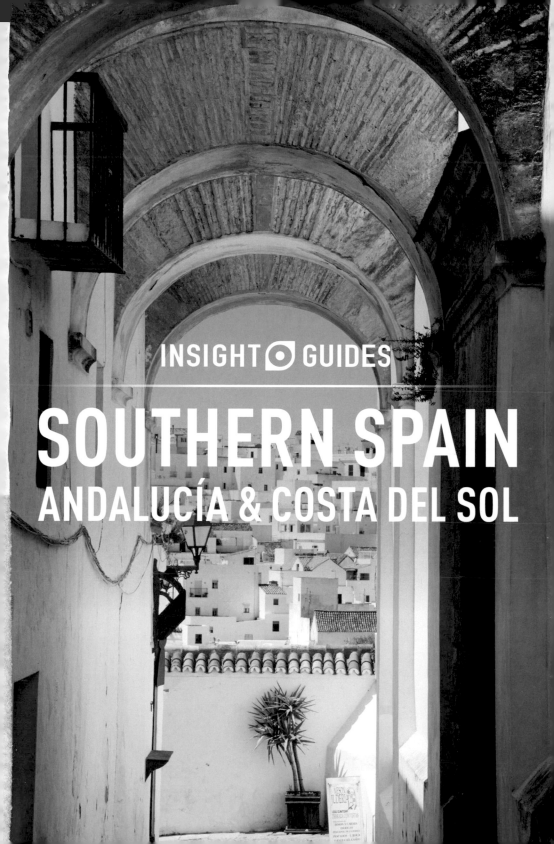

INSIGHT ○ GUIDES

SOUTHERN SPAIN
ANDALUCÍA & COSTA DEL SOL

⊙ Walking Eye App

YOUR FREE DESTINATION CONTENT AND EBOOK AVAILABLE THROUGH THE WALKING EYE APP

Your guide now includes a free eBook and destination content for your chosen destination, all for the same great price as before. Simply download the Walking Eye App from the App Store or Google Play to access your free eBook and destination content.

HOW THE WALKING EYE APP WORKS

Through the Walking Eye App, you can purchase a range of eBooks and destination content. However, when you buy this book, you can download the corresponding eBook and destination content for free. Just see below in the grey panels where to find your free content and then scan the QR code at the bottom of this page.

Destinations: Download your corresponding essential destination content from here, featuring recommended sights and attractions, restaurants, hotels and an A–Z of practical information, all for free. Other destinations are available for purchase.

Ships: Interested in ship reviews? Find independent reviews of river and ocean ships in this section, all available for purchase.

eBooks: You can download your free accompanying digital version of this guide here. You will also find a whole range of other eBooks, all available for purchase.

Free access to travel-related blog articles about different destinations, updated on a daily basis.

HOW THE DESTINATION CONTENT WORKS

Each destination includes a short introduction, an A–Z of practical information and recommended points of interest, split into 4 different categories:

- Highlights
- Accommodation
- Eating out
- What to do

You can view the location of every point of interest and save it by adding it to your Favourites. In the 'Around Me' section you can view all the points of interest within 5km.

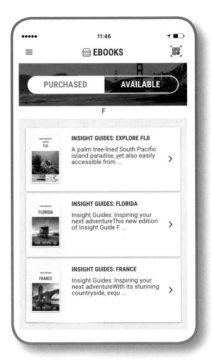

HOW THE EBOOKS WORK

The eBooks are provided in EPUB file format. Please note that you will need an eBook reader installed on your device to open the file. Many devices come with this as standard, but you may still need to install one manually from Google Play.

The eBook content is identical to the content in the printed guide.

HOW TO DOWNLOAD THE WALKING EYE APP

1. Download the Walking Eye App from the App Store or Google Play.
2. Open the app and select the scanning function from the main menu.
3. Scan the QR code on this page – you will then be asked a security question to verify ownership of the book.
4. Once this has been verified, you will see your eBook and destination content in the purchased ebook and destination sections, where you will be able to download them.

Other destination apps and eBooks are available for purchase separately or are free with the purchase of the Insight Guide book.

CONTENTS

LEGEND

  ⚲ Insight on
  📷 Photo Story

THE BEST OF SOUTHERN SPAIN: TOP ATTRACTIONS

△ **Seville**. The quintessential Andalusian city, with a Unesco-listed cathedral and Alcázar, and more tapas bars than you can shake a stick at. The April Feria should be on everyone's bucket list. See page 77.

▽ **Granada**. Home to one of the world's great monuments – the Alhambra – and the medieval winding streets of the Albaicín. Famous for its cave-dwelling gypsies and poet Federico García Lorca. See page 187.

△ **Córdoba**. As a result of its cultural and intellectual importance under the Romans and Moors, the historic centre with its magnificent mosque is now Unesco-listed. Pretty patios add to the charm. See page 161.

△ **Málaga**. The birthplace of Pablo Picasso has undergone a renaissance in recent years and now boasts some world-class museums. The Soho district is a must visit for fans of street art. See page 142.

△ **Cádiz**. One of the oldest cities in Europe, jutting out into the sea, helped shape modern Spain. Soak up the atmosphere of its ancient streets and savour some wonderful seafood. See page 118.

△ **Las Alpujarras**. This mountainous region to the south east of Granada is dotted with time-forgotten villages, inhabited these days by those in search of the good life. Great walking too. See page 205.

◁ **Doñana National Park**. Home of the endangered Iberian Lynx, this important wetland site offers some stunning scenery and experiences to nature lovers. Best explored on the back of a horse. See page 103.

▷ **Jerez de la Frontera**. With a clutch of sherry bodegas and a lively flamenco scene, this town is good for a lively day and night out. Don't miss the white horses either. See page 111.

◁ **Cabo de Gata**. One of the driest parts of Europe, this protected area in Almería province has wonderful remote beaches where visitors can get away from it all. See page 219.

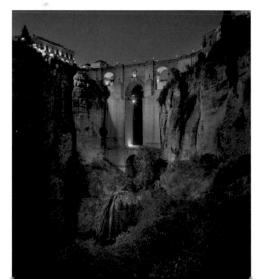

▷ **Ronda**. Perched on a cliff overlooking the Tajo gorge, this is one of Andalucía's oldest and most stunning towns. No wonder it attracted famous artists and writers like Ernest Hemingway. See page 131.

THE BEST OF SOUTHERN SPAIN: EDITOR'S CHOICE

SOUTHERN SPAIN FOR FAMILIES

Spain is an ultra-child friendly country and even boisterous toddlers can be taken almost anywhere that grown-ups go at any time of day or night without raising an eyebrow.

Waterparks. These are generally open May to September, and can be found at Mijas, Granada, Torremolinos, Córdoba, Seville, Puerto de Santa María (Cádiz), Torre del Mar, Almuñécar, Cartaya (Huelva) and at Vera (Almería).

Theme parks. Visit Seville's attraction-packed Isla Mágica (see page 94), Almería's Wild West-themed Oasys Mini-Hollywood (see page 218) and Tivoli

World (see page 145) on the Costa del Sol.

Zoos and Aquariums. Three of the best are on the Costa del Sol: Selwo Aventura at Estepona (see page 149) and Selwo Marina and Sea Life, both in Benal-mádena (see page 145).

Cable cars. Take the *Teleférico* at Benal-mádena for wonderful views, falconry displays plus elevated walking and cycling routes. See page 145.

Shows. The Real Escuela Andaluza del Arte Ecue-stre at Jerez is famous for its dancing horses (see page 111). Oasys Theme Park (see page 218) in Almería exploits a Wild West theme.

The Wild West in Almería.

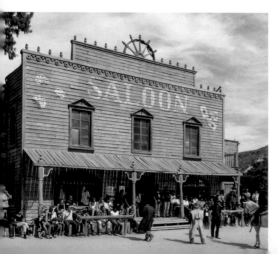

The Alhambra's distinctive pillars.

BEST BUILDINGS

The Alhambra, Granada. This magnificent example of Moorish architecture dating from the 11th century is one of Spain's most visited attractions. See page 189.

The Mosque, Córdoba. This vast mosque, complete with a 16th-century cathedral in the middle, is one of the world's greatest works of Islamic art. See page 162.

Reales Alcázares, the Cathedral, Archivo General de Indias and the Maestranza bullring, Seville. Seville has much to offer but these four buildings sum up its essence: Moors, Catholics, Christopher Columbus and bull-fighting. See pages 83, 80, 85 and 88.

Arab baths in Ronda, Jaén and Granada. The Moors certainly knew how to live and these baths highlight their love of luxury. See pages 135, 181 and 201.

Castles of Málaga and Almería. Due to its turbulent past, Andalucía is dotted with castles and these are two of the best. See pages 142 and 215.

Menga and Romeral dolmens, Antequera. These dolmens are some of Spain's best examples of prehistoric building. See page 154

Ruins of Itálica and Medina Azahara. A showcase of the advanced civilisations, planning and building know-how of the Romans and Moors. See pages 95 and 169.

THE BEST PLACES FOR ART

Museo de Bellas Artes, Seville. Housed in a 17th-century convent with a superb baroque chapel, Seville's Fine Arts Museum holds works by El Greco, Goya, Murillo, Zurbarán and Velázquez (see page 91).

Hospital de la Caridad, Seville. This 17th-century charity hospital is known for the great artworks in its chapel, including ghoulish works by Valdés Leal (see page 87).

Museo Picasso, Málaga. Picasso was born in Málaga. This collection of 233 paintings, drawings, sculptures and ceramics spans his career (see page 142).

Centre Pompidou Málaga. This branch of the Centre Pompidou

Paris brings some of the world's best contemporary art to the Costa del Sol. See page 143.

Museo Ruso, Málaga. Top-class Russian art from the 16th–20th centuries at this offshoot of St Petersburg's Russian State Museum. See page 143.

Museo Carmen Thyssen, Málaga. An exquisite private collection of 19th-century Andalusian art. Highlights include *Bullfight at Éibar* by Ignacio Zuloaga. See page 143.

Museo de Cádiz. Fine examples of Spanish art from the 19th and 20th century. See page 118.

Julio Romero de Torres Museum, Córdoba. See his paintings of sultry Andalusian women (see page 168).

Bullfight at Éibar by Ignacio Zuloaga.

BEST BEACHES

Costa de la Luz. In Cádiz, the best are Caños de Meca (Barbate), Bolonia, Zahara de los Atunes and Cabo de la Plata. In Huelva, head for Punta Umbría, La Casita Azul (El Hoyo), El Asperillo, Torre del Oro, El Alcor.

Costa del Sol. There are still a few nice beaches between the resorts: Costa Natura (Estepona), Lindavista (San Pedro de Alcántara), Tajo de la Soga (Benalmádena), Almayate-Bajamar (near Torre del Mar); Cala del Cañuelo, Cala del Pino,

Las Alberquillas and Molino de Papel (all near Nerja).

Costa Tropical. Try Ensenada de los Berengueles (Marina del Este, La Herradura), Cabria (Almuñécar), La Rijana (near Calahonda).

Almería. Recommendations include Cala de En Medio (near las Negras), Cala del Bergantín (Rodalquilar), Cala de las Hermanicas and La Negrita (near San José), Los Genoveses, Cala Chica Cala del Barronal and Monsul.

Kite-surfers at Caños de Meca.

PICTURESQUE PUEBLOS

Arcos de la Frontera. The quintessential white village offers great views from its clifftop location. See page 125.

Capileira. The highest and largest of the villages in the Alpujarras is a good base for walkers. See page 208.

Casares. A Cézanne-like cluster of little white houses climbing up the hillside. See page 122.

Cómpeta, Comares, Frigiliana, Salares. These white towns offer an insight into authentic Andalucía and great hiking. See page 157.

Grazalema. Gateway to the Sierra de Grazalema, it is noted for its local produce and events. See page 126.

Guadix. Famous for its 2,000 cave dwellings and tapas. See page 198.

Priego de Córdoba. Hilltop town with a fine baroque church and medieval castle. See page 172.

Zahara de la Sierra. Near the Sierra de Grazalema, it has great hiking and canyoning. See page 127.

Zuheros. Known for its cave, Cueva de Murciélagos, and cheese. See page 172.

GREATEST GOLF COURSES

Andalucía has more than 60 golf courses, most of them 18-hole. Half of them are on or near the Costa del Sol, aka the 'Costa del Golf'.

Desert Springs Cuevas de Almanzora, Almería. This is Europe's first 'desert golf course', a splash of green on Almería's east coast.

Granada Club de Golf. With stunning views of the Sierra Nevada, this flat course is a good option for lower levels.

Dunas de Doñana Matalascañas, Huelva. Between the beach and the Doñana National Park, this club with a hotel in the middle of the greens is a good place for golf fanatics.

Montecastillo Jerez de la Frontera (Cádiz). Designed by Jack Nicklaus, this course has been used for the Volvo Masters and is considered to be one of the best in Europe.

Club de Campo de Córdoba. A demanding course in the hills north of Córdoba. The pine and cork trees add to the charm.

Westin La Quinta. This beautiful 27-hole course located near Puerto Banús was designed by Ryder Cup golfers and suits all abilities.

Guadalmina, San Pedro de Alcántara. Made up of two parts, north and south, the latter being only for experts because of its thick vegetation.

Los Naranjos. Long-established course 7km (4 miles) from Marbella, designed by Robert Trent Jones. 'Hard par, easy bogey' is the name of the game here.

Antequera Golf. Set at an altitude of 650 metres (over 2,000 ft) and surrounded by mountains. The fairways are separated by 200-year-old olive trees and the lakes act as both obstacles and reservoirs.

Salmorejo, a speciality from Córdoba.

A TASTE OF SPAIN

Fish and seafood. Order fish fried or *a la plancha* – cooked on a griddle and therefore much less oily. Málaga (see page 145) has some of the best fish restaurants in the region, as does El Puerto de Santa Maria near Jerez on the Costa de la Luz (see page 113).

Sherry. The world-famous fortified wines are made in Jerez de la Frontera (see page 111). The less well known Montilla-Moriles *denominación de origen* (see page 171) makes similar, equally good wines but without fortifying them with grape spirit.

Gazpacho. This tasty cold soup of pulped tomatoes and garlic, is served all over Andalucía, but some regions have their own versions, such as

salmorejo in Córdoba and *porra* in Antequera. Another good cold soup is *ajo blanco*, made with garlic and almonds.

Olives and Olive oil. These are the specialities of Jaén province (see page 178). Be sure to try the traditional Andalusian breakfast of toast dribbled with olive oil rather than spread with butter.

Jamón serrano. Dry-cured ham needs clean mountain air for its preparation and the best in Andalucía comes from Trevélez in the Alpujarras (see page 208) and Jabugo in the Sierra de Aracena (see page 108).

Tropical fruits. Grown on the coast of Granada (see page 200). Depending on the season, they include avocados, mangoes and *chirimoyas* (custard apples).

A golf course in Málaga.

FAVOURITE FIESTAS

Carnival, Cádiz (February). This is mainland Spain's biggest carnival celebration. Ten days of music and revelry culminate in a firework display on La Caleta beach.

Easter Week (Semana Santa). Celebrated everywhere but at its most sensual in Seville; *pasos* (religious sculptures) are pushed or carried through the streets during some 50 processions.

April fair, Seville (second or third week after Easter). This is virtually a semi-private party with lots of flamenco dancing, groomed horses and sherry. Córdoba, Granada and Almería have smaller summer fairs, which are more accessible to visitors.

Romería de la Virgen de la Cabeza, northern Jaén (last Sun in April). The biggest of Andalucía's many *romerías* – mass pilgrimages to country shines.

Festival de los Patios, Córdoba (May). Many of the pretty patios that are normally concealed behind wrought iron gates are opened to the public for a week.

Fería del Caballo, Jerez (May). A horse fair with equestrian competitions, decorated carriages, sherry in abundance and flamenco dancing.

El Rocío (Whitsun: May/ June). A colourful and exuberant mass pilgrimage to the town of El Rocío on the edge of the Doñana National Park.

Virgen del Carmen, (16 July). On this day Andalucía's various coastal communities parade a statue of the patroness of sailors on a flower-decked boat in order to bless the local waters for the coming year.

For more information about Andalucía's numerous festivals, see the photo feature on page 58.

TOP ACTIVITIES

Hiking. With no less than 19 long-distance walking routes, covering the coast and the mountains, plus good weather, Andalucía is a hiker's dream. See page 65.

Windsurfing. Thanks to its windy location, Tarifa is a renowned centre for windsurfing and kitesurfing. Several outfits offer hire and lessons. See page 114.

Taking the waters. From replicas of Moorish baths to hot springs, Andalucía is a popular place to relax or recover in the water.

Horse-riding. Both the Doñana National Park and the Alpujarras region are wonderful spots for exploring on horseback. See pages 103 and 205.

Sherry tasting. Taste some of the region's finest sherries at one of the many bodegas in Cádiz province. See page 113.

Cooking. Learn to cook Andalusian cuisine with the finest local ingredients at Annie B's Spanish Kitchen in Vejer de la Frontera. See page 117.

Watching wildlife. The region's natural and national parks offering numerous opportunities for wildlife watching, especially migrating birds. See page 61.

Skiing. Andalucía isn't just about sea and sun: the Sierra Nevada near Granada is one of Spain's most popular ski resorts in winter. See page 199.

Lining up in Pradollano, a ski resort in the Sierra Nevada.

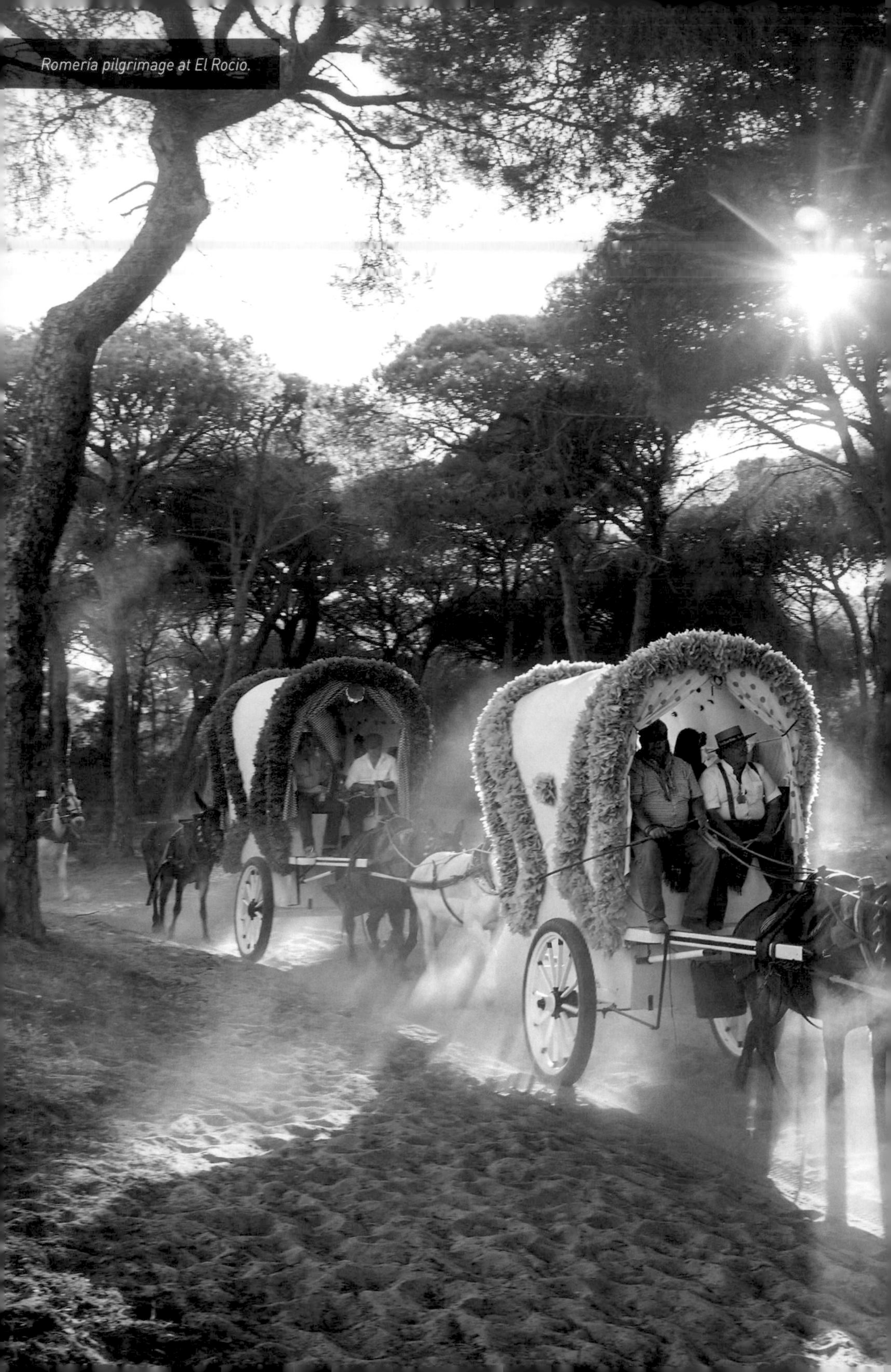

Romería pilgrimage at El Rocio.

Sunset in Frigiliana.

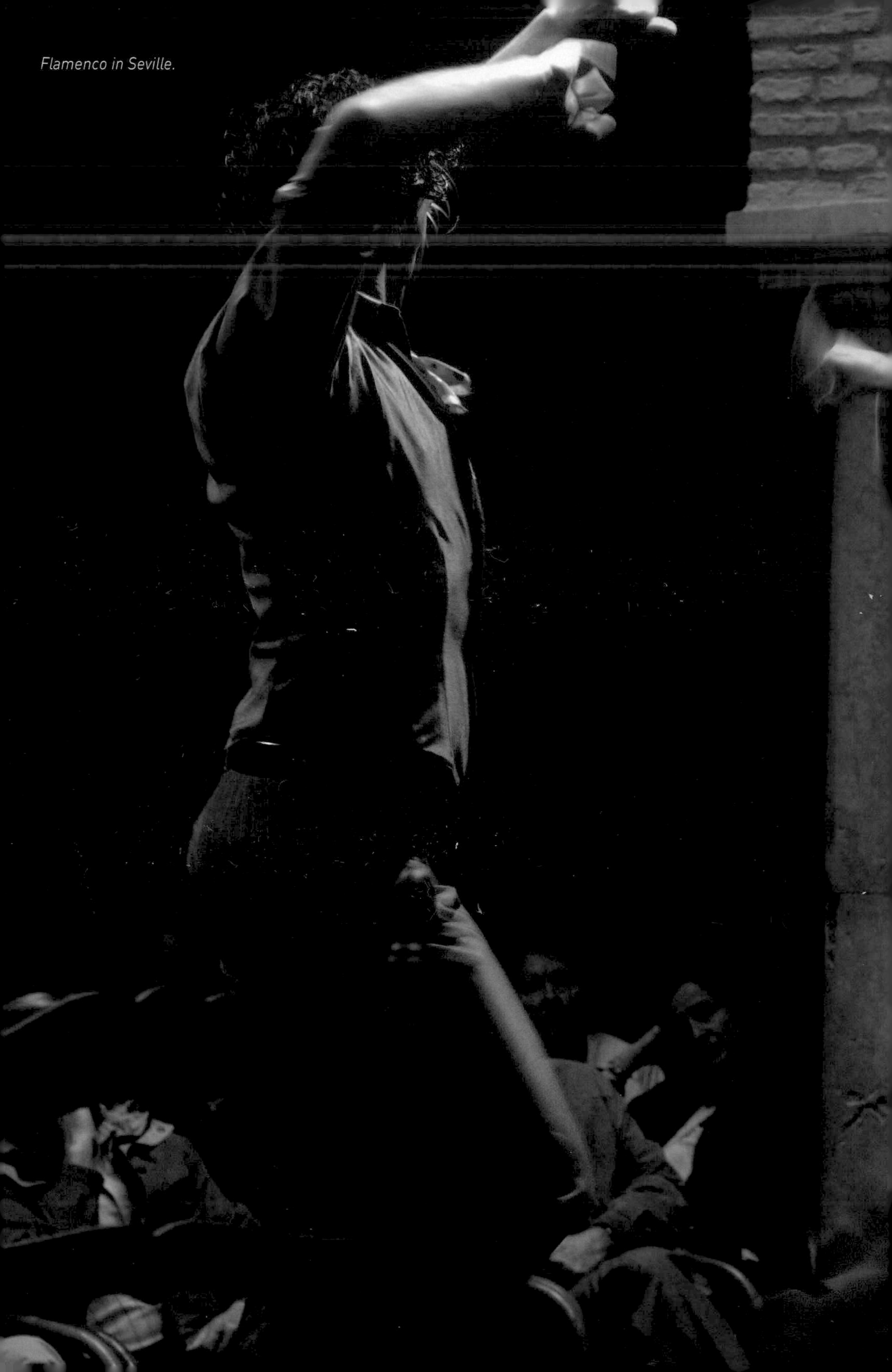

Flamenco in Seville.

Seville's Plaza de España
dazzles at night.

THE SOUL OF SPAIN

Andalucía is the source of many Spanish clichés, but this vast region has many less obvious attractions to entice visitors.

Dresses for sale.

Andalucía is the largest region in Spain, covering around 17 percent of its total area. As such it is scenically diverse and culturally rich, offering a vast array of attractions for visitors. For many package holidaymakers, it is synonymous with the Costa del Sol, the ultimate Spanish *costa*, a 180-km (110-mile) long chain of marinas, golf clubs and white urbanisations. For cultural visitors, however, the highlights of the region are the cities of Seville, Córdoba and Granada, with their glorious Moorish monuments – the Giralda, Mezquita and Alhambra – and the *pueblos blancos* (white towns), the perched villages of the sierras. For lovers of wild, open spaces, Andalucía offers some of the highest mountains in Europe, crossed by hiking trails (and ski slopes near Granada), and the watery marshes of the Parque Nacional de Doñana, a haven for migrating birds.

Moorish domination for more than 700 years left a permanent imprint on the region and its people. The year Granada fell, 1492, heralded a new era for Spain. Christopher Columbus's historic voyage across the Atlantic turned Seville into a flourishing city, enriched by the wealth of the New World, though this did not filter through the surrounding region.

Spring blooms.

Centuries of stagnation followed, and the poverty and lack of opportunity forced large numbers of Andalusians (*Andaluces* in Spanish) to emigrate. Many helped populate the Americas, while in the 1950s and 1960s thousands went to work in the factories of northern Spain and other European countries. On the edge of Europe, between the Third World and the First, Andalucía continued to drift in a cultural and economic limbo. Change was slow, at first confined to the Costa del Sol, where the package-holiday industry was taking off. But, following Franco's death, the advent of democratic government and membership of the European Union, Andalucía was booming – a trend stimulated by the colossal spending on infrastructure that preceded Expo '92 in Seville.

And despite the economic crisis of 2008, which brought to the region the highest unemployment in Spain, the tourism industry goes from strength to strength.

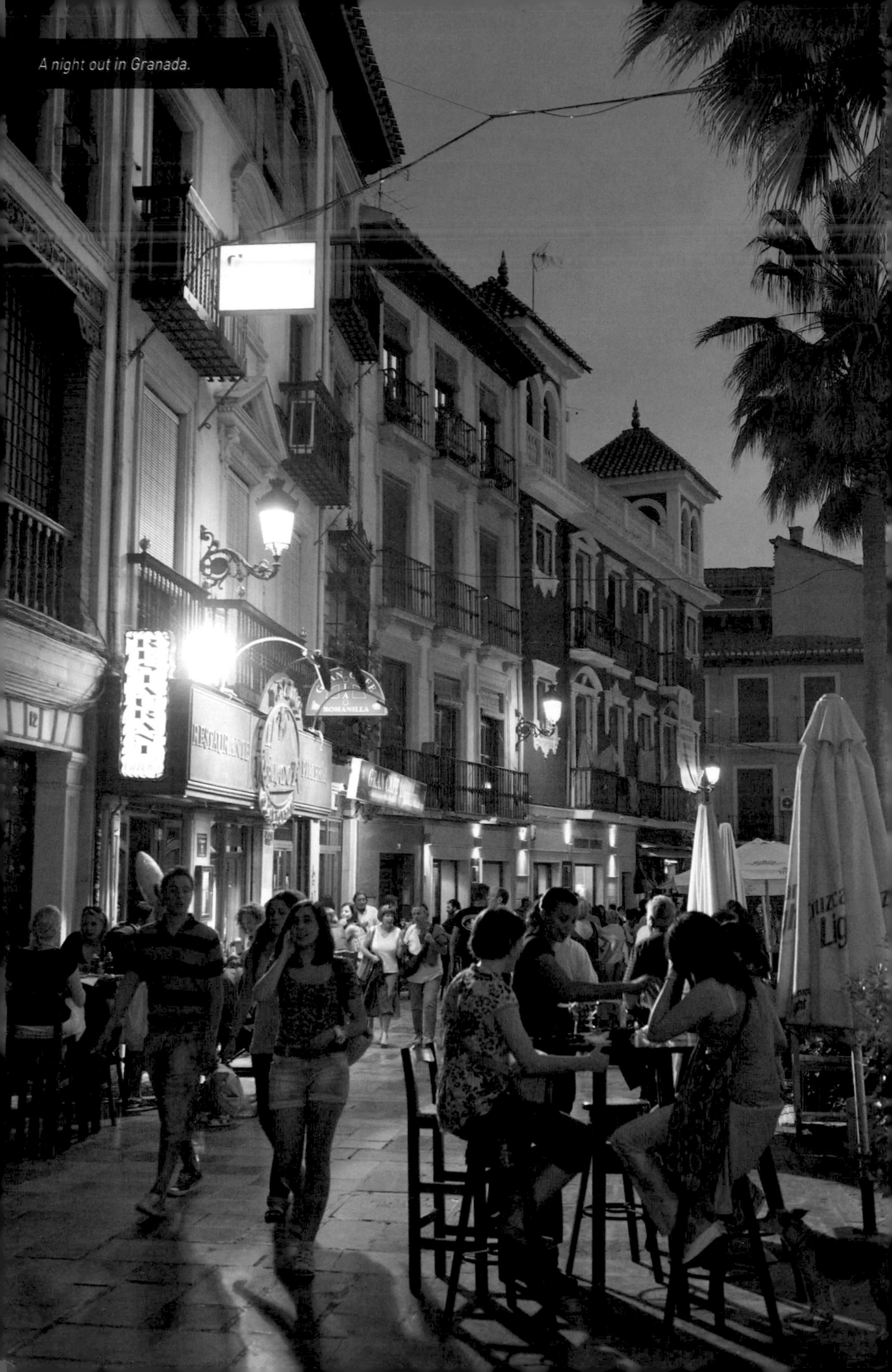

A night out in Granada.

THE ANDALUSIANS

Andalucía's apparent nonchalance of its people's live-for-today *informalidad* belies a complex society with a deep appreciation and love of life.

The Andalusians *(Andaluces)* have much to live up to – or live down. In the imagination of the world, theirs is a region of all things typically, desirably Spanish: flamenco music strummed on guitars accompanied by rattling casta-nets; brave bulls and even braver bullfighters; inscrutable, twinkle-eyed gypsies; philandering Don Juans beguiling sultry, fiery-eyed Carmens behind their filigree black grilles; stunning white hill towns under intense blue skies; minaretted palaces straight from *The Thousand and One Nights*; wild sierras inhabited by bandits with a picaresque sense of honesty – in short, a place of vivacity, sensuality and life-or-death passion, the antidote to the mediocre and banal.

Since at least the 17th century, foreign travel-lers have been descending on southern Spain in search of all these things, and returning home to add to the picture of Andalucía as an animated Elysian Fields where the sun always shines, nature is generous and people are dedicated to living life to its fullest. Only a few admitted to disappointment – like Hans Christian Andersen, who was dismayed when his party was not held up by *bandoleros*, picaresque or otherwise, while crossing the mountains into Andalucía.

Modern tourists still expect to find here the age-old ingredients of a good holiday: tapas, paella, sangria and the rest, all served up in resorts where anything goes, day or night, in the eyes of its hedonistic, *mañana*-shunning, siesta-sleeping, ever-partying people.

Every Spanish stereotype, cliché and hyper-bole comes to roost here, and, whether through a secret pride in their reputation or a sense of canny commercial self-promotion, Andalusians don't do much to dispel the misconceptions. Andalucía may be the best-known part of Spain

Serenading in the Barrio de Santa Cruz, Seville.

– the monuments of Seville, Granada and Cór-doba and the excesses of the Costa del Sol are world-famous – but in a more important sense, most visitors don't get to know it at all.

TERRITORY AND IDENTITY

Although geographically Andalucía is the most clearly defined *comunidad autónoma*, or autono-mous region, of Spain, it has a surprisingly poor sense of its own identity. Its territory begins in the west on the banks of the Río Guadiana, the natural frontier between Spain and Portu-gal, and stretches across the rest of the Iberian Peninsula, all the while incontestably defined to the north by the broad mountains of the Sierra Morena, separating it from La Mancha and the rest of Spain. On three sides there is sea: it is lapped by the Mediterranean in the east and pounded by the breakers of the Atlantic in the west. Only in its northeast corner is Andalucía's frontier at all fuzzy, falling rather arbitrarily somewhere between Vélez Rubio and Puerto Lumbreras in Murcia.

Yet the notion of Andalucía is a relatively recent one. It was only with the move towards devolution on the death of Franco that the eight traditional provinces of the south were rounded up as the country's second-biggest region under

with a distinctive accent which clips off the final 's' of words.

Andalusians identify more with their provinces than their region, and are much more interested in the differences that divide them than the common causes that could unite them. It doesn't take much to get a group of Andalusians laughing about the characteristics attributed to the people of each province: *Sevillanos*, for instance, are often regarded as showy and hedonistic, whereas *Granadinos* have a reputation for their sour tempers.

Iberian pig farmer in Aracena.

the Junta de Andalucía in Seville – an uncentred capital if ever there was one. Within the heavily devolved country that is modern Spain, Andalucía, holding 8.4 million people or 18 percent of the population, is one of the least cohesive, least nationalistic of regions – far less vociferous in its demands for autonomy than the much smaller Basque Country and Catalonia. This is largely because of economic underdevelopment – Andalucía has always been a place where outsiders have come to from other parts of Spain or abroad to plunder resources – and also because of the lack of a unifying culture. Whereas the other two regions have their own indigenous languages, Andalusians speak Spanish, a language imported from Castile, albeit

HIGHS AND LOWS

Andalucía manages to fit in a bit of everything into its territory, from desert to subtropical valleys. Its central zone is made up of the fertile basin of the Río Guadalquivir, but to all sides there are mountains. Indeed, a third of the region is over 600 metres (2,000 ft), which inhibits communications and historically has engendered communities little interested in the world beyond the horizon.

A MIXED BUNCH

The population is as multifarious as the landscape. Andalucía has always been and continues to be a melting pot of races. A few of its inhabitants may be distantly related to the original tribes of southern Spain, but most are of mixed ancestry. In particular, many people almost certainly descend from the Moors who dominated Andalucía's history for so long.

When the Muslims were forced to leave Spain, there was an influx of migrants from central and northern Spain as the abandoned countryside was repopulated. Later, when Spain was an empire, settlers from Central Europe were brought in to create new towns in northern Jaén, adding a starkly different strain to the gene pool. It is not uncommon to meet Andalusians – according to stereotype full-blooded Latins – who have blond hair and piercing blue eyes.

GATEWAY TO AFRICA

Ever since Spain became part of the EU, uncounted immigrants from the Maghreb countries and black Africa have been entering southern Spain illegally. Most cross the Straits of Gibraltar however they can, landing on the beaches of Cádiz and making a run for it. Some do not complete the crossing but are apprehended by the police or, sadly, drowned at sea. Those that do fan out through Spain and Europe but inevitably many stay in Andalucía to take what work is available and legalise their situation when they can.

While wanting to be seen to defend Europe's borders, Andalusians have a vague sense of sympathy and solidarity towards these new arrivals – and accept them as a cheap source of labour to fill jobs in agriculture and construction that many locals no longer want to do.

FOREIGNERS WITH MEANS

If poor, powerless workers make up one part of the quarter of a million foreign residents of Andalucía, an even bigger chunk is composed of individuals from the other end of the economic scale. These are the rich and relatively rich – mostly from the countries of northern Europe, but also from the US and, more recently, from Eastern Europe – who have chosen to settle in or near the Costa del Sol. Some of them live ordinary humdrum lives gardening in the sunshine, but the coast is also a magnet for celebrities, people evading the tax authorities and officialdom in general, even criminals on the run. Not many of the coast's residents learn fluent Spanish or integrate in any meaningful sense; rather, they are content to live in a multilingual sub-community with its own newspapers and

radio stations, a community that overlaps mainstream Andalusian society but barely touches it, like some phantom fourth dimension. Some of them, however, earnestly embrace the country they have chosen to live in; the more discerning are to be found doing up old farmhouses inland or writing books about their adopted region.

THE YOUNG ONES

Almost a more important determinant than racial provenance in 21st-century Andalucía is age. Conditions of life have changed dra-

Southern belles, Málaga.

matically within living memory, so much so that the old and young can barely understand each other's experiences. Those generations formed after the Civil War and under Franco were born into a world at worst of dire hardship and at best of little choice. Conformity to social and religious mores was the norm, and no one expected to live like the pampered foreign tourists who were beginning to litter the beaches of the Costa del Sol. Many people migrated to the industrialised Basque Country or Barcelona, or even France or Germany, in search of work – with or without their families.

But young people who have come of age in democratic Spain have grown up not only used to political freedom but expecting comfortable lives with unlimited options, including same-sex marriage. However, they were in for a rude awakening following the economic crisis of 2008: approximately 57.9 percent of 16–24 year olds in Spain are now jobless (Andalucía has the highest unemployment rate in Spain) with a new wave of young people moving abroad in search of work. As the GDP continues to fluctuate, only time will tell what effect this will have. Encouragingly, the International Monetary Fund (IMF) forecasts that unemployment will steadily fall during the next few years.

A RETURN TO TRADITION

Until now, not many Andalusians chose to leave their native region, except for a brief spell or unless compelled to for their work. Even a greatly boosted salary did not necessarily compensate them for the loss of an enviable climate and a friendly lifestyle. And, interestingly, some young people opt for the traditional ways rather than the glamour of modern life. Two signs of this are the number of charming small hotels being opened in the Andalusian countryside by young entrepreneurs wanting to stay close to their roots, and

Bullfighter Sebastián Castella in action during the Feria de San Miguel in Seville.

⊙ ROMANCE OF THE RING

Nowhere in Spain, with the possible exception of Madrid, is bullfighting as exalted as in Andalucía. To be a *figura de torero* earns huge respect and status. Indeed, for some bullfighting goes to the heart of the Andalusian character, epitomising courage, artistry and refinement.

The region has about 70 bullrings altogether. Seville's is the most important, while Ronda's, which is one of the oldest in Spain, hosts the much-esteemed Goyesca bullfight in September, when the matadors are dressed in elaborate costumes from the Goya era. Top *toreros* perform in up to 70, 80 or even 90 corridas a year, for wages varying according to their level of

popularity and celebrity, which can be up to €500,000 per appearance. These apparently impressive fees are reduced considerably after the salaries of a minimum of eight employees are deducted, along with all their hotel, food and travel expenses, the manager's commissions, taxes and the cost of publicity, sequinned suits, capes, swords and other paraphernalia.

In the summertime the schedule is extremely pressing, and bullfighters criss-cross the country with barely enough time to rest before the corrida. To learn more about this fascinating but controversial aspect of the culture, visit the bullfighting museums in Seville, Córdoba or Ronda.

the number of inhabited caves that have been restored with pride by new owners as more desirable places to live than modern flats.

Within two or three generations, Andalucía has gone from being an essentially rural society to one in which most of the population live in cities. The economy has correspondingly shifted from a dependence on agriculture to a dependence on the service sector, as if the age of industrialisation had passed the region by completely. One of the main motors of change has been tourism, which has transformed Anda-

today – an effect attributed to the consumer society and improved opportunities for women.

The Catholic Church, meanwhile, has seen congregations slump in the face of the same consumer society, but it still manages to insinuate itself into all corners of life. Most children still carry Christian forenames (María and Jesús are perennially popular); the shrines of saints everywhere are maintained and visited on key days of the year; and annual fiestas, for all the fun they seem to be, are essentially sober religious feast days at heart.

Women wearing the traditional mantilla at the procession of Los Gitanos brotherhood during Semana Santa, Málaga.

lucía's coast from a poor strip of wasteland into a playground for the affluent.

FAMILY AND CHURCH

Surprisingly, perhaps, two principal institutions of Andalusian society – the family and the Church – have so far survived the changes. Even the footloose young feel strong links to their families, and often they keep their attachments to the *pueblo* – the country town the family originally hails from. But there may be a crisis around the corner, as the average Andalusian family is shrinking fast. In common with the rest of Spain, the birth rate in Andalucía has plummeted from an average of over three babies per woman in the 1970s to less than one-and-a-half

⊘ GYPSY MINORITY

Andalucía's 300,000 gypsies *(gitanos)* comprise the region's largest ethnic minority. Gypsies often proudly reject the values of *payo* (non-gypsy) society and as a result are often marginalised, with high rates of illiteracy and other forms of social deprivation. But many seamlessly integrate into society, running businesses and holding down jobs like any other citizens. It is impossible to overestimate the impact they have had on the region, and sometimes – as seen in flamenco music and dance and all its derivatives – it is impossible to differentiate between gypsy and Andalusian culture.

LIVING IN THE PRESENT

In this rich and complex mosaic it is not easy to say exactly how Andalusians differ from other Spaniards. As communications quicken and customs become more nationalised and globalised, it could be argued that Andalusians are merely the extrapolation of general Spanish traits – the southern end of a continuum of national characteristics. But taken together, these traits still constitute an unmistakable Andalusian identity.

Chief among them are sociability and gregariousness. Andalusians like to be in the street, to

Above all, Andalusians are zealous about living life in the present – which can be either charming or frustrating to the outsider. This comes across mainly in the Andalusian habit of *informalidad*. It is hard to define this term exactly, but it reduces to an understanding that everyone does what they feel like doing when they feel like doing it, and no one has the right to tell them otherwise.

A typical aspect of *informalidad* is unpunctuality – as when a friend turns up an hour or two late, without apology or excuse, assuming that those he is meeting will have felt free to behave in the same

Busy Plaza del Siglo at dusk, Málaga.

see and be seen – and they have the climate for it. They have no reservation about making noise and have no shame in showing their emotions, as can be seen in any of their many exuberant fiestas.

They are, with exceptions, a generous, hospitable and straightforward people who do not play mind games or keep a score of social debts and obligations. Theirs is a world of unspoken and unenforced honour, in which it is assumed that anyone they are introduced to by a friend, relation or business partner is to be trusted to uphold their own sense of honour. It can be hard to pay for a round of drinks when out with a group of Andalusians – especially men; even when entertaining a visitor clearly wealthier than themselves, they would never ask or expect him to reach into his pocket.

way. Another common example is when a tradesman promises to come on a certain day but doesn't show up. He might have meant to come at the time but his plans then changed; more probably, he knew full well he couldn't come at the time of asking, but simply felt it would be bad manners to refuse.

Rather than considering *informalidad* something to be ashamed of, Andalusians are adamant that it is the only sane way to live, especially in a world in which stress and overwork are regarded as the inevitable price to pay for material gain. Take away the urgency and obligation, they will point out, and everything still gets done, just in a more enjoyable way. The concept of *mañana* has always been misunderstood beyond the Sierra Morena. All it means is that life is to be lived in full, today.

FLAMENCO

From Andalucía to Madrid and beyond, Spain's most famous attribute is still going strong and has even been recognised by Unesco.

The earliest origins of flamenco, a synthesis of music and dance which has come to be identified with the essence of Spain, are unclear. Flamenco crystallised in the gypsy communities of southern Andalucía in the mid-18th century (its historic heartland is the delta between Seville, Jerez and Cádiz), and features in common with Indian and Arab song attest to this migratory heritage. There are traces, too, of Jewish and Byzantine Christian religious music, as well as regional folk styles.

The rise of flamenco to an art appreciated by the educated and moneyed fits the pattern familiar from forms like the Blues, which started as rough but vital lower-class entertainment. The word 'flamenco', both an adjective and a noun, denotes a way of life, and a person who is unsettled, emotional, unpredictable, in every sense anti-bourgeois.

The flamenco repertoire is based on songs with specific contexts – songs about work or religion, dance tunes, expressions of life's joys and sorrows. The oldest are sung unaccompanied, or with basic percussion; some are still recorded with the clang of a simulated hammer and anvil, after the blacksmiths' forges where they originated.

The numerous styles of flamenco are sometimes divided into *cante grande* (great song), *cante intermedio* and *cante chico* (little), the last brighter, lighter and often accompanied by dances such as the *bulería*, *alegría* or *tango*. The pinnacle of the flamenco singer's art is the body of great songs – often called *cante hondo* (deep song) – which are expressive of the profoundest emotion and are most difficult to perform. It is here that the quality known as *duende*, literally spirit or demon, is crucial: a form of involuntary inspiration that takes over a performer, provoking a murmur – or roar – of '*olé!*' from the audience.

The development of flamenco into a public entertainment started in the 1850s, with the growth of *cafés cantantes* featuring gypsy artistes such as El Planeta and El Fillo. By the 1920s, the so-called Golden Age of flamenco had become a tinsel age, with its popularity leading to increasingly gaudy spectacle. Associations with Franco alienated large numbers of youthful, progressive Spaniards in the 1960s and 1970s, until a number of developments finally

A typically spirited display.

heralded flamenco's return to form. The first was the emergence of the Cano Roto sound, a fast blend of guitars, bass and drums based on the rhumba rhythm and expounded by young gypsy-dominated groups such as Los Chorbos and Los Grecas. Also establishing themselves were the brilliant guitarist, Paco de Lucía (1947–2014), and a charismatic singer from Cádiz, El Camarón de la Isla (1950–92).

Today, flamenco in its numerous forms continues to exert a huge influence on the culture of Andalucía and Spain in general. In 2010, flamenco was added to Unesco's list of Intangible Cultural Heritage. The best way to find out more about it is to visit Seville's Museo del Baile Flamenco (Museum of Flamenco Dance, Calle Manuel Rojas Marcos 3; tel: 954-340 311; www.museoflamenco.com).

Alfonso VII of Castile conquering Almería, a tiled mural in Seville's Plaza de España.

eria.

he Almeria

DECISIVE DATES

800,000 BC
Earliest evidence of human habitation on the Iberian Peninsula dates from this time.

1100 BC
Phoenician traders settle in Cádiz.

800–550 BC
The Tartessos civilisation thrives near Huelva and Cádiz, then vanishes.

218–201 BC
Romans occupy Iberia.

61–60 BC
Julius Caesar is governor of present-day Andalucía.

AD 99
Itálica-born Trajan becomes Emperor of Rome.

407–415
Germanic tribes, including the Vandals, occupy Spain; Visigoths take over most of the Peninsula at the behest of the crumbling Roman Empire.

711
Tariq ibn-Ziyad, a Berber commander, lands at Gibraltar and launches the Islamic conquest of the Iberian Peninsula.

720
Christians defeat Muslims at Covadonga in northernmost Spain, initiating the 'Reconquest' of Iberia, which was to take 772 years.

756
Abd al-Rahman I establishes an independent Emirate in

Entrance to the Dolmen de Menga at Antequera.

Córdoba, ruling most of the Iberian Peninsula.

1010–13
The city-palace of Medinat al-Zahra is destroyed by rebellious Berbers; the Caliphate of Córdoba breaks up into petty kingdoms.

1147
Almohads invade Spain from North Africa.

1211
Christian armies cross Despeñaperros Pass into Andalucía and defeat Moors at Las Navas de Tolosa.

1236
Córdoba conquered by Fernando III.

1248
Fernando III conquers Seville.

1340
Islamic forces are defeated at the battle of Río Salado near Seville, ending all efforts of invasion from northern Africa.

1348
Black Death sweeps through Spain.

1391
Widespread pogroms against Jews.

1474
Isabel becomes Queen of Castile.

1481
Inquisition instituted in Spain.

1485
Columbus arrives in Spain.

1492
Fernando and Isabel conquer Granada, last Moorish kingdom in Spain; Columbus sails from Palos de la Frontera (Huelva) in search of the Indies.

1519
Magellan sets sail from Sanlúcar de Barrameda to circumnavigate the world.

1587
Sir Francis Drake attacks Cádiz and sets fire to the Spanish fleet.

1599
Diego de Velázquez is born in Seville.

1701–13
Spanish King Carlos II dies childless, sparking War of Spanish Succession; Treaty of Utrecht grants throne to the Bourbon pretender; Gibraltar is ceded to Great Britain.

1779–83
Great Siege of Gibraltar by Spanish and French.

1805
Admiral Nelson defeats combined Spanish–French fleet off Cape Trafalgar in Cádiz.

1808
Napoleon replaces Spanish king with his brother, Joseph Bonaparte; Spaniards revolt against occupying French army.

1812
Spain's first constitution is drafted in Cádiz.

1885
Devastating earthquake kills hundreds and destroys thousands of homes in the provinces of Granada and Málaga.

1923
Primo de Rivera seizes control as dictator, with Alfonso XIII remaining as king.

1929
Ibero-American Exposition in Seville.

1931
Spain becomes a republic.

1936
Spanish army revolts, led by General Franco, and three-year Spanish Civil War begins; the poet Federico García Lorca is shot in Granada.

1939
Spanish Civil War ends with Franco's victory.

1953
Spain agrees to US military bases on Spanish soil, ending 15 years of isolation.

1955
Spain joins the United Nations.

1969
Spain closes border with Gibraltar.

1975
Franco dies, and Spain becomes constitutional monarchy under King Juan Carlos.

1977
First free elections in Spain following restoration of monarchy.

1982
Andalucía becomes an autonomous region.

1985
Gibraltar border reopens after 16 years.

1986
Spain joins European Community.

1992
Seville hosts Expo '92.

2002
The euro replaces the peseta.

2008
Global financial crisis: Spain is the worst affected country in Europe after Greece.

2012
Spain records its highest unemployment rate (24.6 percent) since 1976.

2014
King Juan Carlos I abdicates; his son is crowned Felipe VI.

2016
Following a second general election in six months, the PP forms a minority government; Andalucía receives its highest ever number of international tourists (10.6 million).

2017
The Spanish government clamps down on Catalonia's bid for independence.

Expo '92 in Seville was a real success for the region.

Eighth-century BC statuette of the Phoenician goddess Astarte, found among a hoard of ancient artefacts at El Carambolo near Seville in 1961.

EARLY DAYS

Andalucía was conquered many times over the centuries, but the Andalusians won a more subtle victory over their invaders.

The south of Spain was originally settled by the Iberians, a Mediterranean race of uncertain origin. However, the first inhabitants for whom there is firm historical evidence were the Tartessians of the Bronze Age in the 2nd millennium BC.

The lost city of Tartessos has never been found. Nevertheless, quite by accident in 1957, Mata Carriazo, a professor of archaeology at the University of Seville, picked up a bronze of a fertility goddess in a Seville junk shop and identified it as being of Tartessian origin. This was followed by the discovery of a sculpture, the 'Mask of Tharsis', by a mining company near Huelva; and in 1961, during construction work in the hills across the river from Seville, a workman's pick struck a metallic object, the first in a hoard of Tartessian plates, bracelets and necklaces, which came to be known as the Carambolo Treasure.

During recent years archaeologists have unearthed thousands of other artefacts, testifying to a knowledge of mining, industry and agriculture in Andalucía at a very early date, bearing out the Greeks' description of Tartessos as a veritable El Dorado.

A Tartessian vase.

TRADING PLACES

The Tartessians ventured far afield, fishing along the Atlantic coast and around the Canaries. Their sailors are reliably said to have sailed the 'tin route' to Galicia and possibly as far as Cornwall. It was largely because of the abundance of tuna and the availability of tin, used in making bronze, and of other metals from the mines of Huelva that the Tartessians' trading partners and allies, the Phoenicians, established a factory at Gadir around 1100 BC.

There was peaceful competition from the Phocaean Greeks, who founded a trading post at Mainake near Málaga, and Tartessos was at its most prosperous in the 6th century BC. But it suffered an abrupt change of fortune after the battle of Alalia around 535 BC, and from then on Carthage, founded as a North African colony of Tyre, had a free hand in Spain and supplanted the Phoenicians. The Kingdom of Tartessos disintegrated, and in the 3rd century BC, in spite of defeat by Rome during the First Punic War, Carthaginian forces unified most of greater Andalucía and proceeded up the Valencian coast.

The Romans watched events in Spain with growing anxiety. The Carthaginian general Hannibal's attack on the city of Saguntum, which was under Roman protection, led to the outbreak of the Second Punic War (218–201 BC), in which

Hannibal famously crossed the Alps on elephants and invaded Italy itself. Slowly the Romans fought back. A new Roman commander, Publius Cornelius Scipio, was sent to Spain in 209 BC. He seized the Carthaginian base of Carthago Nova (Cartagena) by a surprise attack, and by 201 BC had driven out the last of the Carthaginians.

ROMAN RULE

The Roman occupation of Spain was to last for some seven centuries, during which agriculture was reorganised, bridges, roads and aqueducts

Hannibal crossing the Alps with his elephants.

⊘ SPANISH EXPORTS

The Romans expanded the production of wheat, olives and wine. They introduced the large earthenware jars or *orcae* still used in Montilla for storing wine, and by the 2nd century some 20 million amphorae of Spanish wine had been shipped to Rome. Another export, from Cádiz (named Gades by the Romans), was *garum*, a paste produced by the tuna-fishing industry. Made by marinating the belly meat of the tuna, and as expensive as caviar is today, it was believed by some, including Pliny the Elder, to have curative powers. Another type of *garum*, a smooth paste of anchovies, black olives, capers and herbs, is still available in Catalonia.

The Andalusians were, in the words of the Roman historian Livy, "Omnium Hispanorum maxime imbelles" (of all the Spaniards, the least warlike).

were built, and the Roman legal system was introduced. The country was divided into three provinces, of which the most southerly, Baetica, corresponded roughly to present-day Andalucía. Hispania, and especially Baetica with its flourishing agriculture and mineral resources, was to become one of the Empire's richest provinces.

Roman cities the length and breadth of the Empire were built to a pattern, and many of those in Andalucía preserve the remains of temples, forums, aqueducts, bridges and theatres. Bridges survive at Córdoba (Roman name Corduba) and Espejo (Ucubi); aqueducts at Seville (Hispalis) and Almuñécar (Sexi); theatres at Málaga (Malaca) and Casas de la Reina (Regina); an amphitheatre at Écija (Astigi); a temple and baths at Santiponce (Itálica); while at Bolonia in Cádiz province the ruins of Baelo include a fortified precinct, streets lined with columns, and the remains of a forum, temples, an amphitheatre and houses.

THE VISIGOTHS

With the decline of the Roman Empire the first 'barbarians' entered Spain via the Pyrenees in AD 407–9, but left little mark on the south. They were shortly followed by the Visigoths, a Germanic people, theoretically auxiliaries of the tottering Roman Empire until the Visigothic king, Euric, broke with Rome in 468. The Visigoths passed quickly down through the peninsula, meeting little resistance in the south. The Hispano-Roman nobility, dependent on a slave society, quickly came to terms with the new rulers. After the conversion of Visigothic King Reccared to Christianity in 568, the Church played a central role in unifying the country.

However, the lack of a law of succession resulted in instability. Of the 33 Visigothic kings who ruled Hispania from 414 to 711, three were deposed, 11 assassinated and only 19 died a natural death.

THE MUSLIMS MARCH IN

In 711 Tariq ibn-Ziyad, Governor of Tangier, an outpost of the Damascus Caliphate, crossed the

Straits of Gibraltar with some 7,000 men at his side and established himself on the flanks of Mount Calpe (subsequently known as Gibraltar, from the Arabic Jebel Tarik, 'the mountain of Tariq'). King Roderick, the last Visigothic king, massed a large army and launched a frontal attack on the Muslims, now reinforced and in a strong position near the present-day city of Algeciras. The king fought bravely, but the flanks of his army, commanded by renegades, treacherously turned tail. Roderick was either killed or took flight, never to reappear.

fast, pressing northwards until al-Andalus, as the Muslim-occupied part of Spain was known, covered virtually all of modern Spain and Portugal.

The invaders were, however, split into different factions, the Qaysites and Kalbites of pure Arabian descent, and the North African Berbers, on whom Tariq and his successors largely relied in the conquest of the country. Al-Andalus was eventually united by the establishment of the Umayyad dynasty of Córdoba, which was to control its destiny for some 300 years.

Annihilation of the Visigoths by the Arabs under Tariq ibn-Ziyad in AD 711.

The levying of tribute from converts to Islam was not permissible, so had there been conversions to Islam on a large scale the invaders would have suffered severe loss of income.

The advance into Spain was the tip of an Arab thrust along the North African coast. It had begun in 642 with the annexation of Egypt by the second of the Umayyad caliphs of Damascus, and was to be halted only in France at the battle of Tours in 732. During the 30 years after the first incursion, Moorish governors of al-Andalus followed thick and

THE NEW REGIME

It has been argued that the Muslim invasion of Spain was a jihad (holy war). In truth, the victorious Moors did not display much enthusiasm for converting the indigenous Christians and Jews, let alone putting them to death for refusing. But in granting a large degree of religious freedom, the invaders were not as disinterested as might appear at first sight. Some were desert nomads with no bent for cultivating the lands they had seized, men who preferred to move on to fresh conquests and quick booty. Others settled in the cities, leaving agriculture to the original owners. Providing that they were People of the Book (i.e. Christians or Jews and not polytheists), the conquered people enjoyed local autonomy and freedom to pursue their own religion, subject to the payment of taxes.

In all probability, no more than 40,000 Arabs crossed into Spain with the invading armies. As time went on they married the local women, and as a result the later Umayyads were more Spanish than Arab. However, the lustre of their royal origin survived, and they remained fiercely proud of their Arab descent. This was to prove a two-edged sword, since in the eyes of both Christians and Berbers they remained a foreign dynasty.

GLORIOUS ERA

Al-Andalus reached its zenith under Abd-al-Rahman III (912–61). On his accession he found it in a disturbed and rebellious state, but he worked quickly to pacify the kingdom and secure its border. He settled accounts with dissidents within al-Andalus and then directed equally forceful operations against the Christians of the Marches to the north. In 929 he took the important step of declaring himself Caliph, thus asserting his rights as sovereign. As a symbol of his new status, in 936 he embarked upon the

Abd-al-Rahman III and his court.

⊘ A PALACE FIT FOR A CALIPH

The construction in 936 of Abd-al-Rahman III's Madinat al-Zahra (now known as Medina Azahara), near Córdoba, was a massive project. According to Henri Terrasse in *Islam d'Espagne*, it involved '10,000 to 12,000 workmen; 15,000 mules and 4,000 camels... each day called for 6,000 items of dressed stone and 11,000 loads of lime and sand, without counting bricks and gravel'.

The centrepiece of the great pillared reception hall was a pool of quicksilver, reflecting a quivering light over the whole interior and giving an exhilarating overall impression of constant movement.

Medina Azahara, a magnificent palace 8 km (5 miles) west of Córdoba. It lay on three levels, with a mosque below, gardens in the middle and the palace above. Unfortunately it was destroyed by Berbers just 70 years after its completion.

The overflowing wealth of al-Andalus was rooted in agriculture and the exploitation of mineral resources, rather than on foreign trade. The most important crops, as in Roman times, were cereals, beans, peas, olives and vines, though many new crops, herbs and fruits were introduced, notably bitter oranges and lemons, almonds, saffron, nutmeg and black pepper. The Arabs also planted semi-tropical crops that depended on efficient irrigation, and greatly extended irrigation systems instituted by

> *Wine was openly drunk, even by the emirs and caliphs, though in deference to the Koranic prohibition of the consumption of alcohol it was made and sold by Christians.*

the Romans. Gold, silver, copper, mercury, lead and iron had also been worked by the Romans, but the mines had fallen into disuse during the Visigothic period. They were reopened by the Moors, who also mined cinnabar (a source of mercury) at Almadén near Córdoba.

For all its brilliance, the Caliphate suffered from an infrastructure that was to lead to disintegration and downfall. The sharp division of social classes into the monied and influential and an amorphous proletariat subject to the least whim of the Caliph and his deputies resulted in a passivity and lack of initiative amongst the mass of the population – a state of affairs that the Arabs had themselves exploited when overrunning the earlier Visigothic kingdom. As time went on, the inhabitants of al-Andalus, enjoying ever-increasing prosperity, preferred a life of peace and plenty, and paid mercenaries to fight the belligerent Christians of the north.

CHRISTIAN RESURGENCE

By the end of the Caliphate in 1013, al-Andalus had disintegrated into some 30 small principalities governed by so-called *reyes de taífas* or "party kings". In the east the Slavs (mercenaries from northern Europe) and the eunuchs of the palace guard carved out kingdoms for themselves in Valencia and the Balearics; Granada and Málaga were taken over by Berbers; while in the western heartland of Seville and Córdoba, Muslims of both Arab and Spanish descent held sway.

Meanwhile, the Christians of the north, inspired by a new religious zeal, began making inroads into al-Andalus under leaders such as Fernando I of León-Castile, his son Alfonso VI of León-Castile and, scourge of the Moors, the freebooting El Cid. The most brilliant soldier of his generation, El Cid, having quarrelled with his liege lord Alfonso VI, began his private campaign against the Moors, culminating in the capture of Valencia in 1094. In a sudden reversal of roles as the Reconquest got under way, it was increasingly

the Muslims who became tributaries of the Christian kings. Impoverished as they were, these kings were, to begin with, only too pleased to accept this arrangement. The adjustment seems to have been made without much difficulty, since Muslims and Christians had been used to living side by side and pursuing their different religions.

Of all the *taífas*, the Abbasid Kingdom of Seville most nearly approached the fallen Caliphate in the extent of its territories and the splendours of its court. Its founder, al-Mutadid (1042–69), extended his realm as far as southern Portugal. Ruthless,

Pyx with the name Al-Mughira, son of Abd-al-Rahman III.

⊘ SUPREME VICTORY

Perhaps the greatest conquest of the Muslims was the great expedition of 997 undertaken by the general and statesman al-Mansur (938–1002), which, striking at the heart of Christian Spain, destroyed Santiago de Compostela. The city and its cathedral were razed to the ground, with only the tomb of St James left intact (at the express command of al-Mansur). The army marched back to Córdoba with an enormous booty, including the bells and doors of the cathedral, carried by Christian captives and used to embellish the Great Mosque. Later, when Córdoba fell to the Christians, the bells were carried back to Santiago, this time by Moorish prisoners.

cruel and sensual, he planted flowers in the skulls of his decapitated enemies, using them to decorate the palace gardens, and had his first son put to death on suspicion of plotting against him.

He was succeeded by the gifted and intellectual al-Mutamid, under whom 11th-century Seville saw a remarkable flowering of culture. But the initial idyll was not to last. Al-Mutamid might be as a lion to the rulers of the other *taífas*, but was no match for Alfonso VI of León-Castile. Alfonso captured Toledo in 1085, declared himself Emperor of Spain and issued a peremptory demand for the surrender of Córdoba. The writing was on the wall, and after much heart-searching al-Mutamid took the momentous step of summoning aid from the fanatical Yusuf ibn-Tashufin, the leader of the Almoravids in North Africa.

THE ALMORAVIDS FIGHT BACK

The Almoravids, a warlike and puritanical sect devoted to a return to the original purity of the Koran, had swept across half of North Africa. Their leader, Ibn-Tashufin, already 70 years old, dressed in wool, partook only of barley bread, milk and the flesh of the camel, and viewed with repugnance the wine-imbibing, the music and culture of al-Andalus.

Caught unawares by the landing of the Almoravids in June 1086, Alfonso marched to meet the invading army, which was swelled by the forces of al-Mutamid and other party kings, at Sagrajas near Badajoz. Here, for the first time, the Christians faced the tactic of compact and well-ordered bodies of infantry, supported by lines of Turkish archers and manoeuvring as a unit to the command of thunderous rolls from the massed tambours of the Moors.

Used, as they were, to single combat, where personal valour counted above all, the Christians broke and fell into confusion. Only 500 horsemen, most of them wounded, survived, among them Alfonso.

The battle of Sagrajas set back the cause of Reconquest in al-Andalus for some 60 years, but the rulers of the *taífas*, soon to be expelled from their kingdoms, were equal losers. All al-Mutamid's misgivings about Ibn-Tashufin were justified. In September 1091, after heroic resistance and a desperate plea for help to the erstwhile enemy Alfonso VI, Seville was overrun by the Almoravids. Al-Mutamid and his queen were exiled to Aghmat in the Atlas Mountains, where he lived in penury until the end of his life.

In spite of a publicly proclaimed austerity, even the Almoravids fell victims to the easy lifestyle of al-Andalus. A new Christian champion had meanwhile arisen in the shape of Alfonso El Batallador ('The Fighter') of Aragón, who in 1125 struck deep into the south, reaching the Mediterranean near Málaga.

By now the power of the Almoravids was spent. Once more al-Andalus seemed ripe for

El Cid, campaigner against the Moors.

⊘ RULE OF IRON

Under the zealous and puritanical regime of the Almoravids, Seville was shorn of its former glories. The common people initially welcomed their new rulers, but quickly found that they had exchanged the flamboyant liberalism of the Arabo-Andalusian aristocrats of the *taífas* for the uncompromising rules of Muslim theologians, the fanatical *faqihs*. It was now the Christian kingdoms of the north that tolerated a symbiosis of religions and cultures; and although the Christians and Jews suffered most under the Almoravids, Muslim poets, philosophers and scientists also soon experienced the full force of a religious Inquisition.

reoccupation by the Christians, but they were to be thwarted for another century.

The Almoravid Empire in North Africa was overturned in 1145 by that of the Almohads, also religious in inspiration but with a broader interpretation of Islam and bitterly opposed to the narrow doctrines of the Almoravids. In 1171 Abu-Yaqub Yusuf embarked on the systematic subjugation of al-Andalus. The rulers of a second generation of *reyes de taífas*, who had filled the vacuum left by the downfall of the Almoravids, trimmed their sails to the wind and

the Moors. By May of that year Alfonso VIII had assembled a huge army, swelled by some 60,000 crusaders from beyond the Pyrenees, and in July he faced the Moors at Las Navas de Tolosa in the Sierra Morena.

It was a fiercely fought battle. According to one account, the Caliph had a premonition of disaster and his negro guard was hemmed around him with iron chains. At the end of the day the Moors were routed, the plucky Archbishop Arnold of Narbonne, who took part, putting their dead at 60,000, against the loss of 40,000 Christians.

Alfonso X (the Wise) referred to the conflicts between Muslims and Christians in his famous work of poetry, Cantigas de Santa María.

swore allegiance to the new Almohad Caliph, one of whose achievements was the building of the Great Mosque of Seville.

THE RECONQUEST

Al-Andalus, extended by the conquest of most of present-day Portugal, remained firmly in Almohad hands for the rest of the century. In 1195 at Alarcos the Christians suffered one of their worst defeats in the history of the Reconquest. Undaunted, Alfonso VIII, the lion-hearted King of Castile, worked tirelessly with the Archbishop of Toledo to cement a grand alliance, and his efforts were recognised by Pope Innocent III, who in 1211 declared a crusade against

During the 13th century, Moorish resistance in al-Andalus crumbled under the hammer blows of James the Conqueror of Aragón, of Fernando III of Castile and of his son Alfonso X (The Wise). Baeza and Úbeda in the east were taken in 1233, Córdoba in 1236, Jaén in 1245 and Seville in 1248.

The lands retaken from the Moors were made over to the knights and barons who had fought beside the kings. Many land grants were small or medium-sized, but vast tracts of land were also ceded to families such as the Guzmáns, forebears of the dukes of Medina Sidonia. Initially, the new Christian rulers reverted to the tolerant policies of the earlier Moorish regimes, Muslims and Jews remaining free to practise their religions, subject to a capitation tax. Mudéjars (Muslims living in the reconquered Christian areas, as distinct from *Moriscos*, Christian converts from Islam) formed most of the agricultural workers, and estates were taken over by their new Christian owners without changing the pattern of country life.

GRANADA, THE LAST BASTION

By the time the Catholic Monarchs, Isabel and Fernando, became joint rulers of Spain in 1479, the sole remaining Moorish enclave was the Kingdom of Granada, which also comprised

Ibn-al-Ahmar nevertheless took the precaution of constructing a chain of watchtowers along the mountainous borders of his kingdom. Remains of these defences can still be seen in the village of Alhama de Granada on a small road between Granada and Málaga (C340).

THE INQUISITION

The fall of Granada in 1492 cannot be explained simply by internal weaknesses or by the feud between its leaders leaving it prey to the advancing Christians. By the beginning of the 14th cen-

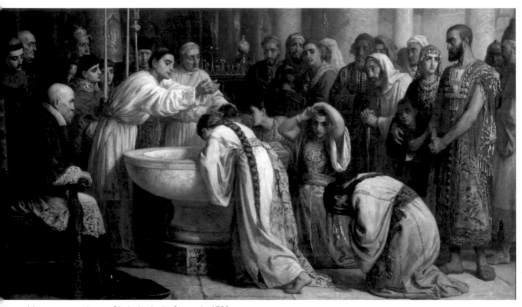

Moors converting to Christianity in Granada, 1500.

Málaga and Ronda. At its peak it extended only 180 km (112 miles) from east to west and 80 km (50 miles) from the sea to its inland border. Towards the end of Moorish rule, as many as 100,000 people crowded into this small area.

That Granada lasted so long was because Ibn-al-Ahmar, the founder of its Nasrid dynasty, had become a vassal of Fernando III of Castile and had assisted in the capture of Seville in 1248. Ibn-al-Ahmar further helped Fernando's successor, Alfonso X, to overthrow the remaining emirates in the south.

Thereafter the Nasrids cleverly played off their North African allies against the Castilians and, by keeping a low profile and by the payment of tribute, staved off a frontal attack.

tury, signs of religious and racial conflict began to appear, which grew increasingly bitter during the reign of the Catholic Monarchs.

The Christians in the reoccupied territories were aware of the abilities of the Mudéjars as workmen and artisans, and of the Jews as administrators, doctors and merchants. From this, it was a short step to postulate that such employment was unworthy of a Christian, and any attempt by the Jew or Mudéjar to better his status was fiercely resented. Once the doctrine of *limpieza de sangre* (purity of blood) had been declared, it became a disgrace for any convert to Christianity to be remotely tainted by Jewish blood. Only those who could claim purity of blood were admitted to positions of public authority.

> *Two thousand heretics were burned in Seville in the year 1481. The Jews were suspect both because of their religion and their wealth, which provoked jealousy.*

The setting up of the Inquisition and the first *auto-da-fé* – the pronouncement of sentence on heretics and their burning at the stake – in Seville in 1481 was followed by the Catholic Monarchs' decree in March 1492, giving Jews a choice between baptism or expulsion, and allowing unbaptised Jews four months to liquidate their property and possessions.

When it became apparent that the Jews were emigrating en masse, even the harsh conditions of the decree were dishonoured and many of the *emigrados* were stripped of their possessions and forced to leave the country destitute. The *Moriscos* were soon to suffer the same fate as the Jews. Spain was thus deprived of the services of its best doctors, administrators and financiers, large numbers of skilled *Morisco* artisans and a sizeable part of its agrarian labour force.

By 1482 the Catholic Monarchs began to make plans for the overthrow of Granada, and another crusade was declared by the Pope.

Meanwhile, a family feud had broken out in Granada. The Amir, Abu'l-Hasan, returned from a military expedition to find that the Alhambra's garrison had declared in favour of his son, Muhammad Abu-Abd-Allah, known as Boabdil. Abu'l-Hasan was forced to take refuge with his brother, al-Zaghal, the only member of his family still loyal.

The campaign against Granada began disastrously for the Christians. So confident were they of success that their army was accompanied by a train of merchants anxious to profit in the anticipated spoils. In the event, the invading force was routed in March 1483, and the merchants spent their gold in buying their own freedom.

UNLUCKY KING

Boabdil's reign began as disastrously as it was to end – not for nothing was he named 'the Unlucky' by his subjects. Overreaching himself in an attack on the Christians, he was taken captive and released by King Fernando on condition that he acknowledged vassalage to Castile and

took the part of the Christians against his father and his uncle, al-Zaghal.

During the next 10 years, Fernando's forces moved in on Granada. Málaga fell after an epic resistance in 1487, and Fernando decided to make an example of it. The town's citizens were deported en masse to other parts of Spain and those unable to pay crippling ransoms were sold into slavery. Boabdil had been living under the delusion that he would be left in possession of Granada, but after the final defeat of al-Zaghal was bidden to deliver up the city. This caused an immediate public out-

Torture was commonplace during the Spanish Inquisition.

cry, and Boabdil belatedly decided to fight.

In 1491 a Christian army of 40,000 foot-soldiers and 10,000 cavalry invaded the lush *vega* below the city. They were beaten off by the Moorish general Musa ibn-Abu'l-Ghazan, and Fernando then decided to sit it out and set up a huge tented encampment outside the city. It was only a matter of time before the besieged town was starved into submission. After prolonged negotiations the capitulation was signed on 25 November 1491. So, in a minor key, almost 800 years of Moorish rule in the Peninsula came to an end. Boabdil had surrendered the last outpost without a fight to the end, and the bitter reproach of his mother, Aisha, rings down the centuries: 'Weep like a woman for what you could not defend like a man'.

Seville in the 19th century.

THE MAKING OF MODERN ANDALUCÍA

Columbus's discovery of the Americas transformed Seville into a glittering centre of world trade – but reversals of fortune followed.

In January 1492, with the surrender of Granada signed and the Christian army about to enter the city, Christopher Columbus, a lonely and Quixotic-looking figure on a mule, rode into the encampment of Santa Fe. It had been six years since he had first petitioned Queen Isabel for support in his project of reaching the Indies by sailing to the west. The project had been ridiculed and rejected by a commission of inquiry; Columbus was in despair and staying at the monastery of La Rábida near Huelva before sailing for France.

While there, he discussed his hopes with one of the friars, Juan Pérez, who had previously served as the Queen's confessor. Pérez wrote to Isabel; as a result, Columbus was recalled to court, and seven months later his three ships set forth on their epic voyage of discovery.

Andalucía was thus associated from the outset with the discovery of the New World. The three ships were crewed with sailors from Palos, Moguer and Huelva; many of the conquistadors and most of the first colonists were from Andalucía or neighbouring Extremadura. By 1503 Seville was playing such a central role in trade with America that Queen Isabel established a Casa de Contratación in the city to regulate all trade with the New World.

GATEWAY TO A NEW WORLD

Seville (and from 1717 Cádiz) thus acquired a virtual monopoly of the trade with America. The ships of the time were limited in range, and depended on the trade winds and a staging post in the Canaries to make the voyage at all; the Andalusian ports were therefore much better-placed than those of the north or the Mediterranean.

Christopher Columbus.

Another compelling reason for routing ships through Seville or Cádiz was to organise convoys. To begin with, ships sailed singly or in groups unguarded; but as buccaneers and pirates began preying on the treasure ships off the Spanish mainland, fleets were assembled at Seville, Cádiz or Sanlúcar de Barrameda, and sailed under the protection of heavily armed galleons.

The practice survived until the mid-18th century, when even eight or 10 galleons could no longer protect the fleets against the depredations of the British Navy. The attacks on Spanish shipping by Sir John Hawkins and Sir Francis Drake during the 1570s and 1580s contributed to Felipe II of Spain's decision to embark on the ill-fated invasion of England with his massive Armada.

RIVERS OF GOLD

During the early years of trade with the Americas, 'rivers of gold' poured into Seville, and there was lavish spending on public works, palatial houses and churches. Perhaps the most grandiose project was the construction in the late 16th and early 17th centuries of the Lonja de Mercaderes, or Exchange, now the Archivo de Indias, which was financed with just one-quarter of one percent of the silver arriving from the Americas.

Another source of wealth was the export to the colonies of olive oil and wine; in return, Andalucía received new plants and foodstuffs, such as maize, tobacco, peppers and chocolate.

That said, historians believe Seville failed to take advantage of the enormous opportunities afforded by its near trading monopoly during the early period. This has been put down to its lack of industry, except on a small artisan scale, such as the manufacture of textiles and tiles. The textile industry could not compete with that of northern Europe, and most of the textiles exported to the Americas through Seville were not made in Spain but came from England and the Low Countries.

The Victory being towed into Gibraltar with the body of Nelson, by Clarkson Stanfield (1854).

⊘ GIBRALTAR: THE ROCK AND A HARD PLACE

The issue of Gibraltar has soured relationships between Spain and Britain for three centuries. The dispute dates from the War of the Spanish Succession (1701–13), when Carlos II of Spain died without an heir, and the choice of a successor lay between Archduke Charles of Austria and Philip of Anjou. After Philip was crowned with the support of Louis XIV, war broke out between Spain and France on the one side and Austria on the other, supported by Britain, Holland and Portugal.

In 1704 the allies decided to open a new front by seizing Gibraltar. The Spanish garrison was hopelessly outnumbered and outgunned by an Anglo-Dutch fleet, and after a siege of only three days the governor surrendered.

Gibraltar was ceded to Britain in 1713 as part of the Treaty of Utrecht, by which the war was brought to an end. The Spanish were soon to question Britain's right to its possession. During 1779–83 Gibraltar underwent one of the most famous sieges in history, when it was beset both by sea and land by the armies and fleets of Spain and France. It was, however, well prepared, with storage galleries cut into the rock and the latest types of artillery capable of raking the attackers at low angle.

The argument over Gibraltar rumbles on, with Spaniards resenting the presence of a foreign enclave on Spanish soil.

By the time of Felipe IV (1621–65), inflation was rampant, not least because of a decision of Count Duke of Olivares to squander American silver and human resources on a fruitless war in Flanders. By this time the Atlantic trade had declined considerably, and Andalucia's most valuable export was its own people.

Emigration from Andalucía and neighbouring Extremadura was 40 percent from 1493 to 1600. The result is a prevalence of Andalusian customs in South America and the close resemblance of Latin American Spanish to that of Andalucía.

THE NAPOLEONIC WARS

European history through much of the 18th and beginning of the 19th century was dominated by the British–French struggle for supremacy, and Spain allied itself according to its best interests. Disastrously, it allied itself with France at the battle of Trafalgar, fought off the Cádiz coast in 1805 and resulting in a masterful British victory, albeit at the cost of Nelson's life. But Napoleon's attempts to occupy the whole of Spain and Portugal in the 1807–14 Peninsular War saw the British and Spanish for once on the same side. The French assault on Andalucía began in January 1810 after a series of Spanish defeats. Marshal Soult and Joseph Bonaparte, with 40,000 men, were faced by 23,000 Spanish along a front of 240 km (150 miles).

Córdoba fell without a fight on 24 January. The junta which had been ruling the country from Seville decamped for Cádiz on the 23rd, followed by the military commander, the Duke of Albuquerque, with his troops. The city fell into the hands of an excited mob; nothing was done to destroy the arsenals, the largest in Spain; and vast quantities of munitions, as well as tobacco to the value of £1 million, were lost to the invaders when they took over on 29 January.

Soult lost no time in despatching General Victor to take Cádiz, but he arrived too late to intercept Albuquerque's 12,000 troops, who had entered the city two days before, blowing up the bridge over the channel between the mainland and the Isla de León on which Cádiz is built.

Despite a French blockade lasting for years, Cádiz was under no serious threat thanks to the presence of gunboats in its harbour and larger units of the Spanish and British navies further out. In the hour of their peril the Spanish forgot

earlier fears about the landing of British troops, and in February 1810, 3,500 men under General William Stewart landed to reinforce the garrison.

Sweeping as the French victory had been, their hold on Andalucía was tenuous and confined to the larger towns and cities. The French were never safe from the activities of the guerrillas, which tied down huge numbers of troops.

Fernando VII's repudiation of the liberal constitution of Cádiz was far from being the end of the matter. A first fruit of his autocratic policies was the revolt and loss of the American colo-

An attempt to break the siege of Cádiz.

nies between 1810 and 1824; and the struggles between liberals and absolutists rumbled on through the 19th century. The Liberal-inspired disentailments of 1836 and 1855 stripped the Church of much of its land and property (resulting in the further loss of artworks). In 1873 a Liberal government proclaimed Spain a republic, though it lasted only 11 months before the monarchy was restored by the army.

THE END OF THE MONARCHY

Spain entered the 20th century minus most of its remaining overseas possessions, lost in the Spanish-American War of 1898. Alfonso XIII, at the head of a shaky constitutional monarchy, was king of a country plagued by increasing civil unrest. In 1923, the Jerez-born General Miguel Primo de Rivera seized power, although the king retained the throne. Primo de Rivera was a more or less benign dictator who counted on considerable popular support, but he was an incurable optimist and hopeless at economics. He drove Spain to the brink of bankruptcy, and was ultimately deposed by more constitutionally correct Spanish military. The Spanish king was forced into calling municipal elections, which were won overwhelmingly by proponents of a Spanish republic. Taking the hint, the cha-

> *During the terrible depression of the post-war years, hundreds of thousands of Andalusians emigrated to factory jobs in France and Germany.*

García Lorca. Málaga was captured in 1937 after bombardment from navy ships and the arrival of Italian troops seasoned by the wars in Abyssinia. The support of Italy and Nazi Germany, and Franco's superior firepower, were decisive

Nationalists patrolling the region around the Río Tinto (Huelva) in 1936.

grined king headed for exile, and Spain's Second Republic was born.

THE RISE OF FRANCO

However, confrontation between left- and right-wing supporters gathered steam. In 1936, the Spanish army posted in Morocco rose up against the government, under their commander General Francisco Franco. The word was sent out to military commanders all over Spain, many of whom joined the revolt. Andalucía was split in two. The sanguine Queipo de Llano seized control of Seville, and Granada fell shortly afterwards, leading to reprisals in which thousands of Republican supporters were executed, including the Granada-born poet Federico

in the insurgents' final victory in 1939. At a cost: it's estimated that 350,000–500,000 Spaniards died in the Civil War.

Franco, who was ruthless and incorruptible in equal measure, was to decide the destiny of Spain for the next three-and-a-half decades. Although officially neutral, Spain was sympathetic to the Axis during World War II, and afterwards Spain was an outcast from the community of nations. Franco's government preached an extreme form of isolationism, hoping against hope to rely on the country's own resources. The devastation of war was followed by a prolonged drought, which led to the 'Years of Hunger'. Andalucía was especially hard hit. Things were to change in 1953 when Spain agreed to cooperate with US efforts in the Cold War, and allowed four American bases to be built, including an enormous naval base at Rota, near Cádiz.

Fuelled by a fresh inflow of cash, Spain edged its way into the 20th century. Franco still held the country in his iron grip, but a number of the more repressive rules were relaxed, and Spaniards began to enjoy a measure of middle-class comfort.

A NEW ERA

But the true revolution was triggered by the arrival of curious foreign visitors. The first were artists and writers seeking an inexpensive life in the sun. Next came the hippies. Finally, the first planeload of package holiday-makers landed at Málaga airport in the late 1960s, and there was no stopping the flood. Hotels sprouted along the Andalusian coast, farmers abandoned their land to become waiters. More importantly, Spaniards came into contact with foreign ways and ideas, and they were perfectly prepared when Franco died in 1975 and the newly proclaimed King Juan Carlos led Spain into democracy. The first democratic elections were held only two years after Franco's death, and Spain was welcomed back into Europe, joining the European Community (now the European Union) in 1986.

THE ECONOMIC CRISIS

Economic development was rapid, with motorways replacing Andalucía's old, winding roads and a high-speed AVE train line linking the region to Madrid. The success of Expo '92, a world fair held in Seville, was seen as proof that Spain had caught up with other Western European countries.

Change, however, came at a cost. One long property boom led to chronic over-development, leaving few spaces between the tower blocks, and the price of housing rocketed – both of which eventually led to the economic crisis of 2008. Spain was the worst affected country in Europe after Greece, with Andalucía suffering the worst unemployment figures in Europe. A new wave of emigration hit the region, as young people moved abroad in search of work. Thankfully the economy has picked up over the last few years, and in 2016 Spain's unemployment figures were at a seven-year low. Although Andalucía remains the country's worst hit region, jobs in the booming tourism industry have eased the burden slightly.

PUBLIC UPS AND DOWNS

The Spanish monarchy has had its fair share of drama in the past few years. In 2014, King Juan Carlos I abdicated due to increasing unpopularity as a result of various activities in his personal life. His son was crowned Felipe VI, and one of his first jobs was to strip his sister Cristina of her title, Duchess of Palma: both she and her husband faced trial for tax fraud – he was given a six-year prison sentence, while she was cleared.

The Spanish government has had an equally turbulent time. The 2015 general election resulted in

1960s sun-worshippers in Málaga.

the most fragmented parliament in Spain's history, with the centre-right People's Party (PP) losing its absolute majority. Although the Spanish Socialist Workers Party (PSOE) won in Andalucía, it had its worst election defeat in recent history. The two largest parties seemed to have had their day, with votes going to smaller parties such as the anti-inequality and corruption Podemos, and centre-left, post-nationalist Citizens. As a result of a hung parliament, another election was held in June 2016, with the same result but the PSOE voted to allow the PP to form a minority government.

Reigniting the fire in 2017 was Catalonia's referendum and subsequent declaration of independence – all fiercely clamped down by Madrid. Spain faces unsettling times once again...

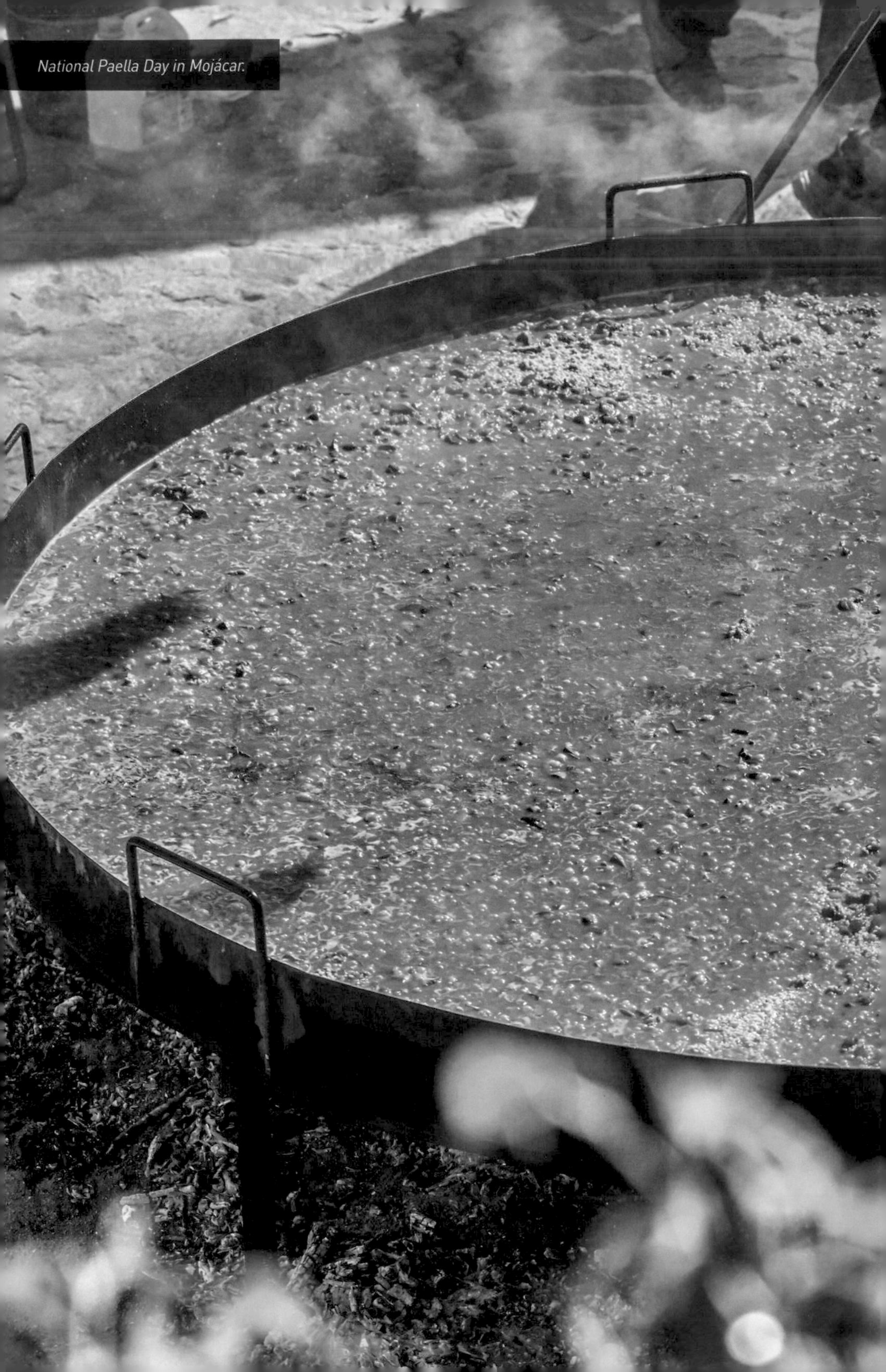

National Paella Day in Mojácar.

Simple tapas in Úbeda.

THE ANDALUSIAN KITCHEN

Sardines grilled on an open fire; home-cured olives; a bowl of gazpacho...
sensational tastes abound in Andalucía's restaurants and bars.

From its jagged mountains to the golden beaches of the Mediterranean, from dry, scrubby hillsides to lush river valleys, Andalucía covers a vast and diverse landscape. The region's food and drink reflects this diversity. In fact, in 2010 'Mediterranean Diet' was added to Unesco's list of Intangible Cultural Heritage. Not only does each province have its own culinary character and signature dishes, but the experience of eating out offers endless variety: it can be as subtle and refined as a cool sherry sipped in the dappled shade of a grape arbour, as brash as a noisy tapas bar; or as simple as the aroma of bread baking in wood-fired ovens.

TASTER SESSION

The best introduction to authentic Andalusian food – in fact, to the southern Spanish way of life in general – is the tapas bar. Here wine, sometimes served from the barrel, is dispensed along with small saucers of snacks, both hot and cold, which are usually consumed while standing at the bar.

Tapas themselves may be the simplest of delicacies: a plate of fat, herb-scented olives; toasted almonds; paper-thin slices of salt-cured *serrano* ham; prawns in their shells; or sliced sausages like paprika-red *chorizo*, peppery *salchichón* or smoky *longaniza*.

Then come *tapas de cocina*, cooked dishes such as croquettes, battered prawns, ham rolls stuffed with cheese *(flamenquines)*, bite-sized pieces of crisp-fried fish or vegetables. Salads include roasted peppers or tomato and onion *(pipirrana)*; *campera*, made with sliced potatoes, onions and olives in a lemon-flavoured dressing; *remojón*, an exotic combination of oranges,

Gazpacho with jamón ibérico and diced cucumber.

onions and cod; and *pulpo*, diced octopus with tomatoes, garlic and parsley.

Seafood selections might include *gambas al pil pil*, prawns sizzled with garlic; clams or mussels *a la marinera* and *boquerones al natural*, fresh anchovies dressed with garlic and vinegar. Other favourites are meatballs, rabbit, chicken in garlic, tiny pork cutlets, stewed tripe with *garbanzos* (chickpeas), kidneys in sherry, and *tortilla*, a thick potato omelette.

Some tapas bars specialise in just a few dishes, others may have up to 40 different choices, sometimes listed on a blackboard. A tapa really is just a nibble – in some bars, served free with a *copa* of wine. Those wanting a larger serving should ask for a *media* (half) or *ración* (full serving).

The drink of choice is dry fino, either sherry or Montilla, both of which are fortified wines made in Andalucía.

Mealtimes are late in Andalucía: 2–3pm for the *comida*, or midday meal, which for Spaniards is the main meal of the day, and 9–10pm for the *cena*, evening meal. So tapas bars are places to pass a pleasant few hours snacking before dinner.

Other popular eating places are *chiringuitos*, shanty restaurants set up on the beach. Here you should try *espetones*, a simple speciality of

the subtlety of flavourings and the freshness of the ingredients make it special.

The simplicity is hardly surprising, given the intense poverty the region witnessed in previous centuries. People learned to exist on the barest essentials and still make them palatable. Gazpacho, the classic cold soup, originated in Andalucía and is little more than bread, oil, garlic and a few vegetables. Equally uncomplicated is *cocido*, also called *puchero* or *olla*, in which chicken, hambone, pulses and vegetables are all cooked together. The broth is served with rice or

Bodega in Ronda.

fresh sardines speared on sticks and grilled on an open fire.

FRESH INGREDIENTS

The basics of Andalusian cooking are olive oil, tomatoes and peppers (both from the New World), garlic and onions, together with fish on the coast and pork products inland. Potatoes are a staple, either fried as a side dish, or cooked in a casserole with other ingredients. Rice features in all sorts of recipes, including paella – but not the long-grained variety grown locally, which is mostly exported to northern Europe. Dried beans and lentils, usually cooked with locally made sausages and vegetables, are also daily fare. It is simple food but

⊘ FRUITS OF THE EAST

The Arabs brought the first orange trees to Spain. These were bitter oranges, sour as lemons, but wonderful in marmalade. These are still used ornamentally in southern Spain, where their blossoms perfume courtyards and their juice is used in cooking, but the fruit is not eaten.

These invaders from the East also contributed rice and spices such as saffron, cinnamon and nutmeg, as well as aubergines and many other fruits and vegetables. For the wealthy with access to new, exotic ingredients, cooking evolved into a high art, and Andalusian cuisine was soon enjoying a reputation as the most refined in Europe.

noodles as a first course, followed by the meat and vegetables.

ESSENTIAL EATING

Gazpacho is just one of the specialities to savour on a visit to Andalucía. *Serrano* or mountain ham is another. Salt-cured and aged from seven months to several years, it is served raw as an appetiser. The most sought-after hams are those that specify their village of origin, such as de Jabugo (from Huelva), de Pedroches (Córdoba) and de Trevélez (Granada), and, most

In the wine-making regions of Jerez and Montilla, vast quantities of egg whites were once used for the clarification of the new wine. The remaining yolks were donated to convents, where the nuns devised ways of turning them into sweets.

time, as are *roscos*, ring-shaped biscuits either fried or baked.

You will find these delicacies throughout

Tasty tapas.

expensive of all, those from *pata negra*, a breed of black-footed, brown Iberian pigs which roam semi-wild and feed on acorns.

Even more irresistible are the sweets of Andalucía, richly flavoured with aniseed, cinnamon and sesame, and drenched in honey – a lavish celebration of the Moorish influence on the region's cuisine. Biscuits, too, cram every bakery shelf. Try *tortas*, round, flat cakes studded with aniseed, often eaten for breakfast; *soplillos,* almond macaroons, and *huesos de santo* ('saint's bones'), shaped like bones and baked for All Souls' Day. *Borrachuelos* and *pestiños* are fried pastries, dipped in honey or sugar syrup; *polvorones*, *mantecados* and *perrunas* are crumbly biscuits shared at Christmas

Andalucía. But each province also has its own local specialities.

SEVILLE: CITY OF TAPAS

Seville, cosmopolitan heart of Andalucía, is famous for its olives, generally served with sherry, but also cooked with meat, chicken and duck. Keep an eye out, too, for home-cured olives, which have been cracked open and cured in brine with garlic, thyme and fennel. This is the city where tapas originated, and you'll probably eat better in tapas bars than in most restaurants. Try *menudo* (tripe); *huevos a la flamenca*, a fancy version of baked eggs with ham, peas, asparagus and *chorizo* sausage; and authentic *yemas de San Leandro*, from the convent of the same name.

Huelva's Iberian pigs supply delectable pork loin *(lomo de cerdo)*, while its famous *pata negra* hams can be purchased straight from the producers in Jabugo, Cortegana and Cumbres Mayores. The province also has excellent game and lamb, and much-prized wild mushrooms and white truffles, not to overlook plentiful fish and seafood. Dishes to ask for are *chocos*, tiny cuttlefish stewed with beans, and *mojama* ('ham of the sea'), salt-cured dried tuna, served in slivers as an appetiser. Many of the strawberries imported into northern Europe

fried sole tastes as if it had jumped straight from the sea into the pan.

Restaurants and tapas bars here and in Cádiz offer a number of interesting variations on fish stew, including *abajá de pescado* and

> *Menú in Spanish always refers to the fixed-price meal of the day. If you want the à la carte menu, you should ask to see la carta.*

Sea urchins for sale at the fish market in Cádiz.

come from the beds of Huelva, which also has its own wine region, Condado, producing light white table wines.

SEAFOOD IN CÁDIZ

Cádiz is a wonderful place to eat fish and seafood, both in the city and the coastal environs. Here you'll find prawns, lobsters, crabs and oysters at their freshest. For a real treat, take a ferry across the bay to Puerto Santa María; on the promenade facing the port are various *cocederos* and *freidurías* where you can buy 20 or more different kinds of freshly cooked shellfish and fish, wrapped in paper cones to eat as you stroll. Prawns from nearby Sanlúcar de Barrameda are incomparably sweet, and the

urta a la roteña (with bream). 'Dog' soup, *caldillo de perro*, is nothing more sinister than fish flavoured with sour oranges; "cat" soup is laced with garlic. The essential dessert to order in Cádiz is *tocino del cielo*, a rich caramel custard which is truly divine.

Not far from Cádiz is Jerez de la Frontera, home of sherry wine and the now fashionable sherry vinegar. The wine is much used in cooking throughout Andalucía: try it in *riñones al jerez*, kidneys braised in sherry; mushrooms stewed in sherry or sweetbreads with oloroso.

ALONG THE COSTA

With more than 150 km (93 miles) of coast, the province of Málaga is unsurprisingly famous for its seafood. Try *fritura malagueña*, a mixed-fish fry of fresh anchovies, so crisp you can eat them bones and all, rings of tender squid, prawns, and a piece of a larger fish such as hake. Other local dishes are *pescado al horno*, fish baked with layers of potatoes, tomatoes, onions and peppers; *rape a la marinera*, monkfish with tomato and garlic; and *lubina a la sal,* a whole sea bass baked in a case of coarse salt.

Besides gazpacho, Málaga has a delightful summer soup of its own, *ajo blanco con uvas*, a tangy white concoction of crushed almonds,

or fresh trout sautéed with ham. Other favourites include *tortilla sacromonte*, an omelette made with sweetbreads, kidneys, red pepper and peas, and *choto al ajillo*, young goat or lamb laced with garlic.

Lovers of game should head for the northern reaches of Jaén and Córdoba, and the Sierra Morena, where venison, wild boar, partridge and hare feature heavily on the menu. *Andrajos*, which literally means 'rags', is a game casserole with pasta squares; *perdiz en escabeche* is marinated partridge. Lamb,

Atmospheric taberna in Córdoba.

garlic and grapes. *Cazuela de fideos* is a variation on *paella* – seafood, peas and peppers cooked with saffron and spaghetti.

On the Costa del Sol, you can eat French, Italian, Danish, Thai, Moroccan, Chinese, Indian and many other world cuisines. In fact, you might have a hard job finding any authentic Spanish food.

INLAND BOUNTY

Inland, the almond groves around Granada have inspired a delicious soup, *sopa de almendras*. Ground almonds are also used as seasoning for rabbit, chicken and fish dishes.

From the Alpujarras Mountains come *serrano* hams. Try broad beans fried with chunks of ham

excellent in both these provinces, is usually served braised.

Córdoba is known for its vegetable dishes, especially artichokes, cardoons (similar to artichokes), wild asparagus and aubergine. Summer specialities include *salmorejo*, like a very thick gazpacho, topped with hard-boiled egg, and white gazpacho, made with almonds and spiked with apples or melon.

Pastel cordobés is a dessert of flaky pastry filled with 'angel's hair' – candied threads of apple. Those with a sweet tooth can bring home a jar of *dulce de membrillo,* a quince jelly that originates from the town of Puente Genil. Córdoba also makes world-class wines, in particular those of Montilla and Moriles.

🔍 THE STORY OF SHERRY

From dry Tío Pepe to flavoursome Fundador brandy, Andalucía's liquid gold is one of Spain's most famous – and enjoyable – exports.

Fino sherry, Jerez de la Frontera.

There was a wine-maker in Jerez de la Frontera in the mid-19th century named Manuel González who did a healthy trade exporting the dark, sweet, nutty wine of the region to England. He had an uncle, José Angel de la Peña – Pepe for short – who was fond of a type of wine which, unlike the popular sweet sherry, was crystal clear in appearance and bone-dry to the palate. There was a section in the wine cellar where Uncle Pepe kept a few barrels of the stuff, for his personal enjoyment and for sharing with friends.

One day, one of Pepe's barrels was included in a shipment to England. Word soon got back from the importers. Could they have some more of that rare, clear stuff, please? So the winery started making more of this style of wine, naming it after the vintner's uncle: Tío Pepe. Thus was a Jerez legend born, and today Tío Pepe is one of the top-selling wines.

The land of sherry abounds in such anecdotes. Few tipples have the mystique surrounding those from this corner of the province of Cádiz, where a unique combination of soil, grape, climate and ageing methods gives rise to the world's most popular aperitif wine.

Reposing in the cellars of Jerez are around half a million wood barrels – the large sherry *botas*, or butts, each containing 500 litres (110 gallons) of liquid gold. These veritable cathedrals of wine are the best places to learn about the different types of sherry and how they are made. The wineries welcome curious travellers and have become the town's major attraction.

SHERRY COUNTRY

Sherry is born in what has been called the 'Golden Triangle', a wedge of gently rolling country in western Cádiz. At one corner is Jerez itself. At the two other corners are El Puerto de Santa María, the port from which sherry was traditionally shipped, and Sanlúcar de Barrameda, at the mouth of the Guadalquivir. Each has a distinct character: where Jerez is aristocratic and proud, El Puerto is a workaday port and Sanlúcar a relaxed fishing town. Between them lie the expanses of white, chalky soil, carpeted with the vines.

Most sherry is made with the Palomino grape. It is a high-yielding white grape, but apart from that there is nothing much to be said for it: white wines made from Palomino are thin and prone to oxidation (darkening). Yet in Jerez it reaches new heights, thanks to a combination of circumstances.

First, there is the soil, the chalky *albariza*, which has the characteristic of soaking up the water from the torrential winter rains and storing it so that the deep-rooted vines can survive the long, hot summer months. Then there is the prevailing humidity, due to the area's proximity to the Atlantic and the wetlands of the Doñana park.

When the wine is put into barrel, a coating of yeast – called the *flor* – forms on the surface, thanks to this humidity, and this seals the wine, protecting it from the air, feeding on the sugars and giving the wines their exceptional dryness. In Sanlúcar, the most humid part of the region, the layer of *flor* is thicker and the resulting wine, called manzanilla, even drier.

Every detail of the wine cellar is designed to keep the vital *flor* happy. High vaulted ceilings keep summer temperatures down; windows, covered with esparto mats which can be raised or lowered to control ventilation, are oriented to trap the damp westerly winds. The cellar floors are compacted sand, which is watered down regularly. Even the gardens surrounding the wineries are for a purpose: they help maintain a cool, humid microclimate around the cellars.

After the grapes are pressed and fermented, the wine is aged for a year or two, then it enters the *criaderas*, rows of barrels that hold blends of different vintages. A portion of wine is drawn off from the casks, called the *soleras*, which contain the oldest

Sweeter than French brandy, it acquires its distinctive character when the basic wine spirits (for which grapes from other Spanish regions are used) are left to age in casks that have previously held sherry wine. Its discovery came about quite by accident. In 1860, the Domecq winery received an order for 500 barrels of *'holandas'* (as clear wine spirits were called, Holland being the main customer), but payment was not forthcoming, and the shipment never left the cellar. Instead, it sat forgotten in old sherry casks for five years, until it occurred to the foreman to sample it. He found it had turned a golden colour,

Harvesting the grapes in Jerez de la Frontera.

blend for bottling. These casks are topped off with wine from casks containing the second-oldest blend, which in turn is replenished from another row of casks, right on up to those containing the youngest blend, which are topped off with the most recent vintage. The system evolved from the need to keep stocks fresh and consistent in flavour. Therefore, with one or two exceptions, there is no vintage sherry; practically all are blends.

Sherries are fortified wines, which means extra alcohol is added just before bottling for fino sherries or before they age for olorosos. They should be drunk within a year or two of bottling.

FUNDADOR BRANDY

Just as important to the local economy is Jerez brandy, also produced by the sherry wineries.

with a good flavour and aroma. Thus was another Jerez legend born: Fundador brandy.

Today around 20 million bottles are produced a year, with around 35 percent of that sold abroad. Over the past ten years production has decreased by about 60 million bottles, as the top brands lowered the alcohol volume, which meant they were no longer able to call their products 'brandy'.

Yet when you attend the *feria*, where men and women in traditional costume proudly ride their horses, you know that Jerez will always have some of that old spirit. In a reversal of history, in 1998 members of the González Byass family bought back the 30 percent share of the bodega which they had sold to a British multinational in 1992, the winery thus becoming family-owned once again. Tío Pepe would have approved.

FIESTAS FOR ALL SEASONS

The Andalusian character shines brightest at the region's fiestas, which are some of the biggest and best in Spain.

Andalusian fiestas come in seasonal cycles, and many trace their roots to pagan times. Even the deeply solemn Semana Santa procession has pagan roots, as a celebration of spring. Other celebrations are unabashedly pagan, such as the Eve of San Juan (23 June), when bonfires are lit, effigies are burned, and participants leap through the flames and then cleanse the spirit by bathing in the sea.

Every town holds an annual *feria*, usually in summer, though the most famous is Seville's April Feria. In the harvest season, wine-growing areas host a Fiesta de la Vendimia. Other crops, from oranges to olives, are similarly honoured.

SOLSTICE CELEBRATION

The winter solstice has been celebrated for thousands of years, although we now know it as Christmas. In Spain, Christmas lasts for two weeks, starting with Nochebuena ("the good night"), on Christmas Eve. People greet Nochevieja ("the old night"), New Year's Eve, in front of the clock in the main square, where they eat 12 grapes of good luck, one for each chime. Finally comes the Epiphany, or Feast of Three Kings, when Spanish children receive their presents.

The cycle ends with Carnival, the final fling before the abstemious Lent period leading up to Holy Week and a new round of fiestas.

Carriage at Jerez de la Frontera's annual Horse Fair in May. No town takes its horses as seriously as the sherry town, the birthplace of the Carthusian breed.

Seville's April Feria, El Rocío's romería and the annual Horse Fair in Jerez de la Frontera are all opportunities for parading in traditional Andalusian costume.

Troubadours sing satirical verses during Cádiz's Carnival, one of the biggest in Spain. The 10-day fiesta ends with fireworks and the burning of a witch effigy on Caleta beach.

In fishing villages the image of the Virgen del Carmen, patroness of fishermen, is taken out in seaborne processions in July.

Virgin worship

The story is repeated in countless villages throughout Andalucía: a hunter, a shepherd or a farmer stumbles across an image of the Virgin Mary, hidden in a grotto or in the hollow trunk of an ancient tree, reputedly to conceal it from the heathen Moors. The countryman tries to take it back to his village, but falls asleep and, on waking, finds the Virgin has miraculously returned to her original hiding place. Word of the miracle spreads, a shrine is erected, and it becomes a place of pilgrimage.

Some of these pilgrimages, called *romerías*, after the custom of gathering wild rosemary *(romero)* along the route, have become mass events, such as the pilgrimage of the Virgen de la Cabeza in Andújar (Jaén), the pilgrimage of the gypsies in Cabra (Córdoba), the seaborne processions to honour the Virgen del Carmen or, the biggest of all, the Romería del Rocío, on the edge of the Parque Nacional de Doñana, which attracts around one million people every Whitsuntide (see page 103).

Christ's Passion and death are re-enacted in outdoor plays in many towns, such as Riogordo (Málaga), whose Paso (passion play) spans two days.

Traditionally an agricultural region, Andalucía has numerous harvest festivals. In the September Fiesta de la Vendimia in Jerez de la Frontera, grapes are trodden in front of the main church, recalling wine-making methods of days gone by.

Hooded penitents in one of Olvera's Holy Week processions, an image harking back to the Middle Ages. They are members of a cofradía, the brotherhoods that organise such processions, which can last 8, 10 or even 12 hours.

Griffon vulture in the Sierra de Grazalema.

WILD ANDALUCÍA

Almost one-fifth of Andalucía is protected – a rugged wilderness that houses some of Europe's rarest birds, mammals and plant life.

In a special enclosure high in the Sierra de Cazorla of southern Jaén, five lammergeier vultures (aka bearded vultures) were slowly adapted to the mountainous conditions. Found injured in other parts of Spain and carefully nursed back to health, the birds would never fly again; instead, they formed the basis of an ambitious breeding programme to reintroduce the species to the national park. Although there are now 11 birds here, its species was reassessed as 'near threatened' in 2014, from 'least concern', due to a decreasing population.

With a wingspan up to 3 metres (10 ft), the lammergeier is the biggest bird in Europe, and also one of the rarest. In Spain, its last major refuge, it is known as *quebrantahuesos*, or 'bone-buster', for its habit of dropping bones from a great height to get at the nutritious marrow.

Similar conservation programmes are under way all over Andalucía, as plant and animal species are monitored to ensure their survival, and unspoilt areas earmarked for official protection. It is a reflection of a new awareness among Andalusians that wildlife is something to be treasured.

WAKING UP TO NATURE

A total of 17 percent of the region is afforded official protection as natural wilderness, more than triple the national average. In all, there are more than 80 different locations classified as nature park *(parque natural)*, nature reserve *(reserva natural)* or nature enclave *(paraje natural)* – from small, inaccessible lagoons that are crucial to migrating birds, to vast forested tracts, such as the Cazorla nature park.

Desert landscape, Iabernas.

THE DOÑANA NATIONAL PARK

The jewel in the crown of wild Andalucía is the Doñana National Park, spreading 542 sq. km (209 sq. miles) at the mouth of the Guadalquivir river. About two-thirds of the park consists of marsh and wetlands, the most valuable in Europe, for they provide a breeding ground for more than 100 species of birds, and are a wintering ground or stopover on the migration route for many others. The extremely rare imperial eagle soars in the skies here. Visitors can learn about the birds from ornithologists in the Francisco Bernis Birdwatching Centre in El Rocío (see page 103).

Two thousand years ago, this was a vast brackish estuary, peppered with islands, but gradual silting up of the Guadalquivir river created the marshes. Hunting was the main activity here for centuries, but in the 1960s intensive farming threatened its very existence: water drawn off for irrigation reduced the wetlands from more than 1,800 sq. km (700 sq. miles) to 310 sq. km (120 sq. miles), and only the area's designation as a nature park in 1969 saved it from disappearing altogether.

EUROPE'S DESERT

At the opposite end of the region, Almería's landscape provides a sharp contrast to the wetlands of Huelva. Tabernas is the only true desert in Europe, with less than 20 cm (8 inches) of rainfall a year, and its landscape of parched, eroded hills has served as a backdrop for countless Western films.

The equally arid landscape stretching from the Cabo de Gata, the southeastern tip of Andalucía, up the coast to Carboneras is now also protected as a nature park, with volcanic cliffs, isolated coves of black sand and hillsides covered in prickly pear cactus (a species introduced from the Americas). Even this

Limestone formations at El Torcal, near Antequera.

⊘ BIRDS ON THE WING

The Strait of Gibraltar, where Africa seems so close you could almost touch it, is the crossing point for the many migratory birds that spend their summers in Europe and fly south in the autumn to overwinter in warmer climes.

This is when Andalucía acts like a giant funnel, as tens of thousands of birds converge on the southernmost tip of Iberia to await favourable conditions for the crossing to Africa.

The migration is one of the most spectacular natural phenomena in Europe, and even the lay birder, armed with a simple pair of binoculars and a decent field book for identification, is bound to spot

a few rarities. The birds' arrival in spring is staggered (from February to June), so the best time to observe the migration is on their return flight to Africa. Traffic is busiest at the end of September and throughout October.

In addition to large numbers of storks, some 250,000 raptors make the crossing, including honey buzzards, vultures (Egyptian and griffon), Montagu's harriers, ospreys, kestrels, short-toed eagles, booted eagles, goshawks and many more.

Among the best spots to watch the passage are the lookout points over the Strait of Gibraltar, just east of Tarifa, and from the Rock itself.

moonscape supports wildlife, including types of snapdragon and lily unique to this area.

Not long ago, the coast of Cabo de Gata was accessible only to millionaires on private yachts or via a long trek over goat trails, but roads have opened up the area to travellers, and campsites, hotels and restaurants have sprung up to serve them. The same is happening all over Andalucía, where 'rural tourism' is the latest trend – leading to debates over the compatibility of tourism and conservation.

constant humidity, which it finds here in what is the wettest spot in Spain (an average of 225 cm/ 88.5 inches of rain a year).

FRIENDS AND FOES

Tourists aside, the 20th century brought new perils to Andalucía's wildlife: agricultural pesticides and artificial fertilisers; irrigation systems that depleted underground water sources; reforestation with fast-growing, non-native pine trees and eucalyptus which crowded native species, as did the introduction of alien animal species for

Algerian oaks in the Sierra de Grazalema, Cádiz province.

PRIMEVAL FORESTS

To get an idea of what the primeval forests that covered much of Andalucía looked like before the arrival of man, head for the mountains that straddle the provinces of Cádiz and Málaga. Near the coast is the Parque de los Alcornocales, 1,700 sq. km (655 sq. miles) of cork oak, holm oak and Lusitanian oak. As you ascend towards Ronda, following the old tobacco smugglers' route from Gibraltar, this gives way to the heights of the Sierra de Grazalema, home to peregrine falcons, eagle owls and one of Europe's largest colonies of griffon vultures. Among the trees found here is the *Abies pinsapo*, a fir which grows nowhere else in Europe. It requires shaded valleys at high altitude and

hunting or breeding purposes – everything from mouflons to rainbow trout and Louisiana crayfish.

Fortunately, wild Andalucía has had several things going for it: the sheer size of the region, the fact that much of it consists of inaccessible mountains and, sadly, the social injustices of the past. When Andalucía was conquered by the Christians, and the *Morisco* farmers were ultimately expelled, most of the territory fell into the hands of absentee landowners, who were more interested in counting gold from the New World or hunting for wild boar than in turning their properties into working agricultural concerns. Emigration, uninterrupted for centuries, left much of rural Andalucía under-populated, so nature was allowed to go its own way more or less unhindered.

THE LYNX UNDER THREAT

Some of the wildest terrain is found in the Sierra de Aracena, at the western extreme of the Sierra Morena, the mountain range separating Andalucía from Castile. A string of protected nature areas – the Sierra del Norte in Seville, Sierra de Hornachuelos and Sierra de Cardeña–Montoro in Córdoba, Sierra de Andújar and Despeñaperros in Jaen – form a wild corridor 320 km (200 miles) long. The further east you go, the more rugged the scenery.

These mountains are the home of one of the rarest mammals in Europe, the Iberian lynx. The not long ago on the verge of extinction, is finding new breeding grounds in the lagoons of southern Spain. The chameleon, which for decades had been fighting a losing battle with real-estate developers, is on the increase again, with colonies detected in Almería and Granada.

Some of the most striking examples of Andalusian wildlife are among the smallest. Southern Spain is a botanist's paradise, with over 4,000 different plant species, more than 150 of which are endemic. They have evolved in unique microclimates such as those of Cazorla, where the Cazorla

An elusive lynx in the Sierra de Andújar, Jaén province.

lynx is the animal that best embodies Andalucía's struggle to protect its wildlife. Only around 400 are left in the whole of Spain, in the national parks of Andújar in Jaén and Doñana in Huelva (and the Montes de Toledo, Castilla La Mancha). In 2002 the World Conservation Union listed the Iberian lynx as a Category One Critically Endangered Species, which meant that money was made available for a rescue project. There are now several successful breeding programmes in Andalucía and captivity-born lynx have been released into the wild. As a result, the threat level to the species has been lowered to 'endangered'.

For other species, the future is more promising. White storks returned to nest in Ronda after an absence of 20 years. The white-headed duck,

North of Tabernas, at Sorbas, is one of the world's largest gypsum deposits, occupying what was once an inland sea. When it drained, it carved cavities out of the crystallised gypsum, forming karstic caves whose walls glitter with crystals.

violet grows, or Sierra Nevada. Contemplating the windswept heights around the ski resort, where no trees will grow, you might think the landscape barren following the spring thaw. But look closely, and you might spot the rare Nevada daffodil (*Narcissus nevadensis*) or Nevada saxifrage (*Saxifraga nevadensis*), just two of 70 catalogued.

HIKING IN ANDALUCÍA

With two national parks, 24 natural parks and nine long-distance footpaths, Andalucía offers get-away-from-it-all walking to suit most levels.

Southern Spain's countryside is extraordinarily varied, and while parts are suitable only for hurrying through to get from one place to another, others make perfect walking country. Find the right patch of hillside strewn with wild flowers beneath high-altitude crags overflown by eagles and vultures, or wooded valley alive with birdsong and the trickle of water, and there is no better place to be out of doors.

There are two national parks and 24 *parques naturales* (nature parks) in the region, all of them geared up for hikers, with signposted routes of various length and usually a good choice of rural hotels, bars and restaurants and other services.

The two most popular areas for walking holidays are the Alpujarras (see page 205) south of Granada (together with the rest of the Sierra Nevada National Park) and the Sierra de Grazalema (see page 126) near Ronda. Other good areas are the forested sierras and valleys of Cazorla (see page 182) and the chestnut, cork and holm-oak woods of the Sierra de Aracena in Huelva (see page 108). Beauty spots for short walks include the Doñana National Park (see page 103), El Torcal near Antequera (see page 155), the cliffs and coves of Cabo de Gata (see page 219) in Almería and, close to the Costa del Sol, around the town of Istán (see page 149).

For serious walkers there are 17 long-distance (GR) footpaths crossing Andalucía in two or more daily stages, most famous among them being the 1,280-km long GR7 (E4), or 'Mediterranean Arc' which connects the Aegean Sea with the Atlantic Ocean. Shorter walks, normally between 1 km (0.5 mile) and 10 km (6 miles) long and often circular, are designated PR–A. They are graded according to their difficulty (*dificultad*) from *baja* (easy) to *muy alta* (for experienced walkers only). Tourist offices and visitors' centres will be able to advise on walks.

Spring and early summer are the best times to go walking in Andalucía, when the landscape is smothered in wild flowers but the days are not too hot. The Mediterranean vegetation burns dry in the heat of July and August, although these are good months to go walking at higher, normally snow-capped altitudes. Autumn and winter are good for exploring the

Hiking in the Sierra Nevada.

countryside near the coasts when the access roads aren't clogged with tourist traffic.

Whenever and wherever you go walking, common-sense advice applies: stick to walks on marked paths within your ability; never walk alone; take the best map you can find; and make sure someone knows where you have gone and when you expect to be back. Wear proper walking shoes (boots are best), a hat and something warm if you are going to any altitude. Always carry plenty of drinking water.

Good walking maps are available locally, but it is wise to buy them beforehand. The best are in the 1:25,000 series published by the Centro Nacional de Información Geográfica (CNIG, www.cnig.es). The Spanish army (Servicio Geográfico del Ejército) produces 1:50,000 maps suitable for walking, as does the regional government, the Junta de Andalucía, and several specialist publishers. The best place to shop for maps is Mapas y Compañía, Calle Compañia 33, Málaga (tel: 952 608 815; www.mapasycia.es).

Puerto Banús beach with La Concha mountain rising up in the background.

The Alhambra's exquisite Patio de los Leones, Granada.

The sugar-cube houses of Olvera.

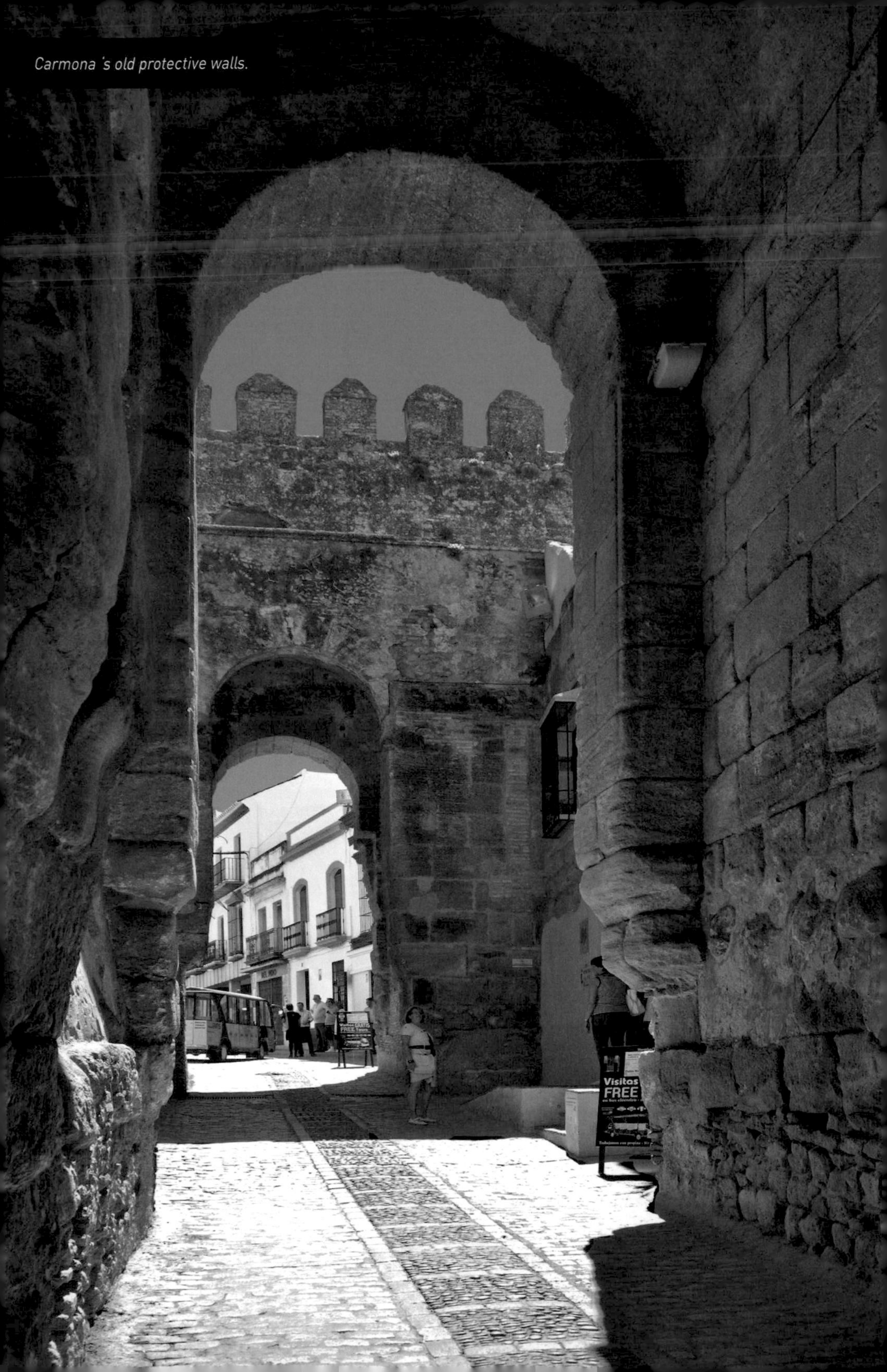

Carmona 's old protective walls.

INTRODUCTION

A detailed guide to the region, with the principal sites
clearly cross-referenced by number to the maps.

Entrance to the Alcázar, Seville.

The autonomous region of Andalucía is Spain's most populous, with over 8 million inhabitants in its eight southernmost provinces. It covers an area of some 87,000 sq km (33,600 sq miles), an expanse the size of Portugal and twice the size of the Netherlands.

Within these confines the variety of landscape is tremendous. To the north is the long ridge of the Sierra Morena, a mountain range that effectively seals the region off from the rest of Spain, where the rich *sevillanos* go hunting; to the south is the Costa del Sol, playground of foreigners, where Europe's working classes rub shoulders with aristocrats and the famous. In the centre lies the flat agricultural plain of the Guadalquivir. To the east are the arid desert lands of Almería and the mountains of Granada, and to the west the marshlands of the Doñana National Park. On the horizon from almost anywhere is North Africa, whose influence is felt in the history and the towns of this southernmost region of Spain and of Europe.

Bolonia beach, Cádiz province.

Each of Andalucía's old cities, Seville, Córdoba and Granada, have major Moorish monuments of international significance. But others have their claims to fame: Cádiz, the home of the Armada and the signing of the first Spanish constitution; Ronda, the birthplace of bullfighting; Huelva, from where Columbus sailed for the New World. Parts of the province of Almería are so desolate that it's a popular location for shooting Westerns; nearby Jaén is the undulating heartland of the olive growing industry, which financed the city's many Renaissance and baroque buildings.

Distances between provinces and cities are not enormous, but travel times may well be longer than expected, either because of the winding mountain roads, or because of the weight of traffic, particularly in the coastal areas (though toll motorways offer faster if less interesting alternatives to the old main roads). However long it takes, the destination will be worth the effort.

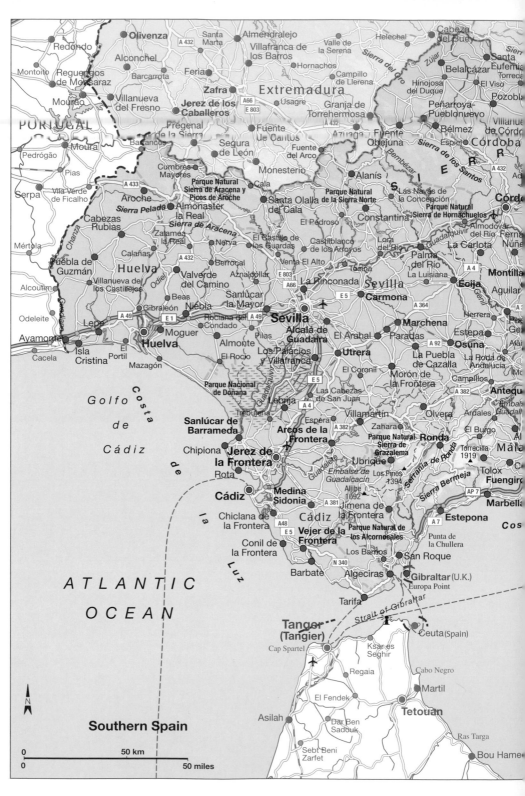

Southern Spain

0   50 km
0   50 miles

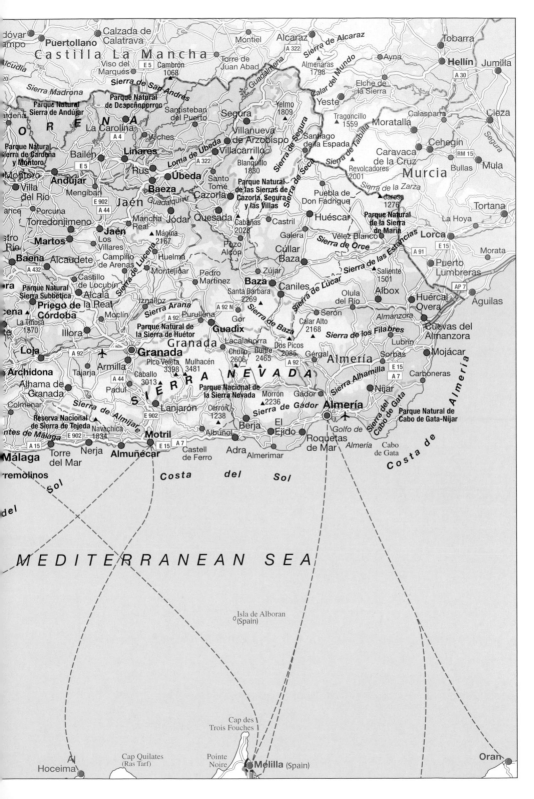

dóvar
ampo
Puertollano
Calzada de Calatrava
Montiel
Alcaraz
Sierra de Alcaraz
Tobarra
Castilla La Mancha
A 322
Ayna
Hellín
Jumilla
lcudia
Viso del Marqués
E 5
Cambrón 1068
Torre de Juan Abad
Almenaras 1798
A 30
20
Sierra Madrona
Sierra de San Andrés
Elche de la Sierra
Cieza
ardeña
Parque Natural Sierra de Andújar
de Despeñaperros
Santisteban del Puerto
Yelmo 1809
Yeste
Tragoncillo 1559
Moratalla
Calasparra
O   R   E   N   A
La Carolina
Segura
Villanueva de Arzobispo
Santiago de la Espada
Sierra de Taibilla
Caravaca de la Cruz
Cehegín
RM 15
Sierra
Parque Natural ierra de Cardeña y Montoro
A 4
Viches
Linares
Villacarrillo
Revolcadores 2001
Bullas
Mula
Montoro
E 5
Rus
Blanquillo 1880
Sierra de Seca
Murcia
Villa del Río
Andújar
Mengíbar
Úbeda
Santo Tomé
Parque Natural de las Sierras de Cazorla, Segura y las Villas
Puebla de Don Fadrique
Jarosa 1276
Tortana
ance
E 902
Baeza
Guadalquivir
Cazorla
Sierra de la Zarza
Porcuna
A 44
Jaén
Mancha Real
Jódar
Quesada
Cabañas 2028
Castril
Huéscar
Parque Natural de la Sierra de María
La Hoya
stro Río
Torredonjimeno
Mágina 2167
Galera
Vélez Blanco
Sierra de Orce
Lorca
Martos
Jaén
Los Villares
Huelma
Pozo Alcón
Cúllar Baza
Sierra de las Estancias
E 15
Morata
Baena
Alcaudete
Campillo de Arenas
Montejícar
Pedro Martínez
Zújar
Baza
Caniles
Saliente 1501
A 91
Puerto Lumbreras
ra
Parque Natural Sierra Subbética
Castillo de Locubín
Alcalá
Iznalloz
Santa Bárbara 2269
Olula del Río
Albox
AP 7
Águilas
cena
Priego de la Real
Moclín
Sierra Arana
A 92 N
Sierra de Búcar
Serón
Almanzora
Huércal Overa
Córdoba
La Tiñosa 1370
Purullena
A 92
Calar Alto 2168
Cuevas del Almanzora
e
Illora
Parque Natural de la Sierra de Huétor
Guadix
Lacalahorra
Sierra de los Filabres
Lubrín
Loja
Granada
A 92
Chullo 2606
Buitre 2465
Dos Picos 2085
Gérgal
Almería
Sorbas
Mojácar
Granada
Pico Veleta 3398
Mulhacén 3481
A 92
Carboneras
Archidona
Tajarja
Armilla
SIERRA NEVADA
E 15
Alhama de Granada
A 44
Caballo 3013
Padul
Parque Nacional de la Sierra Nevada
Morrón 2236
Gádor
Níjar
A 7
Colmenar
Sierra de Almijara
Lanjarón
Cerrón 1238
Sierra de Gádor
Almería
Parque Natural de Cabo de Gata-Níjar
Reserva Nacional de Sierra de Tejeda
Navachica 1834
E 902
Berja
El Ejido
Golfo de
Málaga
ntes de Málaga
E 902
A 15
Motril
E 15
A 7
Albuñol
Roquetas de Mar
Almería
Cabo de Gata
Nerja
Almuñécar
Castell de Ferro
Adra
Almerimar
remolinos
Torre del Mar
Costa   del   Sol
Costa de Almería
del
Costa
del
Sol

M E D I T E R R A N E A N   S E A

Isla de Alboran (Spain)

Cap des Trois Fouches

Cap Quilates (Ras Tarf)
Pointe Noire
Melilla (Spain)
Oran

Al Hoceima

La Giralda at dusk.

SEVILLE

Seville is undeniably romantic, with gracious architecture and avenues of shady orange trees – but it's also an exhilarating modern city.

If Andalucía is the embodiment of the Spanish clichés of flamenco, gypsies, fiestas and bullfights, then **Seville ❶** (Sevilla), its capital, is its heart. This is the home of the sultry temptress Carmen, of the lover Don Juan, and of Figaro, the Barber of Seville.

At one time this was Spain's largest city, through which all the riches of the New World poured. Today, with a population of around 700,000, it is a reasonably prosperous hub of commercial and industrial enterprise, but you wouldn't immediately realise it. Such is the *Sevillanos'* laid-back attitude to life and devotion to fun and fiestas, late nights and sluggish morning starts, that visitors may wonder how they ever accomplish any work. Although, like the rest of Spain, the city's fortunes were affected by the 2008 global economic crisis.

GLORY AND DECAY

Hispalis, the forerunner of Seville, was founded by the Phoenicians in around 500 BC, although native Iberians populated the area from around 700–600 BC. The Romans redeveloped Hispalis and also founded nearby Itálica, the birthplace of emperors Trajan and Hadrian. When the Moors invaded Spain in AD 711, it took them just a year to conquer Seville and make it their cultural centre. They named it

Ishbillya, and by the 10th century it was one of the most important cities in the caliphate of Córdoba.

By the early 11th century the Caliphate had split into some 30 *taíffas*. Ishbillya was the most powerful of these, and it prospered under the reign of al-Mutadid (1042–69) and his son al-Mutamid (1068–91). In 1091 it was taken over by the Almoravids, who reunited al-Andalus, and then by the Almohads, who made Seville the capital of Muslim Spain. La Giralda, the ornate minaret that later became the bell-tower of the

◎ Main Attractions
Cathedral
Alcázar
Archivo General de Indias
Barrio Santa Cruz
Hospital de la Santa
  Caridad
Torre del Oro
Museo de Bellas Artes
Parque de María Luisa
Triana
Itálica

◉ Maps on pages
78, 81, 95

In the Alcázar's tranquil gardens.

Seville

0   500 m
0   500 yds

Pabellón de Andalucía
Isla Mágica
Parque del Alamillo
Pria. Barqueta
Puente de la Barqueta
Andalucía de los Niños

Dr. Leal Castaño
Sor. Fr. Dorotea
Ronda de Pío XII
Pl. de Pío XII

Hospital Universitario
Antiguo Hospital de las Cinco Llagas
Calle Don Fabrique
Calle de Peralan de Ribera
Calle Manuel Villalobos
C. de la Manzana
C. de Fray Isidoro de Sevilla

Torre de los Perdigones
Calle Torneo
Calle Resolana Andueza

Basílica de la Macarena
Murallas
Puerta de la Macarena
Parroquia de San Gil
Convento de los Capuchinos
Cruz Roja

VISTAHERMOSA

Av. del Ombú
Av. del Ombú
Parque Científico y Tecnológico
Av. de los Arces
Av. de los Arces
JARDÍN DEL GUADALQUIVIR

ISLA DE LA CARTUJA

JARDINES DE LA CARTUJA
Auditorio
Centro Andaluz de Arte Contemporáneo
JARDÍN DE LAS AMÉRICAS
Puerta Cartuja

Monasterio de San Clemente
Monasterio de San Jerónimo
Meandro de San Jerónimo

C. de Escobares
C. del Peral
Omnium Sanctorum
Santa Marina
Calle de San Luis
Calle de la Feria
Pl. del Cronista
C. de Relator
C. Amargura
A. Margura
Convento de Santa Isabel
Convento de Santa Paula
Escuelas Salesianas
Pl. Antonio Martelo
FONTANAL
Ronda de Capuchinos
Avenida de Carmona
C. de Alfaro
Pl. del Pelicano
C. María Auxiliadora

Monasterio de Santa María de las Cuevas

Pabellón de la Navegación

Puerto Expo

Torre Sevilla

Pl. de Armas
Plaza de Chapina

Camino de los Descubrimientos
Pasarela de la Cartuja
Calle Torneo
Calle de San Vicente
Calle Juan Rabadán
Calle Alameda de Hércules
C. de Santa Clara
C. de Lumbreras
Gran Poder
C. de Santa Ana
C. Conde de Barajas
C. Pascual de Gayangos
Pl. Blasco de Garay
Baños
C. de los
Parlamento Andaluz
C. de Jesús del Gran Poder

Jesús del Gran Poder
San Martín
Pl. San Martín
Palacio de las Dueñas
San Luis
San Juan de la Palma
Pl. del
San Marcos
Pl. San Román
Santa Catalina
San Andrés
Convento de Espíritu Santo
C. Bustos Tavera
C. Duque Cornejo
Santa Catalina
Recaredo
C. de Urquiza
C. José Laguillo
Pl. C. Gonzalo de Bilbao
C. Amado de los Ríos
C. Juan Antonio Cavestany

Puente del Cachorro
Río Guadalquivir
Calle Marqués de Paradas
Calle de Arjona
Calle de Reyes Católicos
Pl. San Laureano
Plaza San Laureano
Museo de Bellas Artes
Calle Alfonso XII
Pl. del Museo
Santa María Magdalena
Plaza de Armas
Parlamento Andaluz
C. O'Donnell
Casa de la Memoria
Metropol Parasol
Pl. de la Encarnación
Campana
Pab. Sev.
La Anunciación
Casa de la Condesa de Lebrija
San José
Cuna
San Pedro
Casa de Pilatos
San Esteban
San Ildefonso
C. de Ibarra
Pelayo
Ruinas Acueducto
C.A.I. Contreras
Calle de Luis Montoto
C. de San Esteban
C. Conde de Ibarra
C. Madrid
C. Viriato
C. Corral del Rey
C. de las Águilas
C. de Santiago
Pl. C. Escuelas Pías
C. Apodaca
C. Mejías
Pl. de los Terceros
Pl. de San Pedro

Centro de la Cerámica de Triana
Castillo San Jorge
Puente de Isabel II
TRIANA
C. de Castilla
San Jacinto
Parroquia de Santa Ana
C. Rodrigo de Triana
Calle Pages del Corro
C. San Jacinto
Evangelista
Pl. Armando Jannone
C. E. M. Herrera
C. del Salado
Sánchez Arjona
C. del Trabajo

C. Reyes Católicos
C.S. Pablo
C. S. Carlos Cañal
C. de Carlos Cañal
Pl. Nueva
Ayuntamiento
C. Zaragoza
Pl. San Francisco
C. Albareda
C. Moratín
C. Dos de Mayo
Pl. San Molviedro
Argote de Molina
El Salvador
Pl. del Salvador
Cta. Rosario
Museo del Baile Flamenco
SANTA CRUZ
Palacio Arzobispal
Santa Cruz
Santa María la Blanca
Centro de Interpretación Judería de Sevilla
C. de Menéndez
Capitán Vigueras
C. Almirante Apodaca
Calle Demetrio de los Ríos
C. Juan de Zoyas
C. Jiménez Aranda
C. Manuel Pérez
C. Benito
C. de Luis Montoto

Catedral y Giralda
Archivo General de Indias
EL ARENAL
Plaza de Toros de la Maestranza
C. de Adriano
Paseo de Cristóbal Colón
C. Antonio Díaz
Hospital de la Caridad
Teatro de la Maestranza
Torre del Oro
Puerta de Jerez
C. San Fernando
Pl. V. de los Reyes
Pl. del Triunfo
Conv. de la Encarnación
Alcázar y Jardines
Museo Casa Murillo
Monumento a Colón
JARDINES DE MURILLO
C. de Cádiz
C. San Benito

Hotel Alfonso XIII
Universidad (Real Fábrica de Tabacos)
Palacio de San Telmo
JARDINES DE SAN TELMO
Giratoria San Diego
Teatro Lope de Vega
Puerta de Jerez
Av. de Roma
C. San Fernando
Don Juan Sebastián de Austria
Av. de Carlos V
Prado de SAN SEBASTIÁN
PRADO DE SAN SEBASTIÁN
Av. de Portugal
Av. de Málaga
Pl. San
Pl. de Ruiz de Alba
Calle Enramadilla
San Bernardo
C. Doctor Pedro Castro
C. Las Cruzadas
C. Plácido Fernández Viagas
Cuartel de Ingenieros

Plaza República Dominicana
Parque de los Príncipes
Avenida de la República Argentina
LOS REMEDIOS
Calle Virgen
C. del Turia
Plaza de Cuba
C. de Niebla
Calle Lope de Vega
C. de las Delicias
Plaza de Cuba
C. del Mino
Calle López de Gomara
C. Santa Fe
C. Virgen de Olivo
Calle Virgen de la Cinta
Asunción
C. Virgen del Águila
C. del Padre Damián
Carmelo VI
Calle Juan Sebastián Elcano
Monte Carmelo
C. del Salado

Plaza de España
Monumento a Bécquer
Capitanía General
Giratoria de los Marineros Voluntarios
Glorieta de las Cigarreras
Puente de los Remedios
Giratoria Buenos Aires
Gta. Covadonga
PARQUE DE MARÍA LUISA
Pabellón Real
Museo de Artes y Costumbres Populares
Museo Arqueológico
Plaza de América
Paseo de las Delicias
Av. de Hernán Cortés
C. de Santiago Montoto
C. Brasil
C. del Porvenir
C. de San Salvador
C. de Felipe II
Calle Juan Pablos
Calle Bogotá

Av. Blas Infante
PARQUE DE LOS PRÍNCIPES
Av. Alfredo Kraus
Av. Flota de Indias
Calle Gitanillo de Triana
Calle Bienvenida
Calle Joselito el Gallo
Calle J. Belmonte
Av. Presidente Adolfo Suárez

cathedral, dates from the Almohad era, as does the Torre del Oro.

After a 15-month siege by Fernando III in 1248, Seville was recaptured by the Christians. Seville then entered a golden age, and in 1401 construction began on the massive new Cathedral, which was to replace the mosque. The city was the home port for Christopher Columbus returning from his voyage of discovery in 1492. In 1503 Seville's Casa de Contratación was awarded the monopoly on Spanish trade with the Americas, ushering in a period of unprecedented prosperity that lasted nearly two centuries.

By the early 1600s Seville, with a population of 85,000, which included 7,000 slaves, was probably the fourth largest city in the world, after Naples, Paris and Venice. The ships departed and returned in convoys (in 1608 alone there were 283 sailings from Seville to the New World), creating periods of great activity and, inevitably, great inactivity. Seville had a vicious underworld whose gangs were always at each other's throats. And with the gold on the ships came disease. During the most serious epidemics up to 600 people died in the city every day.

By the late 17th century Seville was in decline. A combination of larger ships, an accumulation of silt in the Guadalquivir, improved facilities at Cádiz and a decreasing flow of desirable goods from America resulted in a downturn in trade. In 1680 the Admiralty was transferred to Cádiz, followed by the Casa de Contratación in 1717. In 1810, during the Wars of Independence, French troops occupied Seville, remaining for two years until expelled with the help of the Duke of Wellington (considered a hero in Spain to this day). Subsequently, Seville lapsed into a quiet, almost provincial town.

Nonetheless, 1848 was the inaugural year of the world-famous Feria de Sevilla, and the Ibero-American Exposition was held in 1929. During the Spanish Civil War, Seville was one of the first cities to fall to Franco's Nationalist rebels, who used the captured Radio Sevilla to spread their propaganda. To this day the Guadalquivir forms the basis of the city's prosperity, as it has through the centuries. Indeed, Seville is the only river port in Spain.

ORIENTATION

The most important sights in Seville are clustered around the southern edge of the old city, sandwiched between the Avenida de la Constitución, San Fernando and Menéndez Pelayo. Next to Constitución is the Cathedral and the Archivo de Indias, with the Alcázar, a stone's throw to the south, its walls the eastern border of the labyrinthine Barrio de Santa Cruz, the former Jewish quarter.

Between Constitución and the river are the Hospital de la Caridad, the Torre del Oro and the Plaza de Toros. The Museo de Bellas Artes, the Casa de Pilatos, the Alameda de Hércules and the main shopping area centring on Calle Sierpes lie to the north.

La Gitana, just one of the lively bars in the Barrio de Santa Cruz.

To the south, and still east of the river, the land is more open and the architecture grander; here you will find the old Tobacco Factory, now the University, and the exotic relics the 1929 Ibero-American Exhibition, including Hotel Alfonso XIII, the Plaza de España, San Telmo Palace and the Parque de María Luisa.

West of the river, opposite the Torre del Oro and the Plaza de Toros is the old Barrio de Triana, home to Seville's gypsies until they moved to high-rise apartments on the edge of town, allowing for the slow gentrification of the area. A little further north is the Isla de la Cartuja, the site of the 1992 World Fair, now the site of the Isla Mágica theme park.

THE CATHEDRAL

The **Cathedral** Ⓐ (Catedral y Giralda; Mon 11am–3pm, Tue–Sat 11am–5pm, Sun 2.30–6pm; audioguides available) is listed in the *Guinness Book of Records* simply for being big, but the close-packed streets that cluster around this vast edifice make this hard to

appreciate from the outside. Along with the Alcázar (see page 83) and Archivo General de Indias (see page 85), it's a Unesco World Heritage Site.

A mosque was built on this site in 1172, and 12 years later a minaret was added. The huge Almohad mosque was consecrated for Christian use immediately after the Reconquest, but it was not until the beginning of the 15th century that work began on raising a cathedral.

The bulk of the Cathedral was built between 1401 and 1507; thus the principal structure is Gothic, with later additions, such as the choir, altar and Sacristía de los Cálices, which are late Gothic (1496–1537); the Capilla Real (1530–69) at the eastern end, which is plateresque (intricately ornamented, from *platero*, meaning silversmith) and additions to the southern end, which are baroque.

Independent visitors enter the cathedral by the **Puerta de San Cristóbal** (groups enter via the Puerta del Lagarto). A reception area leads through a small museum containing

Sevillana ladies in colourful costumes at the April Feria.

paintings (including work by Zurbarán and Murillo), church plate and other items of interest.

A faded photocopy of the *Guinness Book of Records* certificate sits in a glass information case alongside the Cathedral's floor plan: 126 metres (413 ft) long by 83 metres (272 ft) wide by 30 metres (100 ft) high, the Cathedral has the largest interior in the world, and is the third-largest cathedral in Christendom, after St Peter's in Rome and St Paul's Cathedral in London.

Inside, the Cathedral's immensity is not instantly apparent, as the centre of the building is filled by the **Capilla Mayor** (Main Chapel). The altarpiece of gilded hardwood contains 36 tableaux of the Old and New Testaments, comprising more than 1,000 figures. Reaching 20 metres (66 ft) in height, almost to the roof, it was begun in 1482 by the Flemish sculptor Pieter Dancart and not finished for another 82 years.

In 1995 it was the dazzling focus for the marriage of King Juan Carlos's daughter Elena and Jaime de Marichalar y Sáenz.

Nearby is the Gothic-Mudéjar **Choir** *(coro)*. Examine the detail in the carving, including the beautifully carved misericords.

On the south side, close to the entrance, is the grand but rather comic monument to Christopher Columbus, the great man's tomb carried by four figures representing the kingdoms that made up the Spanish crown at the time of his voyage – Castile, Navarre, Aragón and León. Many of Columbus's voyages were planned in Seville, as is documented by the Archivo General de Indias (see page 85). It is not certain that the elaborate sarcophagus contains the remains of the great discoverer, as Columbus's widow had these taken to Santo Domingo in the Dominican Republic, from where they were later moved to Havana's cathedral and then back to Spain, a confusing journey that was poorly documented. Attempts to test the DNA of the bone fragments have so far proved inconclusive.

Before climbing La Giralda, the minaret of the original mosque, it is worth exploring the numerous side chapels

Tip

Although the Cathedral doesn't open to tourists until 11am, worshippers can attend Mass at 8.30am. Also, Sevilla Walking Tours (Mon, Wed & Fri 1pm; charge; tel: 902-158 226, 616-501 100; www.sevillawalkingtours.com) offers guided tours of the cathedral in English, which last 70 minutes and leave from the statue in Plaza del Triunfo.

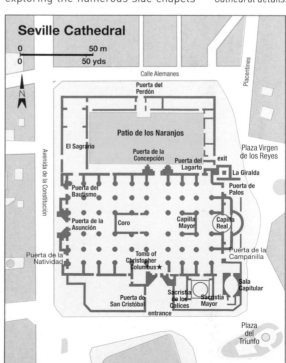

Cathedral details.

Seville Cathedral

0   50 m
0   50 yds

N

Calle Alemanes

Puerta del Perdón

Patio de los Naranjos

El Sagrario

Puerta de la Concepción

Puerta del Lagarto

exit

Plaza Virgen de los Reyes

La Giralda

Puerta de Palos

Puerta del Bautismo

Avenida de la Constitución

Puerta de la Asunción

Coro

Capilla Mayor

Capilla Real

Puerta de la Campanilla

Puerta de la Natividad

Tomb of Christopher Columbus ★

Placentines

Puerta de San Cristóbal

Sacristía de los Cálices

Sacristía Mayor

Sala Capitular

entrance

Plaza del Triunfo

and anterooms (especially on the south side), many of which are adorned with important paintings and statues. The treasury (**Sacristía Mayor**) contains a wealth of silverware, as well as the keys given to Fernando III by the Muslim and Jewish citizens following the Reconquest of Seville in1248.

Next door, the **Sacristía de los Cálices**, which has a fine vaulted ceiling, is hung with paintings by Goya, Valdés Leal and Zurbarán, among others. Look out for Goya's anachronistic painting of Justa and Rufina, Sevillian saints martyred during Diocletian's persecution of the Christians. Behind the 3rd-century saints is the 12th-century Giralda tower.

In the eastern corner of the Cathedral is the 16th-century **Sala Capitular** (Chapter House). Built in elliptical shape with leather seats and marble floor, it was specifically designed for convocations of the Cathedral Council. Poised above the archbishop's throne is Murillo's fine *Inmaculada*, dominant in a series of Murillos incorporated in the dome.

At the eastern end of the Cathedral is the **Capilla Real** (Royal Chapel), the most used and ornate of the side chapels, containing the royal tomb of Fernando III. Fittingly, his remains lie at the feet of the Virgen de los Reyes, the patron saint of Seville. Also here is the tomb of Fernando's queen, Beatriz, and his son Alfonso X (the Wise). On the north side of the Cathedral, don't miss the **Capilla de San Antonio** containing Murillo's *Vision of St Antony of Padua*.

LA GIRALDA

Literally and figuratively, the high spot of the cathedral is the tower, the much-photographed 94-metre (308-ft) minaret, which has been admired ever since its inception on the orders of Moorish ruler Abu-Yaqub Yusuf in 1184. The exterior, adorned with typical *sebka* decoration, is in direct contrast to the bland interior, where a series of 35 gently elevated ramps (designed so that horsemen could ride up them) lead visitors to an observation platform at a height of 70 metres (230 ft). Archaeological finds and other interesting items

Waiting for customers by the cathedral.

are displayed on the landings; they include a pair of 14th-century Mudéjar doors combining Gothic motifs and verses from the Koran.

From the top there are panoramic views of the city, the many patios invisible from street level unveiled in the patchwork below. You can also appreciate the immense scale of the cathedral from here, its soaring pinnacles and flying buttresses.

La Giralda is said to be the finest relic of the Almohad dynasty (although two similar minarets exist in Rabat and Marrakesh). Its beauty reputedly saved it from destruction following the Reconquest in 1248. When negotiating the terms of their surrender, Muslim rulers, tormented by the prospect of the mosque and minaret falling under Christian control, wanted them destroyed. But Alfonso the Wise is said to have refused their plea, threatening to put to death anyone who attempted it.

An earthquake destroyed the tower's original ornamental top in 1356, and it was not until 1558 that it was replaced by the bells and weather vane (*giralda* in Spanish) – a goddess representing Faith by Hernán Ruiz.

Off the north side of the Cathedral, near the access to La Giralda, is the **Patio de los Naranjos**, the courtyard of the original mosque, from where you exit the Cathedral. The nearby **Puerta del Lagarto** (Gate of the Lizard) is named after a life-size wooden alligator hanging from the ceiling, purportedly a replica of a live alligator given to Alfonso X by the Sultan of Egypt.

THE ALCÁZAR

The second architectural jewel in Seville is a short hop from La Giralda. Hidden behind battlemented ochre walls on the Plaza del Triunfo is the **Alcázar** Ⓑ (Alcázar y Jardines; daily, Apr–Sept 9.30am–7pm, Oct–Mar 9:30am–5pm; audioguide available), the fortress-palace of both Muslim and Christian rulers.

The Moroccan invaders built the first fortress on this site in 712. In the 9th century a palace, walls of which are still standing, was added by Amir Abdal-Rahman II. The Moors built additional palaces, though these were still in the

The exquisite Salón de los Embajadores.

Mudéjar motif in the Patio de las Doncellas.

fortress style, and added to the gardens during the 11th and 12th centuries.

Following the Reconquest, the Catholic Monarchs established a court here, and King Don Pedro (known as Pedro the Cruel) built a luxurious Mudéjar style palace on this site in 1364. It was renovated in the 16th century by Carlos V.

The juxtaposition of the contrasting styles has created a particularly intriguing complex. The examples of Moorish architecture are surpassed only by those found in the Alhambra.

VISITING THE ALCÁZAR

The entrance to the complex is through the **Puerta del León**, marked by a heraldic lion, in the original 11th-century walls. Beyond the ticket office are the gardens of the **Patio del León**, a former assembly ground, at the far end of which three arches lead into the Patio de la Montería, the inner courtyard. Before proceeding through here, take the passage in the far-left corner to reach the **Sala de Justicia**, considered to be the first example of Mudéjar-style architecture, built by Alfonso XI, and beyond that

The Moorish Baños de María de Padilla.

the lovely **Patio del Yeso** (Courtyard of Plasterwork), which formed part of the 12th-century Almohad palace.

Regaining the Patio del León, proceed through the arches to the **Patio de la Montería**, faced by the ornate façade of Don Pedro's Palace. On the right hand side is the **Sala del Almirante** (Admiral's Hall), containing historical memorabilia and 18th-century paintings depicting the overthrow of the Moors. It was here that the Catholic Monarchs founded the Casa de la Contratación, for the organisation of expeditions to the New World. Its functions included the furnishing of embarkation permits; the inspection of ships; the supply of mercury for refining silver; the registration of merchandise and the handling of the gold, silver and pearls destined for the royal exchequer. It also administered justice, saw to the despatch of missionaries, and served as a centre for navigational studies.

In the adjacent **Chapel** (which has a fine 16th-century coffered ceiling), the altar painting has a nautical theme appropriate to the rooms, which were specifically built for the planning of naval expeditions. A figure hidden in the Virgen de los Navegantes' skirts is supposed to be Christopher Columbus.

The main entrance to the palace is surmounted by an inscription to Pedro the Cruel. Inside, turn left. The dog-leg vestibule (typical of Arab architecture but here also used to confuse would-be assassins) leads into the **Patio de las Doncellas** (Maids Courtyard). It has a compact grace and quiet beauty. Koranic inscriptions ('None but Allah Conquers') combine with Mudéjar motifs.

Notable in the apartments is the magnificent **Salón de los Embajadores** (Ambassador's Hall), effectively the throne room, dating from the 11th-century palace. It has an intricately carved and gilded dome (15th-century), resting on a frieze of alternating castles and lions, and exquisite geometric and floral carvings on the walls.

Beyond is the small **Patio de las Muñe-cas** (Courtyard of the Dolls), a private family chamber, named after two tiny faces, eroded but still visible, in the decoration on the columns, and the **Cuarto del Príncipe** (Prince's Suite), named after the son of the Catholic Monarchs, who was born here in 1478.

The Christian royal inhabitants also left their mark on the Alcázar in a more predictable manner, notably in the **Gothic Palace**, containing the **Salones de Carlos V** (Charles V's Apartments). The banquet room was the setting for the marriage of Carlos V and Doña Isabel of Portugal; its windows were added by his son, Felipe II, who introduced Renaissance trends. Charles's military campaigns in Tunisia are depicted in faded tapestries by the Dutch artist Juan de Vermayen, who included a self-portrait in his upside-down map of the Mediterranean.

THE ALCÁZAR'S GARDENS

The Salones de Carlos V lead into the **Gardens**, a complex of patios, pools and pavilions. Nearest to the Salones de Carlos V is the Garden of El Estanque (The Pool), Renaissance in style but set around a rectangular pool that once irrigated the Moors' orchards. From here the **Gallery of El Etrusco** (1612–21), with views over the Garden of Las Damas (The Ladies), follows the course of the **Almohad Wall**. Evening concerts are held here in summer.

Before leaving the Alcázar look out for the **Baños de María de Padilla**, the Moorish baths of Pedro the Cruel's mistress, who was said to have had several lovers. Men of the court lined up for the strangely erotic act of drinking her bathwater – all except one who, it is said, excused himself on the grounds that 'having tasted the sauce, he might covet the partridge'.

ARCHIVO GENERAL DE INDIAS

Between the Alcázar and the Cathedral is a square, rather austere Renaissance-style building, once the Lonja (Stock Exchange) and now housing the **Archivo General de Indias** C (Mon–Sat 9.30am–5pm, Sun and holidays 10am–2pm; free admission). Constructed between

The Alcázar Gardens.

Tip

For a modern and luxurious version of the Arab *hammam* (bathhouse) visit Aire de Sevilla, Calle Aire, 15 (www.airedesevilla.com, daily 10am–10pm) in the Barrio de Santa Cruz. The atmospherically lit baths are housed in the Roman foundations of a 16th-century mansion which was built for a wealthy trader.

Archivo General de Indias.

1583 and 1596 by Juan de Herrera, the architect of El Escorial near Madrid, its central patio, main marble staircase, and unusual Cuban wood shelves are of intrinsic interest. The collection comprises some 80 million pages relating to the discovery and colonisation of the New World. A small exhibition of historic and highly colourful documents, including extracts from Columbus's letters and diary, is maintained in one of the long galleries up the stairs. There's also a room containing some works by Goya.

SANTA CRUZ

The northeastern wall of the Alcázar borders on the **Barrio de Santa Cruz** Ⓓ, the former Judería (Jewish quarter), which is entered by an archway in one corner of the Patio Banderas (from which you exit the Alcázar). You can find out about the city's Jewish history in a well put together exhibition at the **Centro de Interpretación Judería de Sevilla** (Calle Ximénez de Enciso 22; www.juderiadesevilla.es; daily 11am–7pm). This corner of Seville unashamedly celebrates a fair few clichés about the city:

the Seville patio is here in super-abundance, with *azulejo*-decorated courtyards glimpsed through wrought-iron gates, and young men playing flamenco in the squares. The Plaza de Santa Cruz is the site of Los Gallos, one of the best-known of the traditional flamenco venues in town.

Calle Justino de Neve or Pimienta will lead you to the Plaza Venerables at the centre of the barrio and the **Hospital de los Venerables Sacerdotes** (Thu–Sat 10am–6pm; free first Thu of the month 10am–2pm; audioguides available), founded in 1675 by Justino de Neve as a home for retired priests. This lovely two-level structure, with its slightly sunken central patio, is considered one of the best examples of baroque architecture in the city. Its most famous asset is the painting Santa Rufina by Diego Velázquez.

Santa Cruz is sometimes criticised for being overly prettified and not much better than a tourist trap, but, with its many bars, restaurants and interesting little shops, it remains an appealing place to wander on a summer evening.

BETWEEN THE CATHEDRAL AND THE GUADALQUIVIR RIVER

Running south of the Cathedral, parallel to the river, is the Avenida de la Constitución. Between here and the river lies an old and characterful area of Seville known as El Arenal, the old port area. It has good traditional bars and restaurants, and includes the Torre del Oro, the Plaza de Toros and the Hospital de la Caridad, a 17th-century charitable hospital with a richly endowed baroque chapel.

From the Avenida de la Constitución, walk towards the river down Calle Almirantazgo, perhaps stopping in the **Plaza del Cabildo**, the scene of a coin-collectors' market on Sunday and the location of **El Torno**, a shop selling biscuits and knitted babywear made by nuns from the convents in Seville. Alternatively, take Calle Santander from Constitución, passing the former **Real Casa de Moneda** (Royal Mint), a fine building which is being restored.

The **Hospital de la Santa Caridad** **E** (www.santacaridad.es; daily 10.30am–7.30pm; free Mon 2–6pm; audioguides available), on Calle Temprado, was founded in 1674 as a charity hospital for the homeless and the sick, a function it still serves to this day. It is best-known for the outstanding artworks in its chapel, which exemplifies such institutions' great patronage of the arts during Seville's Golden Age. In addition to the highly ornate *Holy Interment* altarpiece by Pedro Roldán, considered one of the finest baroque altarpieces in Spain, the walls are hung with remarkable paintings. There are works by Murillo and, above and opposite the entrance, two spine-tingling works by Valdés Leal showing the transitory nature of life, which passes *In Ictu Oculi* (In the Blink of an Eye).

Leaving the hospital you will see in the small garden opposite a statue of Don Miguel de Mañara, a dissolute Calatrava Knight who reputedly established the charitable hospital after experiencing a vision of his own funeral procession. Don Miguel is considered by some to be the role model for the legendary Don Juan, the cynical lover with 1,003 Spanish mistresses. Decide for yourself if this man looks like a reformed seducer or the eponymous hero of Mozart's *Don Giovanni*, who is eventually dragged down to hell by demons.

Just a block away on the riverbank, the **Torre del Oro** **F** (once covered with golden tiles) stands like a chess piece on the bank of the river. Dating from 1220, it was built outside the city walls as a watchtower. It also served a defensive purpose by anchoring a chain that stretched across the river. At other times it was used to store gold brought back from the Americas, and as a prison. The round top and spire were added in the 18th century. Today the tower houses a **Maritime Museum** (Mon–Fri 9.30am–6.45pm, Sat–Sun 10.30am–6.45pm; free Mon; audioguides available) filled with fascinating odds and ends, from a shark's jaws to paintings of the famous navigators.

◉ Where

The Torre del Oro on the east bank of the Guadalquivir is the starting point for hour-long river cruises, which leave every 30 minutes (daily 11am–7pm, until 10pm Apr–Oct). They also run a day trip to Sanlúcar de Barrameda (May–Sept Sat & Sun) which leaves at 8.30am. Buy tickets at the quayside.

The night is young in the Barrio de Santa Cruz.

Murals here show how Seville in the 1700s was a great maritime port.

As well as being the starting point for river cruises, the tower marks the start of hop-on, hop-off bus tours.

A little upstream to the north is the modern **Teatro de la Maestranza** opera house (Calle Núñez de Balboa), built in 1991, and beyond it the **Plaza de Toros de La Maestranza** , the bullring (daily 9.30am–7pm, until 9pm Apr–Oct; free Mon 3–7pm), one of the oldest rings in the country. Guided 45-minute tours (every 20 min) in English and Spanish take in the bullring, the museum, matadors' chapel, operating theatre and stables.

NORTH OF THE CATHEDRAL

North of the cathedral, the Avenida de la Constitución leads up to the **Plaza Nueva** , on which stands the old, plateresque **Ayuntamiento** (Town Hall), dating from 1572. Behind and east of it is the **Plaza San Francisco**. Narrow streets from the top right of the plaza lead to the 17th-century church of **El Salvador** , at a nexus of shops

The 13th-century Torre del Oro.

selling wedding dresses. This church, ramshackle from the outside but with spectacular gold *retablos* (altarpieces), was built on the site of earlier places of worship, including the city's first mosque. Excavations have also uncovered evidence of a Roman temple and early Christian, Visigoth and Mozarbic churches. Notice the Arabic inscriptions above the side door.

From here it is a short hop to busy **Plaza Alfalfa**, a little square with a great patisserie (Horno de San Buenaventura), and the site of a pet market on Sunday mornings. Just south of here, at Calle Manuel Rojas Marcos, 3 (off Calle San Isidoro) is the inspired **Museo del Baile Flamenco** (Flamenco Museum; daily 10am–7pm), which has a performance space (flamenco lessons take place here) and relates the story of flamenco through objects, film, music and art. Nightly shows (7pm & 8.45pm) are held in the courtyard.

A little further east is the 16th-century **Casa de Pilatos** (Plaza de Pilatos; www.fundacionmedinaceli.org; daily 9am–7pm, until 6pm in winter;

audioguide available). Said to have been modelled on Pontius Pilate's house in Jerusalem, a place of pilgrimage for its original owner (hence its name), the house was built in Mudéjar and Renaissance styles. The central patio beyond the *apeadero* (carriage yard) is enclosed by a two-storey arcade of Moorish (bottom) and Gothic (top) arches.

This courtyard contains dazzling *azulejos* in puzzle-book patterns. To the right is the chapel and Pilate's study. A monumental staircase leads up to a late Mudéjar cupola dating from 1537.

Directly north from the Plaza Nueva is the pedestrianised **Calle Sierpes**, lined with stylish shops.

At Calle de la Cuna, 8 (parallel with Sierpes), **Palacio de la Condesa de Lebrija** Ⓚ (Sept–June Mon–Fri 10.30am–7.30pm, Sat 10am–2pm & 4–6pm, Sun 10am–2pm, July-Aug Mon–Fri 10am–3pm, Sat 10am–2pm; guided tours available), is an outstanding palace built in the 16th century and remodelled in the 19th with a Renaissance-Mudéjar patio and mosaics from Itálica, brought here by the late Countess of Lebrija,

who was an archaeologist. Next door in the palace's old stables is the **Casa de la Memoria** (Calle Cuna 6; www.casadelamemoria.es; daily 10.30am–2pm & 5–7pm), a flamenco cultural centre with a museum and authentic nightly shows at 7.30pm and 9pm (reserve in advance).

A short walk northeast of here is Plaza de la Encarnación, which is instantly recognisable by the spectacular **Metropol Parasol**. This curvy, mushroom-like wooden structure, designed by German architect Juergen Mayer H., has seven floors and houses a food market (Mon–Sat 8am–3pm), restaurants, a rooftop walkway (Sun–Thu 10am–11pm, Fri–Sat until 11.30pm) and, in its foundations, the **Museo Antiquarium** (Tue–Sat 10am–8pm, Sun 10am–2pm) where visitors can see the Roman remains uncovered during the building's construction.

Continuing northwest, the **Alameda de Hércules** is a broad avenue marked at one end by two pillars topped by statues of Julius Caesar and Hercules. It hosts a Sunday flea market *(rastro)* and forms the hub of a lingering red-light district. Many of the houses have

The striking Metropol Parasol is all curves.

LOOKING FOR CARMEN

Seville's Royal Tobacco Factory was the setting for one of the world's best-known operas. But who was the inspiration for the sultry cigarette maker?

When it was built between 1728 and 1766, the Real Fábrica de Tabacos (Royal Tobacco Factory), now part of Seville University, was the second-largest building in Spain after the Escorial palace near Madrid.

Here, thousands of women, known as *cigarreras*, worked to produce cigars and powdered snuff. The place was surrounded by tight security, for the Spanish State enjoyed a lucrative monopoly on the tobacco trade.

The tobacco factory, which functioned as such until the 1960s, is known as the home of Carmen, one of the most memorable literary stereotypes Spain has inspired. In the story, by the French dramatist Prosper Mérimée, published in 1845, the brigadier José Navarro becomes smitten with passion for a gypsy

A sultry Carmen, as painted by Miguel Muntanet.

cigarrera whom he must accompany to prison. He risks all by allowing her to escape, then deserts the army and becomes a smuggler and bandit for her sake.

But Carmen isn't faithful to her brigadier, and José stabs her to death outside the Maestranza bullring after he finds her flirting with a *toreador* (bullfighter).

Most people remember Carmen from Bizet's beloved opera, premiered 30 years after Mérimée's story was published. It marked a turning point in the genre, and continues to be the most popular opera in the world. The character Carmen came to represent the classic Andalusian temptress – demure yet defiant, feminine and independent at the same time, capable of turning men mad with desire.

Did Mérimée base his heroine on a real person? To find out, one should to cross the river to the Los Remedios district, where a modern building houses Seville's new tobacco factory. On the third floor are the archives from the old tobacco factory – thousands of ledgers, each containing lists of the women who worked at the factory, with specific descriptions of each one.

The books list quite a few women named Carmen or María del Carmen, any one of whom could have served as a model for Mérimée. One of them, for instance, is 'María del Carmen García, from Seville, unmarried, aged 15, small, light-coloured, black eyes, who was dismissed for having spoken insulting and scandalous words to her companions, and for throwing a pair of scissors at Concepción Vegue'. In fact, the custodian of this peculiar archive believes Merimée's Carmen was most likely a composite of the women who worked there when the author visited in 1840.

The Seville factory, in which up to 3,500 *cigarreras* would be working at one time, was Spain's biggest employer, and provided the first opportunity for women to gain financial independence from their menfolk. These *cigarreras* were the breadwinners in many a household, while their husbands loitered on street corners, smoking the cheroots that their womenfolk had smuggled out of the factory. The women organised themselves well, working in teams, with one member appointed to look after her colleagues' children. Their spirit of camaraderie and their self-confidence must have made a strong and lasting impression on Merimée.

been transformed into bars and clubs, some catering to the gay community.

The church of **Jesús del Gran Poder** **L** (the Powerful Jesus), on Plaza San Lorenzo, has an unusual image of Christ carrying the cross; worshippers kiss or touch the image's heel to help speed their prayers.

At the northern end of the old city, near Puerta Macarena, is the **Basílica de la Macarena** **M**, built in 1949 to house the Virgen de la Esperanza (La Macarena), Seville's best-loved icon. She leaves her pedestal once a year during Semana Santa. A small museum contains her many costumes for the journey and the *paso* (bearer) on which she is carried.

THE MUSEO DE BELLAS ARTES

Northwest of the Plaza Nueva is the **Museo de Bellas Artes** **N** (Fine Arts Museum; Plaza del Museo; mid-June–mid-Sept Tue–Sun 9am–3pm, mid-Sept–mid-June Tue–Sat 9am–8pm, Sun and holidays 9am–3pm; free to EU visitors), housed in the 17th-century Convento de la Merced Calzada, which was closed following the disentailment of many convents and monasteries in 1835. Its architectural highlight is the magnificent baroque chapel with frescoed vaulting and dome. Considered second in national importance after the Prado, its collection is well worth seeing. There are works by El Greco, Goya, Murillo, Zurbarán, Velázquez and Valdés Leal, among others, many expropriated from religious properties. Don't miss the carved Christs, Virgins and saints in gilded and polychrome wood.

SOUTH OF THE CATHEDRAL

South of the Cathedral, the Avenida de la Constitución leads past the Archivo de Indias (see page 85) to the Puerta Jerez roundabout, marking the site of one of the old city gates.

Just off the roundabout is the palatial **Hotel Alfonso XIII** **O**, built in imitation of the Seville patio style specifically for the 1929 Ibero-American Exhibition. The bar, once a favourite haunt of American writer Ernest Hemingway, is a great place to enjoy an early-evening cocktail while listening to the resident pianist.

The grandiose Hotel Alfonso XIII.

Alongside the hotel is one of the biggest buildings in the Western world, erected in 1750 to house the **Real Fábrica de Tabacos** ⓟ (Royal Tobacco Factory), in which the mythical Carmen immortalised by Bizet in his opera of the same name supposedly worked with thousands of other *cigarreras* (see feature). Now this handsome, if austere, building is part of the University (Mon–Fri 8am–8.30pm, Sat 8am–2pm; free tours Mon–Thu at 11am). For a rather idealised picture of life in the factory in its heyday, visit the Museo de Bellas Artes (see page 91), where there are several paintings showing the factory women at work.

Beyond the University are the beginnings of the Parque de María Luisa and the site of Seville's Ibero-American Exhibition of 1929. Some of the pavilions have been put to new uses, such as the biological research station for the Coto Doñana Nature Reserve (Avenida de Chile), which has a striking courtyard in pink marble decorated with animal carvings. The most eye-catching legacy of the exhibition is the semi-circular

Plaza de España ⓠ. The extraordinary moated building surrounding it took 15 years to build and functioned as the Spanish pavilion. Its towers were inspired by the cathedral at Santiago de Compostela, and the elaborately tiled panels below the colonnade depict the Spanish provinces, running in alphabetical order from left to right. The moat has little *azulejo*-decorated bridges and rowing boats for hire.

Across from the plaza is the **Parque de María Luisa** ⓡ, a successful mixture of formal landscaping and wilderness areas, where familiar European plants and flowers are found next to exotic species from Africa and the Americas. Its shady paths are wonderfully cool on a stiflingly hot summer's day and lovely to tour by carriage or bicycle in the early evening (bikes and tricycles can be hired near the gates). It is full of life and surprises: *azulejo*-covered benches; ceramic frogs spouting water; walled patios with frescos; duck sanctuaries full of white doves.

The park once belonged to the **Palacio de San Telmo**, now the headquarters

The moated
Plaza de España.

of the Andalusian regional government, which stands at its northern end. St Telmo is the patron saint of sailors, and this building, which has an elaborately carved baroque main archway, was built in the 17th century as a university for seafarers. In the 18th century it became a naval academy, and was later expanded into the residence of the dukes of Montpensier. Duchess Marie Louise of Orléans donated the grounds to the city in 1893.

TWO MUSEUMS

The **Plaza de América** at the southern end of the park is the location for two museums. The **Museo Arqueológico ⑤** (Archaeological Museum; mid-June–mid-Sept Tue–Sun 9am–3.30pm, mid-Sept–mid-June Tue–Sat 9am–7.30pm, Sun 9am–3.30pm; free to EU visitors) covers local excavation sites, with representative material from Neolithic through to Tartessian, Roman and Moorish times. Pottery, silver and gold work include items originating from the countries of Andalucía's trading partners at the time, such as painted ceramics from Phoenicia. The Roman collection is typical of the significant Roman cities that once surrounded Seville, a map of which is on the wall.

In particular, seek out the replica Caramholo Treasure (the original items are kept in a bank vault), a cache of 21 beautifully worked gold pieces (jewellery and statuettes) found during construction work in Seville in 1961. Dating from around the 5th century BC, the treasure is possible evidence of the mysterious Tartessian civilisation.

Opposite, the sleepy **Museo de Artes y Costumbres Populares ❼** (Arts and Folklore Museum; mid-June–mid-Sept Tue–Sun 9am–3pm, mid-Sept–mid-June Tue–Sat 9am–8pm, Sun 9am–3pm; free to EU visitors) celebrates some familiar aspects of Andalusian culture – famous bullfighters, the Seville Feria, Semana Santa traditions and traditional costumes (with excellent background classical music) as well as tiles from La Cartuja.

TRIANA

A little west of the Plaza de Toros, the lovely **Puente de Isabel II**, with a statue

Parque de María Luisa, Seville's green oasis.

of the famous bullfighter Manolete (1917–47) at its end, crosses the Guadalquivir to the **Triana ⓤ** district, once known as the gypsy quarter but now a lively working-class area visited during the day for the ceramic factories and at night for its restaurants and bars (expensive along the riverside **Calle Betis**, which has wonderful views over to the Torre del Oro on the east bank; cheaper along **Calle Castilla** and nearby side streets). A favourite for local specialities is **Casa Cuesta**, on the corner of Castilla and San Jorge. Opposite, a dark alleyway, appropriately named the **Callejón de la Inquisición** (Seville witnessed some of the Spanish Inquisition's greatest purges) leads down to the river. You can find out more about the area's gruesome history at the **Castillo de San Jorge** (Plaza del Altozano; Tue–Sat 10am–1.30pm & 5–7.30pm, Sun 10am–1.30pm; free), where the first council of the Spanish Inquisition was held in 1481, and its ceramics industry at the Centro Cerámica Triana (Calle Antillano Campos 14; Tue–Sat 11am–5.30pm, Sun 10am–2.30pm).

Fishing along the river, looking across to the Triana district.

EXPO SITE

To the north of Triana, the **Isla de la Cartuja** used to be a swampy wasteland, but was transformed for the Expo '92 Universal Exposition, commemorating the 500th anniversary of Columbus's discovery of the Americas. The area was landscaped and a new outdoor auditorium built, while two new suspension bridges were constructed to connect the 'island' to the rest of Seville, the elegant, wishbone-shaped **Alamillo**, designed by the well-known Spanish architect Santiago Calatrava, and the **Barqueta** bridge, the main link to the Isla Mágica theme park (see below). Afterwards part of La Cartuja was transformed into a technological park.

Isla Mágica (tel: 902-161 716; www.islamagica.es; opening times vary throughout the year) is a 35-hectare (86-acre) fantasyland of roller-coaster and other rides, all with a South American theme, plus live shows with actors in period costume. New attractions are added regularly.

El Pabellon de la Navegación (Camino de los Descubrimientos 2; Apr–Oct

Tue–Sat 11am–8.30pm, Sun and holidays 11am–3pm, Nov–Mar Tue–Sat 10am–7.30pm, Sun and holidays 10am–3pm) was originally built for Expo '92 and has now been turned into a state-of-the-art navigation museum whose permanent collections show what life was like on the ocean wave in times past; climb up the Torre Schindler for some great views over the city. Nearby, the 180-metre (590 ft) Torre Sevilla is Andalucia's tallest building.

The island is named after the 15th-century **Carthusian Monastery**, Santa María de las Cuevas, at its centre. Columbus was a regular visitor, and was temporarily buried here when he died. In the 19th and 20th centuries, the monastery had a ceramics factory, where the prized Cartuja china was made until 1982. Part of the building houses the **Centro Andaluz de Arte Contemporáneo** (www.caac.es; Tue–Sat 11am–9pm, Sun 10am–3pm; free Tue–Fri 7–9pm & Sat all day), showing temporary international exhibitions and a permanent exhibition of modern Andalusian art.

SEVILLE PROVINCE

The industrial and residential influence of Seville extends some way into the countryside, but there are no other towns of any real size in the province. To the north lies the Sierra Morena, a vast belt of hills covered with rough woodland; to the south lie agricultural flatlands dominated by the Guadalquivir; to the west is the province of Huelva; and to the east soft rolling agricultural land, the Campiña, has a chain of ancient settlements.

Visitors heading due south in the winter months may find minor roads frustrating; a combination of heavy rain and high tides can mean many a route is cut by swollen streams. The central town to these flatlands is **Los Palacios**, a quiet, rural place and the site of an agricultural research station.

WEST OF SEVILLE

Once across the Guadalquivir, roads west of Seville swiftly leave the city behind. Up the far bank of the river to the north, near Santiponce, is the Roman site of **Itálica** ② (Tue–Sat,

⊙ Tip

It's easy to get to Itálica from Seville by public transport. Take bus M-170A (20 min journey express) or M-170B (30 min journey) from Plaza de Armas station. Buses leave regularly throughout the day. Ask at the tourist office or station about times.

Apr–mid-June 9am–7.30pm, mid-June–mid-Sept 9am–3.30pm, mid-Sept–Mar 9am–5.30pm, Sun year round 10am–3.30pm; free to EU visitors), built as a resort facility for Roman troops in 206 BC. Later, two Roman emperors, Hadrian and Trajan, were born there.

Excavations have revealed a huge amphitheatre (thought to be the third-largest in the Roman Empire) and an extensive grid-plan of streets, still under excavation. Several fine mosaics have also been revealed: indeed, Italíca was the source of many of the stunning mosaics in the Palacio de la Condesa de Lebrija in Seville (see page 89).

NORTH OF SEVILLE

Roads north from Seville cross the flat river valley and ascend into the **Sierra Morena**, a thinly populated belt of hills which provides the plain with its water. The Sierra's main attraction is its refreshing coolness after the heat of the lowlands; in the winter it is a hunting centre, and the towns of **Cazalla** and **Constantina** ❸ (the latter surprisingly prosperous, with a dramatic

figure of Christ on the hillside above) are filled with well-dressed young men from Seville swapping hunting stories in the bars. The area is protected as the **Parque Natural de la Sierra del Norte**, www.sierranortedesevilla.es, a wonderful place for walking and trout fishing.

EAST OF SEVILLE

Three important historical towns lie east of Seville. **Carmona** ❹, the closest, most interesting and most atmospheric, was an important Roman centre. A Roman amphitheatre and necropolis and museum lie on the Seville side of town; the **necropolis** (Tue–Sat 9am–8pm, Sun 9am–3pm; free), the largest Roman burial ground outside Rome, is well laid out, complete with a crematorium with walls that are still discoloured by the fire, a large numbers of small paupers' tombs as well as a couple of much grander edifices.

The town itself commands an extensive view over the plain. The ancient **Puerta de Córdoba** is well corroded but remarkably intact considering its age (originally 2nd-century, with Moorish

Parque Natural de la Sierra Norte.

and baroque additions). The other gate, the **Puerta de Sevilla** (on the Seville side of town), is gigantic and features a protective double entranceway. The building incorporates another **Alcázar** (Mon–Sat 10am–6pm, Sun 10am–3pm; free Mon) and the tourist office.

Écija ⑤, some 56 km (34 miles) east of Seville, has many such towers. Unlike most Andalusian towns, it sits in a valley bowl rather than on a hill, and therefore has no summer breeze to relieve the heat. The town hall promotes Écija as 'the city of sun and towers'; however, it is better known as 'the frying pan of Spain' on account of its relentless summer heat.

The **Museo Histórico Municipal** (Calle Cánovas del Castillo; June–Sept Tue–Fri 10am–2.30pm, Sat 10am–2pm, 8–10pm, Sun 10am–3pm, Oct–May Tue–Fri 10am–1.30pm, 4.30–6.30pm, Sat 10am–2pm, 5.30–8pm, Sun 10am–3pm; free) has some interesting Roman finds while the church of **Santa María** (southwest of Plaza Major) has a Mudéjar patio filled with archaeological artefacts. The covered market is worth dipping into, and Calle Caballeros (north of the main square) has several rambling and ornate merchants' houses, including the **Palacio de Peñaflor**, which has an unusual curved balcony. The town is littered with crumbling church towers, all of which echo Seville's Giralda.

South of Écija is **Osuna ⑥**, its large collection of merchants' houses reflecting its prosperous history as the seat of the dukes of Osuna. Here the Giralda imitation is built into a grand facade on the Calle San Pedro, next door to the grandly baroque **Palacio del Marqués de La Gomera** (now a hotel).

On the hill is the 16th-century turreted **Universidad de Osuna**, and the Colegiata de Santa María de la Asunción (Tue–Sun, summer 10am–1.30pm, 4–7pm, winter 10am–1pm, 3.30–6.30pm) with a decent collection of fine art. Below the church is the Monasterio de **La Encarnación** (Tue–Sun July & Aug 9.30am–2.30pm, Sept–June 10am–2.30pm & 4–6pm), which houses a museum of religious art.

From Osuna a good road makes for the Sierra Nevada and Granada.

On the outskirts of Carmona.

Carmona has the largest Roman necropolis outside Rome.

📷 FROM LA PILETA TO PICASSO

Artistic treasures abound in Andalucía's museums and churches. In the 17th century Seville was the centre of a Golden Age of Art.

Pablo Picasso was born in Málaga in 1881 and, although his family moved north when he was only 10, throughout his life he considered himself first and foremost an Andalusian. He was heir to a formidable artistic legacy, stretching back 25,000 years to the time when prehistoric man decorated the walls of caves such as La Pileta.

The Moors leaned more towards decorative arts, which adorned their palaces and ceramics. Under the Christians, Andalucía experienced a flourishing in the arts, and in the 17th century Seville was the cradle of Spain's Siglo de Oro ("Golden Age") of art, with masters such as Francisco de Zurbarán, Bartolomé Esteban Murillo and Diego de Velázquez all working around the same time. The Church, profiting from the activities of the Inquisition, grew rich during this period and commissioned grand altarpieces and religious paintings. Recognised artists would gravitate to the court in Madrid, but Seville was always decisive in their careers.

In the 19th century, the age of Romanticism, Andalusian art tended to historical themes and *costumbrista* portrayals of everyday life. One of the most popular artists of the day was Julio Romero de Torres, famous for his paintings of Andalusian women, demure and provocative at the same time.

St Hugo of Grenoble in the Carthusian Refectory (1633), by Francisco de Zurbarán (1598–1664), in the Museo de Bellas Artes, Seville. Zurbarán worked extensively in Seville.

Detail from The Birth of the Virgin (1661), painted by Bartolomé Esteban Murillo for the Chapel of Saint Paul in Seville's Cathedral. The foremost exponent of baroque religious art in his day, Murillo is known for his ethereal virgins wreathed in clouds and cherubs.

Naranjas y Limones (Oranges and Lemons), a classic work by Julio Romero de Torres (1874–1930), who specialised in Andalusian beauties. Córdoba has a museum dedicated to the artist.

Altarpiece in the Church of San Miguel in Jerez de la Frontera. This extraordinary late-Renaissance piece by Juan Martínez Montañes has baroque elements attributed to José de Arce.

Andalucía's icons

One of the most typical manifestations of Andalusian art are the polychrome wood sculptures of the 17th century, an art form that developed from a folk-art tradition. Unlike northern European carving, the general theme was religious, and churches were filled with fine images and carved altarpieces, often used in the Semana Santa processions. The genre was extremely popular because the expressive statues of virgins and martyred saints appealed to the Andalusian sense of drama and pathos.

Two main schools were established around the central figures of Juan Martínez Montañes in Seville and Alonso Cano in Granada. Both artists had numerous followers, such as Juan Gómez and Pedro Roldán in the case of Montañes and Pedro de Mena and José de Mora in the case of Cano, whose work developed increasingly exaggerated, baroque expressiveness.

Many of these priceless images were destroyed in the course of various wars (including the Napoleonic invasion and the Spanish Civil War), but others still survive in the churches of Andalucía and are well worth seeking out.

Sculpture by Salvador Garcia inspired by Picasso's painting Mujeres Corriendo por la Playa (Women Running on the Beach), Torremolinos.

Maternity, by Rafael Zabaleta (1907–60), in Jaen's Provincial Museum.

Bust of Saint Paul by Alonso Cano (1601–67) in Granada's Cathedral.

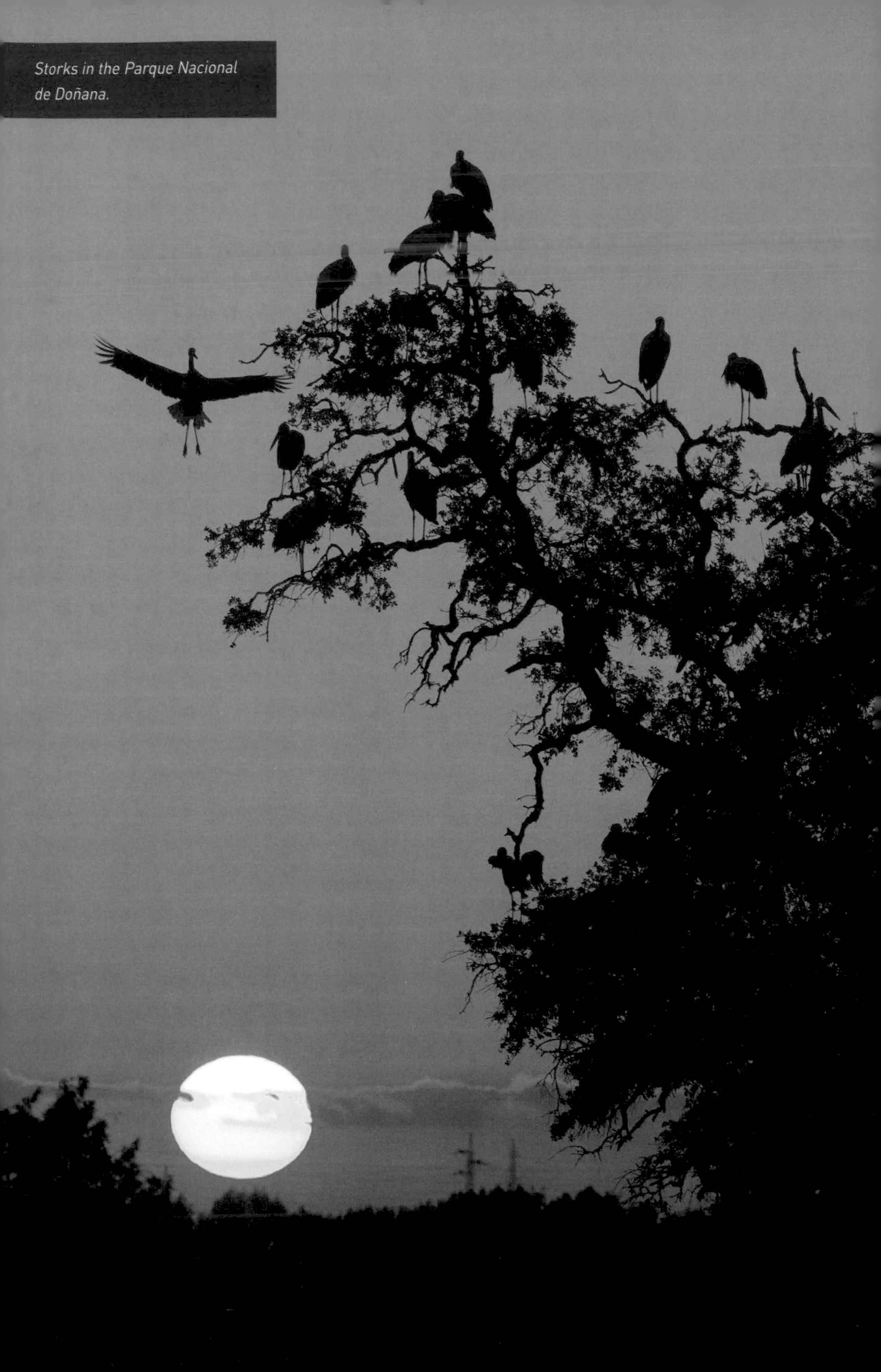

Storks in the Parque Nacional de Doñana.

HUELVA AND THE PARQUE NACIONAL DE DOÑANA

Huelva's towns and estuaries create an ethereal beauty. Its attractions include the Parque Nacional de Doñana and sweeping Atlantic beaches.

Stretching to the Portuguese border, Huelva is one of the less visited provinces of Andalucía. Although quickly and easily reached from Seville, the region has an air of peripheral isolation that can be felt in its remote mountain villages, gloriously empty beaches and the vast, wild Doñana National Park – all of which makes for pure, undisturbed escapism.

Meanwhile, evidence of a more significant past emanates from Huelva's two historical sources of wealth and reputation: the first lying many hundred feet below ground, the second linked to a 'new world' several thousand miles across the sea.

Rich natural deposits of minerals and precious metals (still mined and exported) were reputedly traded by the 6th-century BC kingdom of Tartessos. Akin to Atlantis, this advanced ancient civilisation vanished without a trace, leaving a small number of impressive archaeological relics and a belief that its foundations lie somewhere under Doñana's marshy floodplains.

The same copper and iron on which Tartessos prospered are responsible for the coloured waters of the Río Tinto – a river that has played a pivotal role in world history. From its estuary banks in 1492, Christopher Columbus, with royal sponsorship, set sail on his first epic expedition, to seek a westerly

route to the Orient. Instead, of course, he stumbled upon the Americas.

ORIENTATION

Huelva is sparsely populated, with most development clustered either side of the A49 highway, which bisects the province from Seville to Portugal. To its north, the best and most attractive route into the Sierra de Aracena is the N435. South of the east–west axis is the strictly protected Parque Nacional de Doñana, which, along with the River Guadalquivir, creates an impassable boundary with

Map on page 102

Main Attractions

El Rocío
Parque Nacional de Doñana
La Rábida
Huelva
Isla Cristina
Minas de Río Tinto
Aracena

A riot of colour at the Minas de Río Tinto.

> **◎ Tip**
>
> If you fancy exploring the park on horseback, take an equestrian tour organised by Doñana a Caballo (tel: 674-219 568) based in El Rocío. As well as two-hour rides through the wetlands, they organise evening gastronomic treks stopping at three restaurants. Carriage rides are also available.

Step back in time in El Rocío.

Cádiz province, forcing any southbound traffic via Seville. Points of interest for visitors lie in a cross shape, so a degree of backtracking is inevitable.

WINE COUNTRY

On entering the province from Seville, the first stop is **La Palma del Condado ❶**. Many of the taller buildings within easy flying distance of the Doñana mudflats have been occupied by nesting storks, and La Palma's attractive 18th-century church, San Juan Bautista, is no exception. A tangle of twigs tops its ornate blue baroque tower like a chimney brush.

This is Huelva's wine-growing region, and it has been planted with vines for centuries. Of the three del Condado (county) towns – **La Palma**, **Rociana** and **Bollullos**, the last offers cavernous, high-ceilinged bodegas with trestle tables to accommodate noisy wine-tastings. Typically the region's wines, derived from the local Zalema grape, are amber-coloured, nutty olorosos, similar to dark sherry. However, in recent years, wine-makers have been switching to fruity young whites which go well with the local seafood.

HISTORIC NIEBLA

The red oxides that tinge the soil and waters of Río Tinto can be seen in the crimson walls of ancient **Niebla ❷**. Approached from the A472 via a restored Roman bridge over the river, the town has been important in the downstream movement of extracted metals since perhaps the 9th century BC. Totally enclosed by fortifications incorporating a magnificent *alcázar* dating from 1402 (daily 10am–2pm & 5–9pm), complete with torture museum, the town is virtually sound-proof. At its centre are the attractive **Plaza Santa Maria** and church of the same name: 10th-century, with a minaret, intricate gates and mihrab testifying to its 13th-century conversion from a mosque.

The town has several other ancient churches. The **Iglesia de San Martín** incorporates evidence of Visigothic origins, Muslim conversion and Mudéjar remodelling, reflecting the history of Niebla itself.

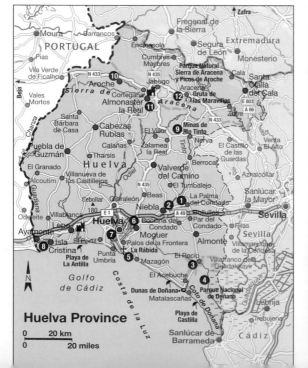

Huelva Province

0   20 km

0   20 miles

EL ROCÍO

Heading south, the A483 enters an extraordinary time warp at **El Rocío ❸**. Tarmac gives way to wide open sandy thoroughfares, and whitewashed stone is replaced by large timber ranches – built to house the large number of pilgrims who come for the annual *romería* (see below). Under a midday sun, shade is hard to come by, and the town is eerily quiet, adding to its Spaghetti Western character. Despite this film-set appearance, shops are selling cowboy hats for local farmers, not visitors. El Rocío was the place from which many Spanish pioneers emigrated for America, and they faithfully exported the look and feel of their home town.

The village is dominated by the bell-tower facade of **Ermita del Rocío**, the focus for one of Spain's largest and most ecstatic annual pilgrimages, the Romería del Rocío. At Pentecost, this sleepy backwater is transformed by festivity, overrun with up to a million costumed, singing revellers, riding in flower-filled carriages. Excitement centres on a tiny wooden effigy of the Virgin Mary above the church altar, Nuestra Senora del Rocío, revered for a miraculous legend about her discovery (see page 59).

Overlooking the beginnings of the protected coastal *marismas* (wetlands), El Rocío is a good spot for watching birds, including flocks of flamingos. Head to the Centro Ornitológico Francisco Bernis (Paseo Marismeño; June–Sept Tue–Fri 9am–2pm Sat–Sun 9am–1pm & 6–9pm; Oct–Apr Tue–Sun 9am–2pm & 4–6pm; free) to learn about local and visiting birdlife from experienced ornithologists.

PARQUE NACIONAL DE DOÑANA

El Rocío is a springboard for the **Parque Nacional de Doñana ❹**. An alternative base, less interesting but slightly closer to the access point at El Acebuche, is **Matalascañas** – a built-up 1960s resort in stark contrast to the 542 sq. km (209 sq. miles) of wilderness it serves.

The park is a World Heritage Site, Spain's largest reserve and a refuge for endangered species. A flooding and

⊙ VISITING THE DOÑANA NATIONAL PARK

To protect its fragile environment, access to the interior of the Coto de Doñana is restricted to organised tours, though you can access the beaches independently. A popular four-hour 4x4 trip can be arranged with Doñana National Park Tours (tel: 959-430 432; www.donanavisitas. es). It is a good idea to book at least a couple of days in advance. Trips depart from the visitors' centre in El Acebuche, just north of Matacasalañas, at 8.30am and 5pm from May mid-Sept and at 8.30am and 3pm from mid-Sept to Apr. The tour begins on the coast then weaves through the pines and scrub along the Guadalquivir river to the seasonal wetlands and then back to the sand dunes along the coast.

Serious nature enthusiasts might like to investigate Discovering Doñana (tel: 959-442 466; www.discoveringdonana.com), which operates a variety of 4X4 excursions (five-hour or 10-hour trips) into the park from their base in El Rocío. Expert guides accompany the group (Tue Mar–May) or private (spring, autumn, winter) tours, which take in a variety of flora and fauna, but place special emphasis on ornithology – if you're lucky, you might also spot an Iberian lynx. They operate in winter and summer and can supply binoculars, field guides, etc. There are also year-round self-guided walking trails, which are ideal for families.

⏱ Eat

For an authentic dining experience, follow the easily accessible paths or boardwalk trails through the Parque Dunar (8am–9pm) on the west side of Matalascañas, then reward yourself with lunch or dinner at one of the beachside seafood shacks (chiringuitos). Great food, chilled vibe off-season (packed in summer) and the freshest seafood.

retreating delta, which creates seasonal wetlands and cyclically shifting and evolving dunes, forms an unusual combination of ecosystems supporting a precious habitat for a huge diversity of birds and mammals.

The coast is home to oystercatchers, dunlins, sanderlings and low-swooping sandwich terns and gulls. Along the Guadalquivir, pine woods and scrub are the habitat of lynx, mongoose and the rare Spanish imperial eagle, though all these are elusive. Inland, vast seasonal wetlands flood in winter, attracting huge numbers of waterbirds. In summer, as the lake shrinks to a cracked, clay plain, flamingos, storks, herons and spoonbills arrive to feast on trapped fish.

Large mammals such as red deer and boar are drawn to a strip of lush vegetation on the edge of the marsh.

MAZAGÓN

If concrete Matalascañas doesn't appeal as a seaside base for Doñana, a more authentic alternative 20 km (12 miles) further along the coast is **Mazagón**. It is an easy going town with an attractive marina, lively restaurants and a long stretch of clean, golden sand and clear water (good for swimming), which truly earns the right to the name Costa de la Luz. To the east of the centro, stretching for 10 km (6 miles), the beach is backed by pine-topped sandstone cliffs.

COLUMBUS WAS HERE

After Mazagón, the coastline is interrupted by the mouths of the rivers Odiel and Tinto. At the point where they meet, against a background of heavy industry on the outskirts of Huelva, rises a giant statue (sculpted in 1929) of Christopher Columbus staring out to the Atlantic. The A494 bends inland to reach the sites associated with the great discoverer.

Hidden by the forests of the surrounding oil refineries, the Franciscan monastery of **La Rábida** ❺ is a tranquil sanctuary (Tue–Sat 10am–1pm and 4–6.15pm, until 7pm in summer, Sun year-round 10.45am–1pm). It was at La Rábida that Columbus met Friar Juan Pérez, the former priest of Queen Isabel, who intervened on Columbus's behalf and persuaded the Spanish monarchy to back his expedition. Murals depicting the events of 1492 and headset commentary in English vividly bring to life Columbus's time at the monastery.

The visit includes the cloister, set around a Moorish courtyard, the early 15th-century church (where one of Columbus's locally recruited captains, Martín Alonso Pinzón, is buried, and the chapel where the explorer is thought to have prayed before departure.

From the upstairs chapter house, in which much of the voyage was planned, there is a view of the river and a reproduction of the 15th-century harbour, **Muelle de las Carabelas** (Tue–Sun, mid-June–mid-Sept 10am–9pm, mid-Sept–mid-June 9.30am–7.30pm). Here, fully accessible to visitors, there are life-size replicas of the maiden flotilla. The surprisingly small dimensions of the wooden vessels and the confined

Red deer in the Parque Nacional de Doñana.

living quarters highlight the remarkable bravery and achievement of the crew.

The tiny fleet set sail in August 1492 from **Palos de la Frontera**, 4 km (2.5 miles) from La Rábida and once a sizeable port. It has since clogged up with silt from the Tinto estuary, so Columbus's precise departure point is hidden under clay. A great source of local pride is that the town was home to the Pinzón brothers, who captained caravels *Nina* and *Pinta*, both constructed in Palos, while Columbus captained his ship the *Santa María*. There is a museum at the Pinzón family home (on Calle Cristóbal Colón) and a monument to Martín Alonso Pinzón in the central square, marking the spot where the royal order for the 'Enterprise of the Indies' was declared.

Upstream from Palos, **Moguer ⑥** also claims a connection with Columbus, as it was the recruiting ground for much of the crew. It is also home to the 14th-century **Monasterio de Santa Clara** (www.monasteriodesantaclara.com; Tue–Sat guided tours 10.30am–12.30pm & 4.30–6.30pm, Sun 10.30am & 11.30am),

where Columbus prayed through the night in thanks for his safe return.

The town retains a distinctly Moorish feel with its whitewashed walls and dead ends. Buildings of interest include the graceful 18th-century **Ayuntamiento** (Mon–Fri 11am–2pm), which has a fine patio, on Plaza del Cabildo. Opposite is a statue of local poet Juan Ramón Jiménez, winner of the 1956 Nobel Prize for Literature. The poet is celebrated in the Casa Museo Zenobia y Juan Ramón (mid-June–mid-Sept Tue–Fri 10am–2.30pm & 4–9pm, Sat–Sun 10am–3pm; mid-Sept–mid-June Tue–Sat guided tours 10.15am, 11.15am, 12.15pm, 1pm, 5.15pm, 6.15pm & 7pm, Sun am only).

PROVINCIAL CAPITAL

Across the Tinto is **Huelva ⑦**, the provincial capital, which celebrates the Columbus connection with the Fiestas Colombinas every August. Beyond its smoky suburbs, parts of the city's historic centre that withstood the 1755 Lisbon earthquake stand elegant and proud. The baroque **Catedral de**

Replicas of Columbus's flotilla at Muelle de las Carabelas.

la Merced dominates a shady plaza (off Paseo Buenos Aires) which has the grand but slightly edgy feel of a South American plaza – a reminder of Huelva's inter-continental influence. Trade with the New World brought wealth, though in time most of this was absorbed by Sevilla.

Conjuring up these affluent times, lofty palms are evenly spaced along wide avenues, casting shadows on the tiled facades of five-storey mansion blocks. A smart pedestrianised shopping district runs south of the central **Plaza de las Monjas**, parallel to Gran Vía. At the eastern end of this main thoroughfare, the **Museo de Huelva** (Alameda Sundheim 13; mid-June–mid-Sept Tue–Sun 9am–3pm; mid-Sept–mid-June Tue–Sat 9am–8pm, Sun 9am–3pm; free to EU citizens) sheds light on the enigmatic Tartessos civilisation, which is thought to have centred on Huelva.

Another prosperous period for the city was the late 19th century, when the British-owned Río Tinto Mining Company brought the industrial revolution to the region. The huge iron Río Tinto Pier, designed by British engineer George Barclay Bruce, is now redundant, but it still arcs out into the estuary like a long broken rollercoaster. The British also built Barrio Reina Victoria, a quintessentially English-style suburb, with neat lawns and tended rose bushes.

BEST BEACHES

In search of a seaside escape, Victorian expatriates travelled by paddle steamer to **Punta Umbria**, the first of the beach resorts dotted along the coast towards Ayamonte on the border with Portugal. It is still a popular, low-key resort, with a long stretch of clean, gently sloping sand backed by holiday homes, a few guesthouses and the occasional *chiringuito*. Today Punta Umbria is reached along the A497, which skirts the **Paraje Natural Marismas del Odiel** (Visitor Centre Anastasio Senra, Ctra. del dique Juan Carlos I; Mon–Sat 9am–3pm), a wetland reserve attracting similar bird species to Doñana.

Continuing east, a spectacular unspoilt beach runs past **El Portil**, hidden by dense pine thickets and

Off to the beach near Punta Umbria.

⊙ THE RÍO TINTO

The Greeks and Phoenicians sailed the length of the Mediterranean to get the ore, and the local tribesmen founded the Tartessos civilisation on the profits. But it was the Romans who developed the potential of the Río Tinto's resources. Roman miners – first slaves, then free men – worked in galleries 1 metre (3ft) in diameter, lit by tiny oil lamps. The problem of flooding was solved by waterwheels that lifted the water from one level to another.

The mines survived the fall of Rome, and Niebla grew into a powerful Moorish enclave through its control of the Río Tinto. Later, the easy pickings that were to be had in the Americas almost put an end to the mines. They were finally bought in 1873 by a consortium of British and German bankers. Mining ceased here in 2001.

bumpy, tufted dunes. The shore looks out onto a flat sandy spit which has accumulated at the mouth of the Río Piedras, forcing the road to detour inland. Where the river meets the ocean, fresh water attracts line-fishermen, and a blustery wind trap makes it a popular spot for kite-surfing. The long beach peters out near the original river mouth at **El Rompido**, an attractive fishing village.

Regaining the coast necessitates a dog-leg through row upon row of strawberry bushes and the town of **Lepe**, Spain's foremost producer of the fruit. In Spanish, to be 'from Lepe' means to be from the proverbial back of beyond. In the chronicles of Columbus's voyage of discovery the first person to see landfall was 'a man from Lepe'.

Turning back towards the sea, **El Terrón**, on the west bank of the Río Piedras is little more than a fishing quay carpeted with colourful nets. Unfortunately this is the last traditional village before modern overdevelopment engulfs the coast at **La Antilla** and **La Islantilla**.

Sharing a degree of this development, but for the time being retaining genuine character, is **Isla Cristina** ❽. As its name suggests, the area was once an island. Today the town is joined to the mainland, lapped by a tidal estuary which serves as an effective base for a commercial fishing fleet that supplies Seville. The *puerto pesquero* (fishing port), a pungent tangle of nets and busy vessels, is a wonderfully animated place to dine on the very freshest seafood. Plaza de las Flores in the town centre is another lively evening spot.

From the harbour, the beach extends east, across crab-burrowed mudflats and past unsightly apartment blocks. It quickly becomes brilliant-white sand crossed by a boardwalk and backed by hotels shaded by a eucalyptus grove. Beachfront action is limited.

Within sight of Portugal is the border town of **Ayamonte**. The pretty palm- and restaurant-lined marina makes it worth a pause before crossing the Río Guadiana (by bridge or ferry) to the Algarve. The town's outlying resort of **Isla Canela** has a good beach, but rapid development has resulted in an expanse of tarmac, modern blocks and box-like hotels.

MINING COUNTRY

Leaving the coast, the N435 climbs steadily up-country towards some of Huelva's best but least known sights. Just northwest of Zalamea la Real on the A461 are the **Minas de Río Tinto** ❾. Carved out like an amphitheatre, open-cast Corta Atalya mine (one of the world's oldest and largest) is a miniature Grand Canyon of exposed earth: sunset-coloured bands of rusty red, orange and yellow contrasts with the deep-blue waters and green pines of the Gossan reservoir. Attractions include a visit to a small mine in Peña del Hierro, a mining museum and a train ride (www.parquemineroderiotinto.es; opening times vary).

The rusty hues of the Río Tinto.

THE SIERRA MORENA

The road lifts and twists into the cool air of the western **Sierra Morena**, a landscape of green woodlands, streams and mountains. Just inside the **Parque Natural Sierra de Aracena**, the Portugal–Seville N433 and quieter A470 cut west to east, taking in a handful of villages.

Jabugo is a tiny place renowned for Spain's finest *jamón ibérico*. A line of bars just outside the centre offers the prized (and pricey) cured ham as tapas. Apart from its pork business, Jabugo is an isolated settlement, centring on the crumbling **Iglesia de San Miguel**. Nearby **Galaroza** is prettier, wrapped in greenery, refreshed by streams and dominated by a baroque church.

The furthest west of Huelva's sierra towns is **Aroche** ⑩. Unselfconscious in its remoteness, its strong identity and sense of camaraderie make for interesting people-watching in the central square. The town receives few tourists, but its cobbled streets are worth exploring, not least for the medieval *castillo*, now an unconventional bullring.

East of here is **Almonaster la Real** ⑪, which rises to the crest of a hill where a 10th-century mosque is a perfect miniature of Córdoba's renowned Mezquita, minus the crowds. Its Islamic features, including brick-pillar horseshoe arches, fountain and minaret tower (that offers a free view of the next-door corrida) are impeccably preserved.

Further along the A470, watched over by a tiny hilltop church, **Pena de Arias Montano**, are **Alajar** and **Linares de la Sierra**: attractive but depopulated hamlets that are not much more than farms.

Aracena ⑫ is the largest market town in the area. There is a good vantage point from Cerro del Castillo, a hill (reached via a steep trail from the cobbled Plaza Alta), topped by a Gothic-Mudéjar church built by the Knights Templar in the 13th century.

Aracena's main attraction lies under the castle. The **Gruta de las Maravillas** (daily 10am–1.30pm & 3–6pm; audioguides available in English) is a labyrinth of grottoes. An hourly tour investigates chilly chambers where pools have collected among fantastic mineral formations. The circuit concludes at the Sala de los Culos (Chamber of the Buttocks), named for reasons that are obvious. You can learn about – and taste – the famous local ham at the Museo del Jamón (Gran Vía; daily 10.45am–2.30pm & 3.45–7pm).

Returning to Seville on the N433, a final detour is warranted by spectacularly sited **Zufre**. Clinging to a slim crag above cliffs of several hundred metres, the isolated village seems bemused by visitors. Horses negotiate steps to drink from troughs outside a 16th-century Mudéjar church, while daily life centres on the Paseo, a garden square with panoramic views of the natural park.

Inside the otherworldly Gruta de las Maravillas.

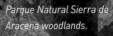
Parque Natural Sierra de Aracena woodlands.

Jerez de la Frontera is famous for its sherry, including Tío Pepe.

JEREZ, CÁDIZ AND THE COSTA DE LA LUZ

Cádiz province has an illustrious seafaring history, a centuries-old wine and sherry industry and a truly stunning coastline.

Occupying a coastal right-angle to the point of Andalucía's most southerly tip, Cádiz province is influenced in character by its proximity to Morocco and elemental exposure to the vast Atlantic. Clues to a confrontational history abound in the names of hill towns carrying the suffix 'de la Frontera', many of which are defensively and dramatically perched atop striking crags of the inland sierra.

The region lived as a frontier for centuries: at the frontline of Moorish invasion and Christian reconquest; violently harassed by Drake and Nelson; its New World riches ransacked by pirates. The strategically located provincial capital, Cádiz city, was once an island gateway to the entire Phoenician trading empire, then named Gadir, meaning 'the defended place'.

Today, the Cádiz coast is affronted merely by incessant ocean winds and the threat, so far repulsed, of an architectural fate similar to that of the neighbouring province of Málaga. It remains resolutely under-developed, facing west to inspirational sunsets and offering its visitors a feast of fresh fish and crisp local sherry, while quietly delighting in the miles of brilliant white sand that earned it the name, Costa de la Luz – Coast of Light.

White dunes on Bolonia's beach, north of Tarifa.

GATEWAY TO THE PROVINCE

Improved flight connections to the provincial airport at Jerez have made this appealing corner of Andalucía accessible.

More affluent and sophisticated than the provincial capital Cádiz, **Jerez de la Frontera** ❶ is gracefully typified by La Real Escuela Andaluza del Arte Ecuestre (Royal Andalucian School of Equestrian Art; tel: 956-318 008; www.realescuela.org; daily 10am–2pm), where dressage training to a soundtrack of Spanish guitar music can be watched,

Main Attractions
Jerez de la Frontera
El Puerto de Santa Maria
Sanlúcar de Barrameda
Tarifa
Baelo Claudia
Vejer de la Frontera
Cádiz

Maps on pages 112, 118

with a stables tour and entry to the museum. The horses give a polished performance in the arena on Tuesdays and Thursdays at noon.

In the old city, to the west of the lively Calle Larga, sophistication is manifest in stylish plazas (notably de Arenal, Plateros and de la Asunción) and a grand Gothic-Baroque cathedral. Nearby, surrounded by orange blossom, the original Islamic **Alcázar** (daily 9.30am–2.30pm, until 5.30pm Mon–Fri July–Sept) incorporates an exquisite mosque, attractive gardens and Arab baths lit by starry skylights. An 18th-century palace has been built within the medieval walls.

There are two good reasons for staying overnight in Jerez. Firstly, there is no better neighbourhood in which to kick off a tour of Cádiz province than the **Barrio de Santiago**. Here, a well-integrated Roma gypsy community keep alive deep-rooted flamenco traditions, dancing a distinctive style of flamenco known as the Buleria. You can find out more about it at the **Centro Andaluz de Flamenco** (Plaza de San Juan; www.centroandaluzdeflamenco.es; Mon–Fri 9am–2pm; free), a resource centre which also hosts exhibitions and shows films. Secondly, a bodega tour (see box), culminating in some sherry tasting and sometimes tapas, is a must.

Jerez has grown rich on its bodegas, the largest of which is González Byass (Calle Manuel Maria González 12; tel: 956-357 016; www.bodegastiopepe.es), the producer and exporter of Tío Pepe, whose advertising you will see everywhere. Its cellar, La Concha, located near the cathedral and Alcázar, was designed by Gustave Eiffel. The fanciest is undoubtedly Bodegas Tradición (Calle Cordobeses 3; tel: 956-168 628; www.bodegastradicion.es), which has an exquisite private art collection and vintage sherries.

Alternatively, near to the equestrian school is **Bodegas Sandeman** (Calle Pizarro 10; tel: 675-647 177; www.sandeman.com), where the guides wear the black cape and *caballero* hat of the trademark Don. For any visit, it is a good idea to book ahead.

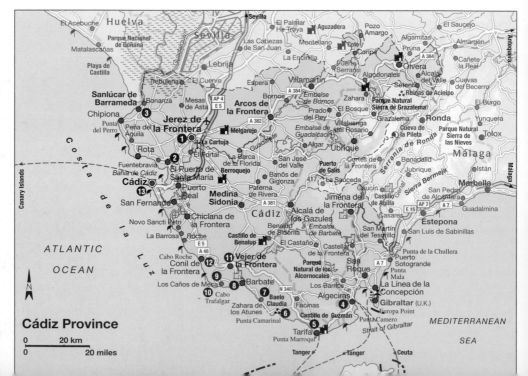

Cádiz Province

THE COAST

West of Jerez, **El Puerto de Santa María** ❷ is a thriving port near the mouth of the River Guadalete. On summer evenings locals and visitors tend to converge on the Ribera del Marisco, to enjoy the sociable atmosphere and first-rate seafood. The town's most famous son was the poet Rafael Alberti (1902–99), one of the Generation of '27 along with Federico García Lorca, and the **Fundación Rafael Alberti** (Calle Santo Domingo 25; www.rafaelalberti.es; Tue–Sun 10.30am–2pm) traces his life and work.

The town is ringed by wineries, including the vast Bodegas Osborne (tel: 956-869 100; www.bodegas-osborne. com), the brand advertised by the iconic black bull, whose silhouette is a familiar feature on roadside hills throughout Andalucía. El Puerto's good beaches are a few kilometres west of town, becoming less crowded the further they are from the centre – the best is **Playa Santa Catalina**.

The coast road northwest of El Puerto detours around a naval base and the small fishing port at **Rota**, then curves round to a jolly holiday-home resort at **Chipiona**.

On the wide estuary of the Río Guadalquivir, **Sanlúcar de Barrameda** ❸ once acted as Seville's port and shared in its New World spoils. Historical wealth accounts for some elegant architecture, focusing on the palm-lined Plaza del Cabildo. The sizeable town includes a laid-back fishing district around Bajo de Guía, which has a nationwide reputation for shellfish. Excellent restaurants front a fine beach, near the departure point for organised 4x4 tours to the Coto Doñana National Park (Viajes Doñana; tel: 956-362 540; www.viajesdonana.es) on the opposite bank.

A festival at the end of May toasts Sanlúcar's local manzanilla wine, considered to be more delicate than sherry. It derives its distinct flavour from the salty, humid conditions that prevail here. You can try it at Bodegas Barbadillo (Calle Luis de Eguilaz 11; tel: 956-385 521; www.barbadillo. com; guided tours in English at 11am Tue–Sun).

Learn all about sherry production at Harveys Bodega.

⊘ SHERRY TOURS

The palomino white grape thrives in the chalky soil and humid, windy climate of northwest Cádiz, a combination of environmental factors that are ideal for sherry production.

A bodega tour through sweetly aromatic, high-vaulted buildings offers a fascinating insight into the biological process that transforms *vino* into *jerez*. Pressed grapes are allowed partially to ferment, creating a skin of yeast called *flor*. Inside 500-litre (100-gallon) oak barrels, this layer forms a natural barrier against oxidisation. The sherry's colour and sweetness depend on how this film is preserved: if it collapses, like an apple left without peel, the result is a sweet, dark oloroso, but when it survives, the sherry is a dry, white fino.

EAST OF JEREZ

Heading east, the plains that carry the road inland from chalky vineyard country lead to Arcos de la Frontera, a springboard for the so-called 'white towns' *(pueblos blancos)*, which straddle the provinces of Cadiz and Málaga (see page 121). To the southeast lies **Medina Sidonia** and **La Ruta del Toro**, so called because nearby lowland pastures are home to herds of fighting bulls bred for the *corrida*.

Southeast of **Alcalá de los Gazules**, another white town (see page 125), the A381 skirts the Barbate reservoir and, leaving behind clear mountain air, descends into the urbanised bay of Gibraltar. In **Algeciras** ❹, a polluted, sprawling port, there is a magnetic seaward pull and a transitory atmosphere. The city's main claim to fame is that it was the birthplace of one of Spain's finest flamenco guitarists, Paco de Lucia (1947–2014); the tourist office runs a guided tour of his associated sites. Ferries for Tangier and Ceuta (a Spanish enclave on the North African coast) leave throughout the day (see box on Going to Morocco).

Windswept Tarifa is beloved by windsurfers.

You might also consider visiting **Gibraltar**: the 5-km by 1-km (3-mile by 0.6-mile) Rock is clearly visible on the far side of the bay. To do this, simply follow signs to La Línea – Spain's border with Gibraltar. You can leave your car in the guarded car park, cross the border on foot and pick up a bus or taxi to take you to the centre.

LAID-BACK TARIFA

A Moorish flavour pervades the town of **Tarifa** ❺, 20km (12 miles) further west. After dark, the streets inside its medieval walls buzz with an eclectic mix of dimly-lit bars, cushion-strewn cafés, aromatic restaurants and art galleries. Laid-back and a touch bohemian, Tarifa relishes its reputation as 'a piece of washed up Africa' and is determined not to go the same way as resorts on the nearby Costa del Sol. From here Tangier is a mere 35 minutes away by hydrofoil (see box).

On the ramparts of the **Castillo de Guzmán** (www.castilloguzmanelbueno.com; 10am–2.30pm & 4–6pm), originally a

Moorish Alcázar, a huge catapult is displayed, seemingly aimed across the Strait of Gibraltar, a reminder that living on Morocco's doorstep has brought friction as well as fusion. Tarifa takes its name from Tarif ibn Malik, who led a reconnaissance mission to Spain preceding the North African invasion in 711.

The earliest surviving part of Tarifa's castle is 10th-century. In 1292 it fell to Christian forces, but as the closest point to Africa it remained a point of conflict. Alonso de Guzmán's heroic defence of the town two years later earned him the epithet 'El Bueno', the Good. Guzmán had sacrificed his own son rather than surrender the castle to the Muslims. Guzmán was subsequently ennobled and became the Duke of Medina Sidonia. Some 300 years later, a descendant of Guzmán led the Spanish Armada.

ON THE WILD SIDE

For all its exotic heritage, Tarifa is also a busy resort, offering surf boutiques, shipwreck dives and organised whale-watching trips. The latter (book a day in advance) are organised by several commercial companies as well as the Foundation for Information and Research on Marine Mammals (tel: 956-627 008; www.firmm.org). Dolphins and pilot whales can be spotted year-round (they are often also seen on the ferry crossing to Morocco). Another natural phenomenon worth catching is the migration of birds between Europe and Africa. Birds migrate south from February to June and return between September and October. Good spots to watch the passage are the lookout points over the Strait of Gibraltar, just east of Tarifa.

WINDSURFERS' PARADISE

The growth in tourism is mainly due to the town's reputation as mainland Europe's windsurfing capital, best appreciated by walking between the town's two beaches, the sheltered **Playa Chica**, on the Mediterranean, to **Playa de los Lances**, on the Atlantic and usually lashed by a sand-blasting gale. Try Spin Out (tel: 956-23 63 52; www.tarifaspinout. com) for lessons and equipment hire.

Further up the coast at **Playa La Plata** the wind, a little more bearable here,

Statue of hero Alonso de Guzmán, known as Guzmán el Bueno, in Tarifa.

⊘ GOING TO MOROCCO

A short hop across the Strait of Gibraltar, Morocco makes an interesting overnight or even day excursion from Southern Spain. Ferries leave throughout the day from Algeciras to Tangier (no need to book), though this is a fairly long voyage at up to two hours, depending on the type of ferry and the prevailing wind (there is also a 30-minute or one-hour crossing to Ceuta, an uninteresting Spanish enclave on the North African coast). It is preferable to take the less frequent but much quicker hydrofoil crossing (35 minutes) from Tarifa to Tangier. Be aware that very windy weather can delay crossings, or even bring the service to a halt. See www.frs.es, www.balearia.com, www.inter shipping.es, http://aml-africa-morocco-link.fr or www.transmediterranea.es.

No visas are required for EU or US visitors to Morocco, but you must fill in an arrivals form and get your passport stamped on board the boat. Tangier's port lies immediately below the medina, the heart of the old town, so it isn't that difficult to find your own way around. That said, you may be badgered by would-be guides offering their services and they can be a good option when time is short. If you go down this route, point out that you want to see the sights (medina, kasbah, Grand Socco), not the shops, and agree a fee beforehand.

gathers dunes under the bluff at **Punta Valdevaqueros**, the venue for international kite-surfing championships based in Tarifa. On the hills to the east, the climate is put to environmental use by an army of giant wind turbines.

ROMAN OUTPOST

North of Tarifa, a stunning coastline unfolds. **Bolonia** is protected from the wind by headlands and the sea is calm. Cattle and cockerels wander aimlessly in front of a handful of *chiringuitos* (beach bars) on the grass behind a curved bay. It is appealingly rustic and unspoilt.

Also at Bolonia are the substantial Roman ruins of **Baelo Claudia ⑥** (Tue–Sat Apr–mid-June 9am–8pm, mid-June–mid-Sept 9am–3pm; mid-Sept–mid-Mar 9am–6pm, Sun year-round 9am–3pm; free to EU visitors), including the remains of an amphitheatre, paved forum and temples. Having prospered on its production of garum, a salted fish paste that was popular across the Roman Empire, the settlement is believed to have fallen into decline following an earthquake in the 2nd century.

Roman ruins of Baelo Claudia at Bolonia.

THE BEACHES

Next along the coast (reached via an inland dog-leg via the N340) is **Zahara de los Atunes ⑦**, an easy-going fishing village, which is a popular summer escape for Sevillian families. Zahara's straight, broad beach is somewhat exposed and weather-beaten, making inroads into the friendly and unpretentious town, where you will find several low-key tapas bars.

Zahara blends into **Atlanterra**, where a string of characterless apartments have sprung up. Keep driving for several kilometres to the dead end at **Punta Camarinal**, to discover a powdery white cove, reached on foot along overgrown footpaths, hidden from the road.

Continuing northwest from Zahara, the road hugs the coastline, crossing marshy wetlands that soak up the estuary of the Rio Barbate, before arriving at the town of **Barbate ⑧**. A hard-working fishing port with canning factories, it is renowned for locally caught blue-fin tuna. Seafood eateries dot the otherwise unremarkable Paseo Maritimo.

Rising from the harbour, a pretty drive (or rewarding five-hour cliff-top walk) leads up through the umbrella pines of the **Parque Natural de la Brena y Marismas de Barbate** and down into to the coastal village of Los Caños.

Los Caños de Meca ❾, tucked under pine-clad hills, was once a hippie resort and an uninhibited mood encourages discreet naturists, who swim from the smaller southern bay. A few hotels and restaurants are scattered along a ridge of sandstone cliffs, with hidden caves and two stunning golden beaches nestled beneath. This spot is captivating at sunset, when the sun sinks into the ocean behind the nearby Cape.

THE BATTLE OF TRAFALGAR

Cabo Trafalgar ❿ was the scene of Admiral Nelson's famous obliteration of the combined fleets of France and Spain on 21 October 1805. Despite being vastly outnumbered, the British fleet won the day through their skill and experience, though Nelson himself was fatally wounded in the battle. The battle was decisive in ensuring Britain's supremacy at sea for the next 100 years. Without reference to the historical significance of the site, a lighthouse topping a breezy, dune-smothered spit marks the spot. North of the cape, **Zahora** offers a secluded swish of soft, toe-wriggling sand.

A detour inland, passing through fields of sunflowers, leads to **Vejer de la Frontera** ⓫, a *pueblo blanco* with the ultimate sea view. Vejer's elevated isolation is impressive, like a suspended white-iced wedding cake, looming above the road. Behind Moorish gates a maze of steep and twisting alleyways lead to the Castillo, 16th-century church of Divino Salvador, built around the minaret of a mosque, and vertiginous vistas. The town is a tangible collision of Moorish and Andalusian character. The central Plaza de España is reminiscent of Seville, with its orange trees and *azulejo*-decorated fountains.

Back at the coast, a bumpy road runs beside a sweep of clean, bright sand at **El Palmar**, a cluster of casual beach-facing developments in elemental surroundings. The stretch peters out at

Plaza de España, Vejer de la Frontera.

the mouth of the Río Salado, facing the town of Conil on the opposite side.

Conil de la Frontera , a down-to-earth fishing community, has managed to embrace tourism while remaining true to itself. Behind its wide concrete promenade and family-friendly beach (Playa de Los Bateles), the village climbs up to an attractive old quarter with an upbeat atmosphere. A kilometre (0.6 mile) to the north is the quieter cliff-bound **Playa de la Fontanilla**, with its own al-fresco restaurants.

As the road approaches the southern suburbs of Cádiz, old seaside towns are replaced by unimaginative blocks of flats. But what **Novo Sancti Petri** lacks in a sense of identity, it makes up for in golf courses.

CÁDIZ

Cádiz  still has the feel of a fortified outpost, almost entirely surrounded by sea, anchored to its province by a finger of land and a high bridge carrying traffic across the bay. The imposing **Puerta de Tierra**, divides the old town from more modern development along the deep

Atlantic beaches. **Playa de la Victoria** offers a relaxed, breezy base as an alternative to the old town. From the lively *chiringuito* bars there is a beguiling view of the city, 30 minutes' walk away – the golden (in reality, yellow-tiled) dome of the cathedral glinting hazily in the sun, flanked by high turreted towers, protected by a bastion of sea defences.

Approaching from Victoria, a stroll around the narrow peninsula serves as useful orientation. On the western side is **Barrio de la Viña**, a fisherman's quarter whose leathery-looking inhabitants can often be seen collecting crabs by the causeway to the military islet of **Castillo de San Sebastián**. They moor their boats in the small **Playa de la Caleta**.

Further on are the **Castillo de Santa Catalina** and two shady parks, **Parque Genovés** and the **Alameda de Apodaca**. The largest, leafiest square is the **Plaza de España** Ⓐ, from where streets delve into a warren of atmospheric, slightly seedy nooks and crannies. A short walk west of here in Plaza de Mina is the **Museo de Cádiz** (mid-June–mid-Sept Tue–Sun 9am–3pm; mid-Sept–mid-June

Cobbled street in Cádiz old town.

Cádiz

Tue–Sat 9am–8pm, Sun 9am–3pm; free to EU visitors) which has a fine collection of art including works by Zurbarán and Murillo as well as Roman relics from Baelo Claudia.

Despite the confusing jumble of back streets, it is impossible to get lost in Cádiz. The city is no more than 2 km (1.5 miles) wide in any direction, so whichever way you walk the ocean soon reappears. It rewards inquisitive zig-zag wandering.

Cádiz entered a golden era in the 18th century, when it overtook Seville as the centre for transatlantic trade. The city's most impressive architecture dates from this time, including its watchtowers, the highest being **Torre Tavira** ® (www.torretavira.com; daily May–Sept 10am–8pm, until 6pm in winter), noted for its camera obscura, and grand avenues such as **Calle Ancha** ('Broad Street').

The city's prosperous heyday produced a discursive middle class, who earned the city a liberal reputation. The **Museo de las Cortes de Cádiz** ® (Tue–Fri 9am–6pm, Sat–Sun 9am–2pm; free) records the short-lived democratic constitution of 1812, declared at the Oratorio San Felipe Neri next door. Liberal attitudes prevail today, displayed most expressively at the city's famous carnival in February (see page 58).

The vast **Catedral Nueva** ®, (Mon–Sat 10am–7pm, Sun 2–7pm) fronted by a wide, open, pedestrianised plaza, is one of the largest cathedrals in Spain and took 122 years to complete (1716–1838), hence the mix of baroque and neoclassical design. Entered separately from the Plaza de la Catedral, a spiral climb inside one of the bell towers, Torre del Reloj, offers a 360° panorama.

In the shadow of the 'new' cathedral, **Barrio del Populo** (the heart of 13th-century Cádiz, with three surviving medieval gates) is home to the old one. The **Iglesia Santa Cruz** ® was virtually demolished by the British in 1596 and later rebuilt. A short walk across **Plaza de San Juan de Dios** leads to the harbour. To this day Cádiz is a significant port for cruise liners and commercial vessels. The docks are also the departure point for a trip across the bay back to El Puerto de Santa María.

⊘ Where

The entrance to the Bay of Cádiz, just beyond the fortified island of San Sebastián, is where the Bucentaure, the flagship of the French fleet at the Battle of Trafalgar (1805), commanded by Admiral Villeneuve, went down. In fact, this area of ocean is littered with shipwrecks that have fallen foul of treacherous weather.

Cádiz Cathedral.

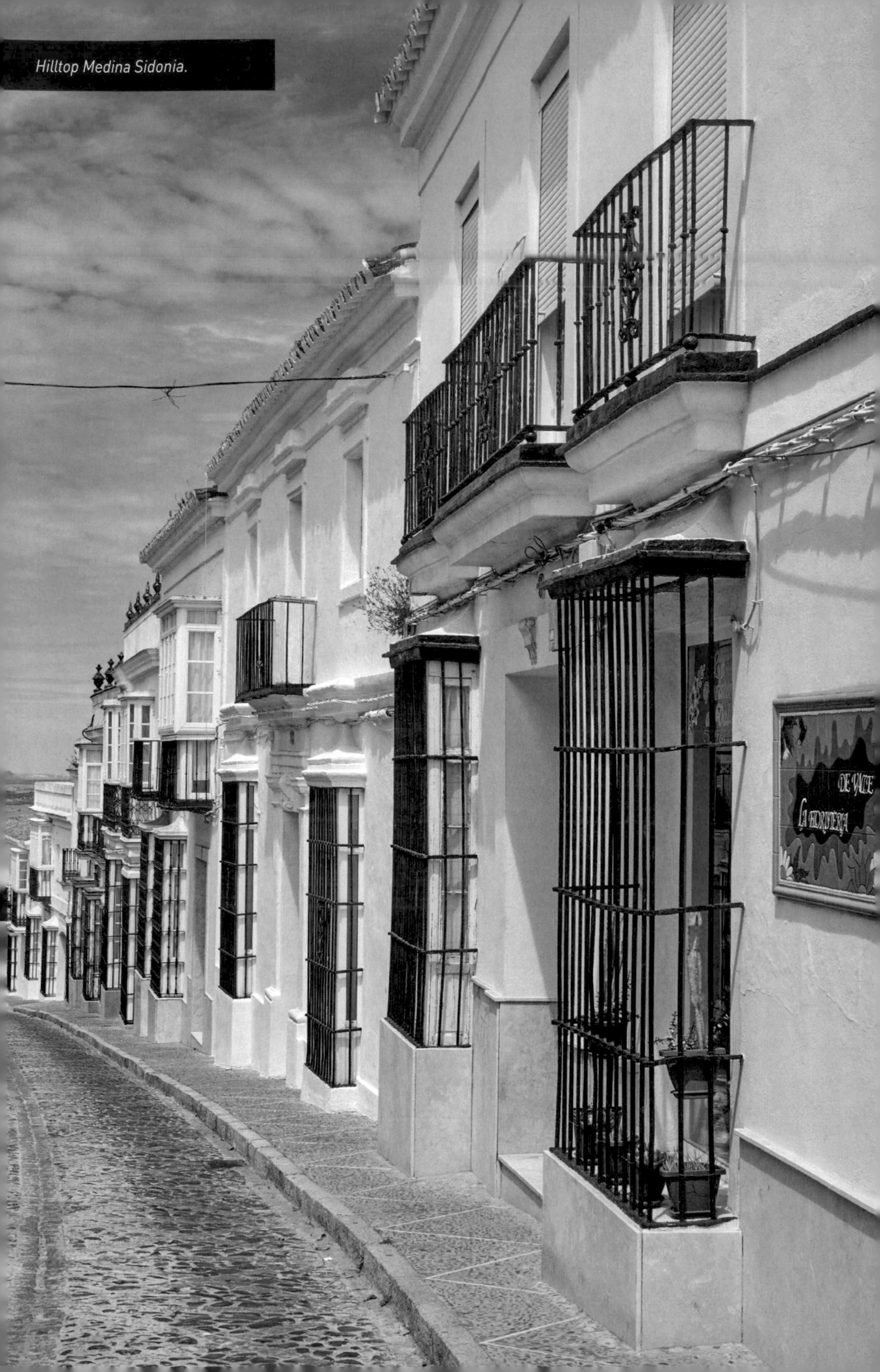

Hilltop Medina Sidonia.

EXPLORING THE WHITE TOWNS

Following a route linking a selection of the
pueblos blancos (white towns) is an excellent
way of sampling Andalucía's interior.

The lowlands of Andalucía are char-
acterised by large whitewashed agricultural villages from which landless
labourers used to go out to till the
big arable farms of the river plains.
Though certainly 'white', these villages are bleak and functional; not all
members of the white town species are
charming or pretty. But the higher you
climb into the sierras, where the terrain is more rugged, the smaller and
more picturesque the towns and villages (both are called *pueblos*) become.

In the hills, large monocultures
give way to smallholdings, herding
and forest crops such as chestnut and
cork. Glimpsed from the road or railway, whether framed in forest green
or tucked under a vertiginous fang of
rock, the mountain *pueblos* are dramatic. They are usually crowned by a
crumbling Moorish fortress and an
imposing church erected as a victory
statement by the Christians following
the Reconquest.

The regional tourist authorities have
striven to establish the white towns as
the great attraction of the Andalusian
interior. Some *pueblos* bear the official
sign 'Ruta de los Pueblos Blancos';
others, often no less attractive, do not.
The major promotion concentrates on
the province of Cádiz and the western half of the province of Málaga. As

*Grazalema, said to be
the wettest town in Andalucía.*

some 50 or 60 *pueblos* are commended
in a number of leaflets, a little inside
knowledge may help.

REGIONAL DIFFERENCES

Some of the *pueblos* netted in the official trawl belong to the Atlantic coast,
running from the Bay of Cádiz to the
Strait of Gibraltar. These tend to be very
different from those accessed from
the Costa del Sol, for here tourism,
though not absent, is less direct. There
is large-scale migration of labour to
Madrid, Barcelona or the coasts; the

Main Attractions

Gaucín
Cueva de la Pileta
Arcos de la Frontera
Parque Natural Sierra de
   Grazalema
Grazalema
Olvera

Map on page 122

remaining townsfolk or villagers pursue a traditional pattern of life and the odd stranger remains a rarity.

That said, great efforts have been made to improve facilities in the villages in recent years, in particular for young people, who are apt to drift away to the cities. You may be surprised to find the occasional nightclub, for example, and also a number of towns with a municipal swimming pool. The mountain roads have also improved considerably.

Tourist infrastructure is still fairly limited in all but the best-known towns and villages, with mainly basic hotels and restaurants. The best way of exploring the *pueblos blancos*, therefore, is to set up base camp in Ronda (see page 131), well placed for the more easterly *pueblos blancos*, Arcos de la Frontera, Olvera or Grazalema, the last also a good base for walkers.

CASARES–GAUCÍN LOOP

Holidaymakers on the Costa del Sol, who want to sample the white towns without travelling too far, can make an easy day excursion to Casares and Gaucín. To reach **Casares ❶**, take the signposted road inland 10 km (6 miles) west of Estepona. The town surges dramatically into view, its white-walled, red-roofed houses rising up the far side of a deep rocky gorge. At the top, in earthy red brick, stand the shell of its ruined church and all that now remains of its Moorish fort.

The town has been discovered, but not spoilt: menus may have English translations but the food is still Spanish. On any summer evening the central plaza will echo with that special Spanish roar, created by most of the town's male population talking to each other at the tops of their voices. From Casares's summit there are some splendid views to the peaks of the Sierra Bermeja and, in the opposite direction, to the valley of the Río Genal.

GAUCÍN

Running on a spine between the Genal and the Río Guadiaro, the Ronda–Algeciras road has a string of white towns. Gaucín, on the main road, with roughly

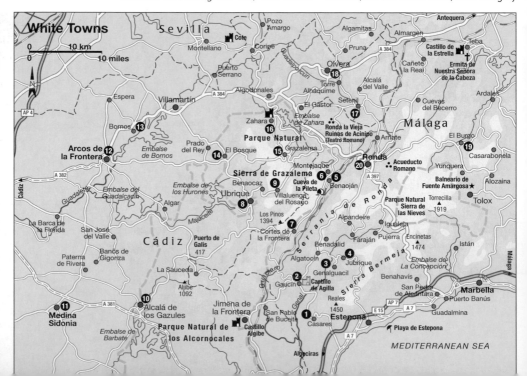

1,600 inhabitants, is the largest of these; most have a population in the region of 1,000, and some, such as Alpandeire, have shrunk well below this figure.

After the Reconquest of 1492 and their nominal Christianisation, these townspeople all joined the *Morisco* (converted Muslim) rebellion of 1570. Resentment smouldered on for centuries and bred a wary people, whose villages were accessible only by steep mule track.

The construction of well-engineered roads has opened up the towns. Their populations increase markedly in the summer months, when migrant workers return to stay with elderly relatives for the holidays and fairs, and in some cases to rebuild and modernise their family homes.

Gaucín ❷ sits high up, spread across a saddle between rocky peaks. It was discovered by foreign visitors long before Casares and has a thriving artists' community, most of whom open their studios to the public in May. It has a well-restored Moorish castle, perched high above the town.

From here you can see Gibraltar and the coast on a clear day. It was in this castle that one of the great heroes of Spanish history, Guzmán the Good (see page 114), sacrificed his son rather than surrender to the Moors.

From Gaucín, continue to **Genalguacil ❸**, off the A369 at Algotocín, in the heart of the Sierra Bermeja. Its name means 'Vizier's Garden', and it exhibits a certain hill-station gaiety, exemplified by the fine municipal swimming pool. There are a couple of hotels, a few self-catering houses, a small posada and a shady campsite down by the bridge over the Río Genal between Algatocín and Jubrique.

From here the route back to the coast at Estepona is bendy but beautiful, taking in a number of tiny white villages, chief of which is **Jubrique ❹**. The village climbs almost vertically up the side of a gorge, with steps in its main streets.

AROUND RONDA

Ronda (see page 131) is another good springboard for exploring the white

Casares, one of the more visited of the pueblos blancos.

Hikers along the Great Path of Málaga in the mountains of Ronda.

On a tour of the Cueva de la Pileta.

towns. The Río Guadiaro (joined lower down by the Genal) rises above Ronda to debouch in the Mediterranean a little north of the Rock of Gibraltar. A railway follows the river from Ronda to Algeciras, stopping at quaint out-of-the-way stations, and this can be a relaxing way to enjoy the fine scenery. Built in the late 19th century by a British consortium, it has only four trains a day in each direction and can be a useful way to get to Ronda from the coast if you don't want to drive.

Minor roads also reach the towns between Ronda and the coast including **Benaoján** ❺ and **Montejaque** ❻, renowned for their *embutidos* (tinned pork products) and mountain-cured hams, then plunging down to the station of Jimera de Líbar before rising again to Cortes de la Frontera.

On the way it is well worth stopping to visit the **Cueva de la Pileta** (www.cuevadelapileta.org; 25 people max at a time, tours daily see website for times; charge), prehistoric caves with spectacular wall-paintings, discovered in 1905 by a local farmer who was looking for *guano* (bird droppings) to fertilise his fields. If there is no one around, wait at the entrance to the caves and one of the caretakers, the grandson or great-grandson of the farmer, will eventually emerge with the previous group of visitors. Inside are paintings of sheep, cattle, horses and fish believed to date from around 25,000 BC, as well as impressive stalactites and stalagmites and a subterranean lake.

Cortes de la Frontera ❼ is a pleasant, medium-sized *pueblo* (pop. 3,200) perched on a high shelf above the Guadiaro. It is clad in the trademark whitewash, with the exception of its distinguished stone town hall dating from the mid-18th century. It also has a bullring of masonry and a fine *alameda* or public promenade. Cortes derives its relative wealth from the cork forests which stretch for over 48 km (30 miles) to the west.

From Cortes, the road winds westwards through the forest, emerging into occasional clearings with fairy-tale cottages (the witches' variety), to the remote crossroads of **Puerto de Galis**.

The most industrial of the sierra towns is **Ubrique** ❽. This is deep in hunting country, as indicated by the great many stag heads and photographs mounted on the walls of the town's bars and restaurants, whose menus are biased towards game. Goats, which are also prolific, are herded for more than their milk, as the town prospers on a centuries-old reputation for leather craft.

A few kilometres east of Ubrique is **Villaluenga del Rosario** ❾, a tiny village carved into the rock that somehow finds space for a bullring. It is a serenely peaceful retreat where elderly locals rest on their sticks in a small, shady square. From here, another 10 km (6 miles) further north is Grazalema, a *pueblo blanco* par excellence and the hub of the Parque Natural Sierra de Grazalema (see page 126).

BETWEEN UBRIQUE AND CÁDIZ

South of Ubrique, a flower-dotted route winds down through the extensive Parque **Natural de Los Alcornocales**, forests of wild olive and cork oak. The source of the cork used to plug sherry bottles, many of the cork oaks are rusty-red from the waist down where their cork has been harvested.

At Puerto de Galis the road splits, offering a choice of routes to the Mediterranean. Secondary roads take in the 'de la Frontera' towns of **Jimena** and **Castellar**, each with a crumbling 13th-century Moorish castle. Indeed, place names that include the word Frontera date from the two-and-a-half centuries before 1492, when the area was the frontier between Christian Spain and the surviving Kingdom of Granada.

Alternatively, the scenic A2304 continues to another hill town at the geographical heart of Cádiz, Alcalà de los Gazules (see below). The undulating arable farms and bull-breeding pastures of the province of Cádiz contain several of the larger pueblos blancos.

Alcalá de los Gazules, Medina Sidonia and Arcos de la Frontera (all on eminences above the plain) are approved White Towns. All three were strongholds of Moorish tribes until the Reconquest, when they passed into the hands of Spanish nobles who then abandoned them in favour of the larger cities.

Alcalá de los Gazules ⑩, with several wayside restaurants on the Cádiz road, is the most Moorish, its flat-topped houses climbing up to the church and fort. **Medina Sidonia** ⑪, bearing the name of the Spanish Armada's admiral, the Duke of Medina Sidonia, excites some expectations. It is in fact a windswept place on top of a conical mound, with a fine main square.

Arcos de la Frontera ⑫, squeezed onto a thin limestone ridge, precariously balanced above a river valley, is the westernmost *pueblo blanco* and one of the most spectacular. Arcos deserves investigation, for though less visited than famous Ronda, it is no less breathtaking, narrowing to medieval lanes so tight that scuffs along sandstone corners testify to the challenge

Arcos de la Frontera enjoys a spectacular setting.

of driving into the centre. A lingering reputation for witchcraft adds to the intrigue of the cobbled labyrinth.

Semana Santa and the Feria de San Miguel (29 September), are celebrated with bull-running, a terrifying thought in Arcos's exceptionally narrow, walled streets.

Easily discovered in the highest, oldest part of town is the **Plaza del Cabildo**. On the lip of the crag's near-vertical precipice, it benefits from far-reaching views across the River Guadalete and beyond. A luxurious parador hotel converted within the Casa del Corregidor, the 11th-century walls of the Castillo de los Duques (privately owned) and a 15th-century Gothic church, **Santa Maria de la Asunción**, flank the square.

Just to the north of Arcos is low-lying **Bornos** ⓭, on the shores of a reservoir squeezed out of the waters of the Guadalete. Above its whitewashed walls rise the remnants of the palace-castle of the Riberas and other grand but gutted buildings. From the desiccated lakeside beach, with its makeshift bars,

there is a superb view of the Sierra de Grazalema. Its decayed grandeur and raffish character make Bornos a perfect foil for the pristine mountains rising across the tranquil water.

THE PARQUE NATURAL SIERRA DE GRAZALEMA

East of Arcos de la Frontera, the A372 tilts up through sunflower fields to **El Bosque** ⓮. This refreshing town, with its tinkling fountains and an old water-wheel, is surrounded by pine trees, sloping down to a clear river abundant with trout a speciality in the local restaurants.

The wooded hills mark the start of the **Parque Natural Sierra de Grazalema** (controlled access). Close to El Bosque's bullring is the park's head office and main information centre (tel: 956-709 733; daily 10am–2pm; closed Mon, June–Sept), where maps are available and free hiking permits, obligatory for the three walks in the park – Garganta Verde, Pinsapar and El Torreón (see page 127) – can be obtained.

The park's rugged terrain, where an unusual microclimate has preserved

Zahara de la Sierra and its reservoir viewed from the ruined castle.

some ancient Mediterranean forest and a precious wildlife habitat, extends almost to the border with Málaga province. At its northern and eastern limits it meets Zahara de la Sierra, which also has a park visitor centre, and Grazalema.

A cascade of pretty whitewashed houses snuggled into the lush foothills of the peak of San Cristóbal, **Grazalema** ⓯ is a welcoming, ebullient place, and a good base for exploring the area. The town lays claim to the region's highest rainfall, and its wrought-iron balconies and geranium-filled window boxes are often coated with snow in winter.

The town earns its living from ceramics and woollen products, crafted according to long-established traditions, as well as tourism. You can see traditional weaving methods at the **Museo de Artsanía Textil** (Mon–Thu 8am–2pm & 3–6.30pm, Fri 8am–2pm; free). For outdoor activities around the town, Horizon Aventura (tel: 956-132 363; www.horizonaventura.com) organises hiking, mountain biking, climbing, caving, paintballing and paragliding.

Alternatively, a rewarding drive through the park follows the spectacular CA531 from Grazalema to Zahara. The route passes the starting point for two of the park's walks (permits required), the **Garganta Verde** – a densely vegetated ravine – and the **Pinsapar** – a conservation area devoted to pre-Ice Age, dark green Spanish fir.

Halfway to Zahara the road twists and climbs to 1,357 metres (4,511 ft) at **Puerto de las Palomas**, where birds of prey (Bonnelli's, booted and golden eagles, griffon vultures and buzzards) circle watchfully, high overhead.

The village of **Zahara de la Sierra** ⓰ wraps itself like a helter-skelter around an isolated, sheer outcrop, twisting down from the ruined 12th-century castle at its peak. An important Moorish town, it was a significant Christian conquest in 1483, and seems little changed. A cared-for place, where a humble pride can be seen in swept steps and immaculately tended flowerbeds, unassuming Zahara enjoys majestic views across olive groves and the reservoir at the foot of its hill.

⊙ Tip

Olvera is the starting point for a 36-km (22-mile) 'vía verde', a hiking and cycling path following a disused railway track. The route runs from Olvera to Puerta Serrano west of Algodonales on the Ronda–Seville road. Visit www.viasverdes-ffe.com for more details or enquire at the tourist office near the Iglesia de la Encarnación.

NORTH OF RONDA

One of the most publicised sights in the region is **Setenil** , a small white town set not on a hilltop as is usually the case but in a ravine of the Río Guadalporcun, 20 km (12 miles) north of Ronda. It has two or three streets of semi-cave houses whose roofs are formed by overhanging rock, giving their neat white facades the appearance of mushroom stems under a spreading crown. It is worth stopping for lunch or a drink at one of its characterful bars.

A few kilometres further north, passing under the walls of the little hilltop village of **Torre Alháquime**, you come to **Olvera** ⓲, a white town par excellence. With around 8,000 inhabitants it is larger than its neighbours. Its silhouette is dramatic: a Moorish keep and the imposing Iglesia de la Encarnacíon rise above tightly packed houses sloping down to a clear perimeter, where the countryside begins. Famous as the refuge for outlaws in the 19th century, Olvera today has a reputation for excellent olive oil and

religiosity. A monument to the Sacred Heart of Jesus on a natural outcrop of rock dominates the lower town, and pilgrims have been known to crawl for miles on their hands and knees, in fulfilment of a vow, to the popular sanctuary of the Virgen de los Remedios.

Olvera's streets are neat and somewhat stern. The handsome facades make few concessions to the floral trimmings so ubiquitous in many *pueblos blancos*. However, the local fair, late in August, is one of the most lavish in the region, lasting for five nights, until 5am or later, with stalls, sideshows, bars, song and dance; during the day there are football matches, clay-pigeon contests and two or three novice bullfights held in a portable ring. Olvera is also the starting point for one of Andalucía's most spectacular Vías Verdes (see margin).

The last white town in this section is **El Burgo** ⓳, out on a limb east of Ronda, on the road to Málaga via Coín, and an alternative base to Ronda for exploring the Parque Natural de la Sierra de las Nieves.

A drink under the rock in Setenil.

The olive groves leading to hilltop Olvera.

Ronda has one of Spain's oldest bullrings.

RONDA

Nothing can detract from Ronda's incomparable setting, above the El Tajo gorge. It also has arguably the finest bullring in Spain.

Dramatically spanning the El Tajo gorge, **Ronda** ⑳, along with the cave-riddled surrounding region, has a long and fascinating history. Prehistoric relics such as the wall-paintings of the nearby Cueva de la Pileta (see page 124) are evidence of human settlement from as early as 25000 BC. Ancient Iberians also populated the area, but it was the Romans who established the first significant settlement here.

The site's impressive geography made the place a natural fortress. After the Muslim invasion of 711 Ronda became one of the Moors' most important towns, known as Madinat Runda, and examples of Moorish architecture can still be seen in the old town.

Early in the 11th century, the Berber Abu Mur displaced the caliphal government, making Ronda an independent *taífa*. Later, after Christian forces had retaken Seville in 1248, the town was at the forefront of tensions between Christian Seville and Muslim Granada. But Muslim rule lasted until 1485 when, as one of the last strongholds of the Kingdom of Granada, it was conquered by the Christians after a seven-day siege. It was soon given a city council with the same rights as Seville.

By the 18th century the old Arab town, La Ciudad, was becoming too small for the growing population, and so, in 1793 the Puente Nuevo (New

Bridge), now the symbol of the city, was built over the Tajo, connecting La Ciudad with a new quarter known as El Mercadillo. The city prospered, and in 1784 Ronda's neoclassical-style Plaza de Toros was also built.

Not long after this, however, the town was practically destroyed by Napoleon's forces during the Wars of Independence.

FAMOUS VISITORS

Ronda was one of the first small Spanish cities (it has around 34,000 inhabitants today) to earn a place on the tourist

Main Attractions
Iglesia Santa María de la Mayor
Palacio del Mondragón
Casa del Gigante
Gardens of the Casa del Rey Moro
Baños Arabes
Puente Nuevo
Plaza de Toros

Maps on pages
122, 132

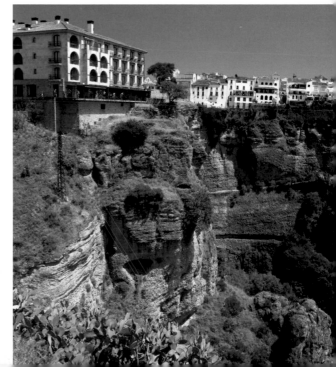

Ronda sits atop the El Tajo gorge.

○ **Tip**

According to Ernest Hemingway, who was a frequent visitor, 'There is one town that would be better … to see your first bullfight in if you are only going to see one, and that is Ronda'. To get a feel for the place and the sport, read his books *Death in the Afternoon* and *The Dangerous Summer*.

map. It was mentioned by early geographers and travellers, from Strabo and Pliny the elder to Ibn Batuta, the 14th-century Arab geographer and explorer, but received its most enthusiastic write-up in Richard Ford's *A Handbook for Travellers in Spain* (1855): 'There is but one Ronda in the world, and this Tajo, cleft as it were by the scimitar of Roldan, forms when the cascade is full… its heart and soul. The scene, its noise and movement, baffle pen and pencil, and, like Wilson at the Falls of Terni, we can only exclaim, "Well done, rock and water, by Heavens!"'

Ford wrote this lyrical description in the heyday of the Romantic movement, when Andalucía drew Scottish artists David Wilkie and David Roberts, Frenchman Théophile Gautier, the great lithographer Gustave Doré, and many others.

In 1906 the Hotel Reina Victoria on the edge of the El Tajo was completed, and it quickly became popular as a retreat for the officers of the Gibraltar garrison. In 1913 the poet Rainer Maria Rilke stayed here for several weeks and wrote *The Spanish Trilogy*, including his eulogistic lines on observing a shepherd tending his flock on the hillside: 'Even today a god might secretly enter that form and not be diminished'.

Later came swashbuckling Ernest Hemingway and Orson Welles to fraternise with the leading matador Antonio Ordóñez, and the painter David Bomberg.

APPROACHES TO THE CITY

With such a legacy of international interest, Ronda has a lot to live up to and probably raises too many expectations in first-time visitors. The inevitable has happened: urban sprawl, an industrial estate and bleak municipal housing have encroached upon the town.

It is therefore wise to approach Ronda with circumspection. The best routes into town, yielding the best views of the old city, are from Algeciras and San Pedro de Alcántara. If you enter from Seville or from Granada, take the ring-road around the town, as if aiming for San Pedro, and then double back into Ronda on the

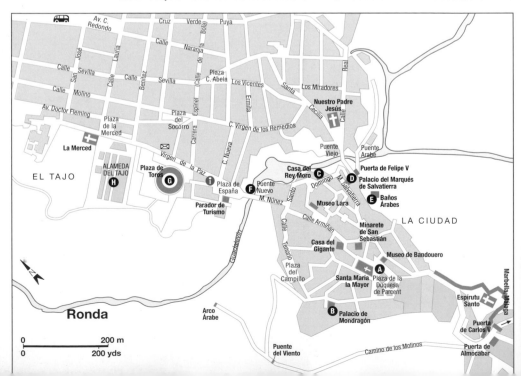

Ronda

unblemished flank, leading into La Ciudad, the old city.

LA CIUDAD

The road enters La Ciudad via the **Barrio de San Francisco**, which is like a small mountain *pueblo* picked up and deposited under the city walls. There is a lively market here every Sunday and an important animal fair early in October. The most striking building, reached through the 13th-century horseshoe arch of the **Puerta de Almocabar**, is the fortress-like church of **Espíritu Santo**, the first to be built after the recapture of Ronda from the Moors in 1485.

The first vehicle-accessible turning on the left as you ascend leads into the **Plaza de la Duquesa de Parcent** **A**, a pretty square with cypresses, medlars and oleanders inside low box hedges. Flanking the plaza are an early 18th-century barracks, now the town hall; a 19th-century boys' school on the site of the Moorish fortress (left ruinous after the Peninsular War); the convents of the Poor Clares and of the Little Sisters of the Cross; the Iglesia Santa María la Mayor; and the law courts.

The 13th-century **Iglesia Santa María la Mayor** (daily 10am–8pm) is built on the site of Ronda's main mosque. Consecrated after the Reconquest, it was later considered too small and was replaced by this church, begun in the Gothic style in the late 15th century and completed in the 18th century. Evidence of the original mosque can be found in the mihrab (niche indicating the direction of Mecca), visible in the entrance, and the minaret, which is now the belltower. Facing the square is an arcade with a gallery, where priests and notables would watch bullfights before the permanent bullring was built.

As you leave the church look out for the quirky **Museo del Bandolero** (Bandit Museum, Calle Armiñàn, 65; www.museobandolero.com; daily 10.30am–8.30pm, until 7pm in winter), dedicated to the region's reputation

for banditry in the 19th century. The museum shop sells replicas of historic knives and guns.

On the same street, the **Museo Lara** (Calle Armiñán, 29; www.museolara.org; daily June–Oct 11am–8pm, Nov–May until 7pm) has an interesting selection of clocks, weapons, torture instruments from the Inquisition, scientific paraphernalia and archaeological finds, as well as a collection of popular art.

Not far from here, on the Plaza Mondragón, is the **Palacio de Mondragón** **B** (www.museoderonda.es; Mon–Fri 10am–7pm, Sat–Sun until 3pm), a grand townhouse of Moorish origins (1314) with a Renaissance stone facade, cobbled porch with mounting block, front patio dating from around 1570 and Mudéjar-style rear patio. Formerly the home of kings and governors, as well as Alistair Boyd (Lord Kilmarnock), author of several books on Spain, including *The Road from Ronda*, it is now the city museum, concentrating mainly on archaeological finds in the region.

There are relatively few remaining examples of domestic building dating

Alfresco lunch on Calle Virgin de la Paz.

View from the Puente Nuevo.

Ronda's Baños Árabes.

from the Muslim era, but the nearby **Casa del Gigante** (Mon–Fri 10am–7pm, Sat 10am–1.45pm & 3–6pm, Sun 10am–3pm) is one of the best preserved outside Granada and has a restored Nasrid ceiling and patio as well as tiles with inscriptions from the Koran. Upstairs is a small museum and film about Ronda's history.

An alley leads from the Plaza de Mondragón into the **Plaza del Campillo** (open on one side to the mountains). Halfway down a steep slope are the remnants of an outer wall and gateway, through which winds a track down to the market gardens and abandoned watermills in the valley.

From the Plaza del Campillo, Calle Tenorio leads back to the main road bisecting the old city. The steep **Cuesta de Santo Domingo** leads down past the **Casa del Marqués de Santa Pola** (with basements preserving some traces of Moorish wall-painting) to the so-called **Casa del Rey Moro** **C** in Calle Santo Domingo. This is an 18th-century pastiche with hanging gardens (designed by the French landscape gardener Jean-Claude Forestier in 1912) through which the **Mina de Ronda**, a long staircase cut inside the rock, descends to the river bed, emerging through a keyhole arch (the gardens and Mina de Ronda can be visited).

The so-called Water Mine is the one feature that is thought to date from the Moorish era. During times of siege, it was manned by a chain of Christian captives, who passed up pitchers of water to supply the citadel, 'whose fierce king' – according to a romantic travel book of 1923 – 'drank only from the skulls of enemies; cutting off their heads and making them into goblets inlaid with splendid jewels'.

Another of Ronda's fine buildings is the 18th-century **Palacio del Marqués de Salvatierra** **D** (not open to the public). Its interesting facade, showing Spanish colonial influences, reflects the fact that it was built for the Marqués de Moctezuma, the Governor of South America. The fine wrought ironwork is a speciality of Ronda; you will see other examples in *rejas* (window grilles) and on balconies throughout the town.

Below the palace, Calle Marqués de Salvatierra leads down to the **Puerta de Felipe V**, a mini triumphal arch built in 1742 and commemorating Spain's first Bourbon monarch. Down the slope, the **Puente Viejo** (Old Bridge) crosses the gorge, offering an impressive upward view of the Tajo.

To the right is the so-called **Puente Árabe** and, a short walk away, the **Baños Árabes** Ⓔ (Arab Baths; Mon–Fri 10am–7pm, Sat–Sun until 3pm), dating from around 1300. Sited at the confluence of two rivers near the city gates, the baths were used by travellers entering the city. As is common in Muslim societies today, they were built next to a mosque, spiritual and bodily purification being interdependent. The baths have been fully restored and comprise a reception area, cold room, warm room and, closest to the wood-fired oven, a hot room. From this point, a rough pebbled track leads up under the Salvatierra palace to the third of the medieval city gates.

THE PUENTE NUEVO

The **Puente Nuevo** Ⓕ (New Bridge) crosses the gorge at its deepest and narrowest point and is a uniquely assertive feat of engineering, more like a solid causeway with apertures than an aerial span over the abyss. The Puente Nuevo was constructed entirely of stone between 1751 and 1793. Once it was open, tightly corseted Ronda spilled out onto the tableland known as the Mercadillo, until then used mainly for markets and fairs.

Many have fallen to their death from the bridge. Indeed, its architect José Martín de Aldehuela plunged to his death while inspecting the structure shortly before its completion. Much later, in the 20th century, the bridge gained notoriety in Ernest Hemingway's *For Whom the Bell Tolls*, which describes local fascists being thrown to their deaths from the bridge by the Republican forces during the Spanish Civil War.

Few can resist the opportunity to peer over the railings at the waters of the Guadalevín river flowing 98 metres

Puente Nuevo, made famous by Hemingway.

(321 ft) below. A small prison (carcel) used to exist in the middle of the bridge.

PLAZA DE TOROS

The **Plaza de Toros**  (www.rmcr.org; daily Apr–Sept 10am–8pm; Mar and Oct until 7pm, Nov–Feb until 6pm; audioguide available) is not the oldest bullring in Spain, as is often claimed, but it is far and away the largest and most elegant of the early plazas. It was inaugurated in 1785, though had been in use before that. Indeed, a corrida held the previous year resulted in a partial collapse of the arena killing 10 spectators. Besides being of architectural beauty, the ring is considerably different from more modern plazas in its technical layout. With a diameter of 66 metres/yds, it is one of the widest rings in the world.

Ronda has produced many notable figures in the bullfighting world. Pedro Romero, of the influential Romero dynasty, laid down the modern rules of bullfighting in the 18th century, starting the tradition on foot, equipped with a sword and muleta (small cloth). Born in Ronda in 1754, Pedro Romero is credited with having killed over 5,600 bulls in his career without ever suffering a major injury. From a family noted for its longevity – his father lived to 102 – Pedro Romero killed his last bull in the Madrid bullring at the incredible age of 79.

The other great Ronda-born dynasty is the Ordóñez family, which has produced several generations of prominent matadors over more than a century.

The bullring's **Museum** is of real interest, detailing the origins and evolution of bullfighting, including Ronda's role in these, with documents, deeds, historic posters, costumes, memorabilia, paintings, and more.

In September, on the Saturday of the feria, the bullring stages a corrida goyesca, introduced by the Ordóñez family in 1954 to mark the 200th anniversary of Pedro Romero's birth. The toreadors, and many members of the audience, dress in the costumes of the period, as shown in Goya's series of etchings, The Tauromachia, which are on display in the bullring's museum.

PASEO PLACES

A little higher up than the Plaza de Toros on the same side of the street is the **Alameda del Tajo** , a shady public promenade dating from 1806, which ends in a balustrade on the brink of a sheer drop. 'The view from this eminence over the depths below, and the mountain panorama,' wrote Richard Ford, in his Handbook for Travellers, 'is one of the finest in the world'. Few will accuse him of hyperbole.

It is not necessary to go beyond the Alameda (or the neighbouring church of La Merced, which once housed the arm of Santa Teresa of Ávila) other than to reach the **Hotel Reina Victoria** on the highest point of the new town. With the coming of newer, more luxurious hotels, including the parador on the edge of the gorge, this once-famous establishment has lost some of its Edwardian atmosphere. However, it

Statue of bullfighting great Pedro Romero outside Ronda's Plaza de Toros.

is worth paying it a visit to see the room in which Rainer Maria Rilke stayed, which has a few mementoes, and to enjoy a drink on the terrace at sunset.

Despite its claim to an aristocratic and warlike past, and its delight in legends of brigands and smugglers, Ronda has for long been a lively commercial centre for almost 30 smaller towns and villages. This is borne out in the **Calle de la Bola**, a traffic-free shopping street running from the bullring due east for more than a kilometre. Ronda's answer to Las Ramblas of Barcelona or Calle Sierpes in Seville, it is packed both before lunch and for the evening *paseo*.

AROUND RONDA

Ronda is a stop on one of the great train journeys of southern Spain, the Algeciras–Bobadilla route, which meanders through the valley of the Río Guadiaro via the white towns of Gaucín and Jimena de la Frontera.

The town is also a good base for excursions by car. Just a few kilometres west of town are the remains – theatre, forum and public baths – of the 1st-century BC Roman town of **Acinipo** (tel: 951–041 452; Wed–Sun 9am–2pm; free) at Ronda La Vieja.

Further afield, southeast of Ronda, the **Parque Natural Sierra de las Nieves** stretches almost to Marbella. It is famous for a rare species of prehistoric fir, the *pinsapo*, which grows only above 1,000 metres (3,200 ft), and also for the *Capra pyrenaica* or ibex; some pairs of golden eagles also survive. Access by jeep trail via the towns of **El Burgo** (see page 128, **Yunquera** or **Tolox** (see page 157) is relatively unrestricted.

West of Ronda, the **Parque Natural Sierra de Grazalema** (see page 126) covers an area of almost 50,000 hectares (120,000 acres), including 13 villages, mainly in the province of Cádiz. The flora and fauna on this side are more varied, but access is strictly controlled, and some of the routes in the *pinsapares* (which also exist here) are closed during the summer months as a precaution against forest fires. The main park office is in the small town of El Bosque (see page 126).

⊙ Drink

They've been making wine around Ronda since Roman times. To try some of the local varieties, accompanied by yummy tapas, head to Bar Siempre Igual (Calle San José 2) or Bar El Convento (Calle San Francisco 140). Both are part of the town's 'ruta de vinos' (wine route; www.ruta-vinos-ronda.com), which promotes local wine-related businesses including vineyards.

Pinsapo trees in Parque Natural Sierra de las Nieves.

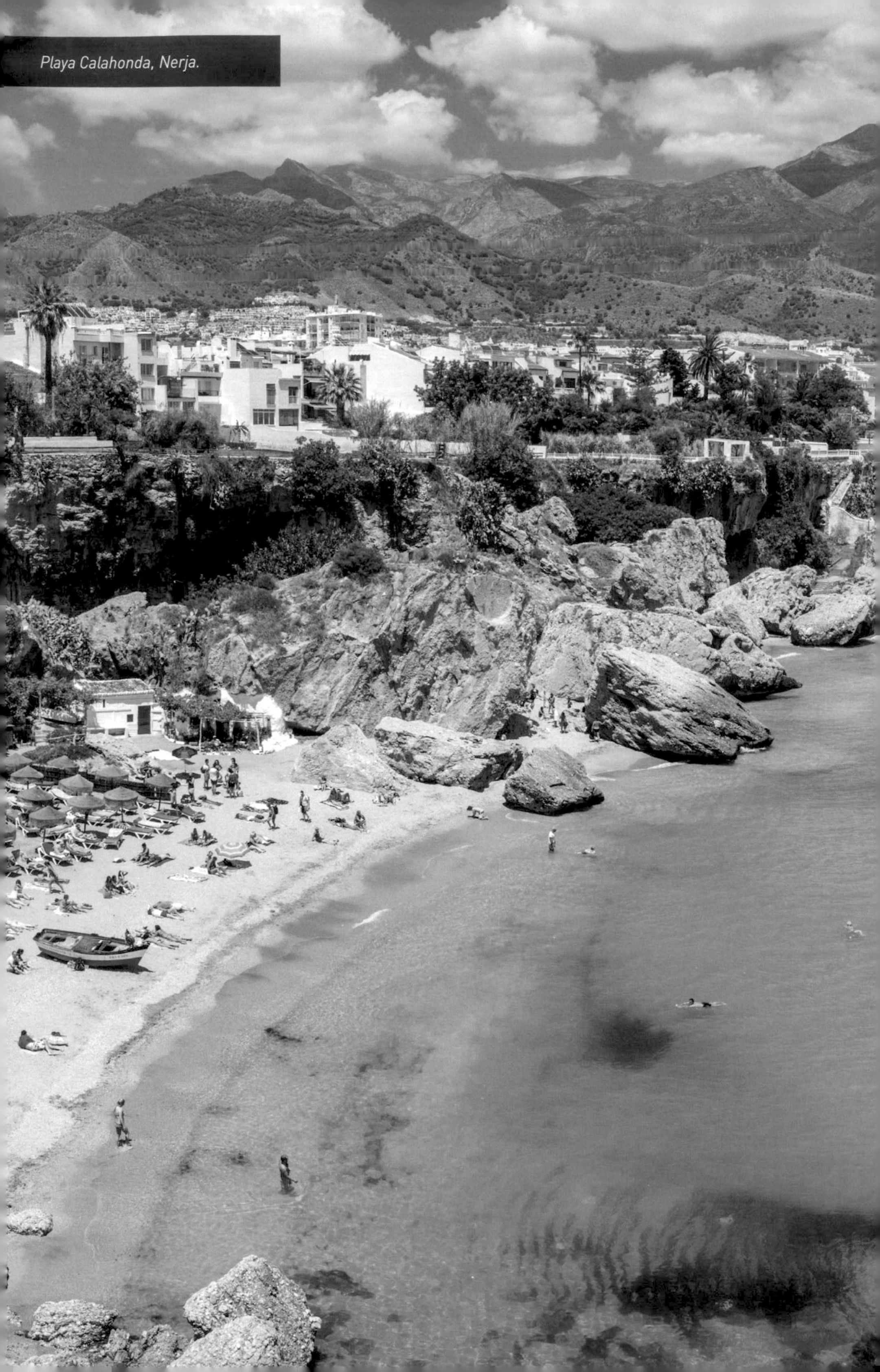

Playa Calahonda, Nerja.

THE COSTA DEL SOL

The Costa del Sol's many resorts offer something for every taste – from glamorous Marbella to brash Torremolinos and family-focused Fuengirola.

It is impossible to write about the Costa del Sol without some degree of regret about what a lovely coast it must have been with its small sandy bays and fishing villages, connected to each other by no more than dirt roads, backed from end to end by a dramatic line of sierras. But that is just a distant memory now, and the only way you will see that scene is on grainy black-and-white photographs sometimes on display in hotels and bars. These days, large built-up resorts lie almost end to end from Sotogrande to Nerja. So many golf courses are found here that it has been dubbed the 'Costa del Golf'.

But if the Costa is scenically and ecologically a disaster, it can still be fun. The climate is good year-round, the sea is warm and the sandy beaches are still there, immaculately maintained by the local authorities. The array of attractions appeals to visitors of all ages, tastes and backgrounds.

MÁLAGA

Málaga ❶ is the largest city, capital and gateway of the Costa del Sol. Although historic and with some interesting attractions, for many years it was largely overlooked by visitors who, for the most part, just passed through the airport on the way to the resorts. In recent years all that has changed,

and Málaga has become a city destination in its own right, with a cluster of world-class museums and a foodie/nightlife scene to rival Seville. The city has been given a thorough make-over. Attractive new hotels have been built in the centre and along the beach, and Calle Marqués de Larios – the main shopping street, west of the Cathedral – is now a pleasant pedestrian zone. There's also a new shopping mall, Muelle Uno, at the port.

For a long time the city had no decent beach, but a massive

Maps on pages
140, 142

Picasso mural in Plaza de la Merced, Málaga.

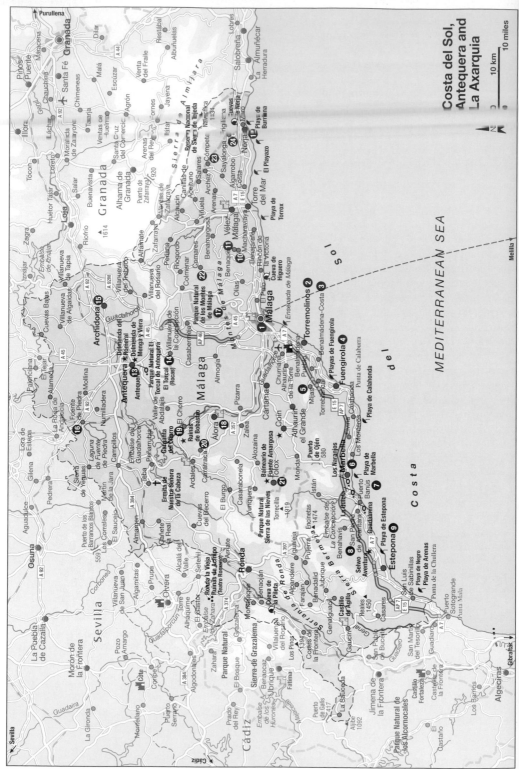

Costa del Sol,
Antequera and
La Axarquía

10 km
10 miles

MEDITERRANEAN SEA

programme involving the import of millions of tonnes of sand and the removal of unsightly shacks vastly improved both Málaga's beaches, which lie east of the city centre, and others along the coast.

MÁLAGA'S HISTORY

Originally Phoenician, Málaga sided briefly with Carthage before becoming a Roman *municipium* (a town governed by its own laws). In 711 it fell to the Moors, and was the port of the Kingdom of Granada until 1487, when it was taken by the Christians after a four-month siege followed by brutal burnings.

On several occasions the city has been a place of revolt. It was on Málaga's San Andrés beach that the rebel General Torrijos and his 52 companions were shot in 1831. In revolt against the repressive government of Fernando VII, this young Spanish general landed on today's Costa del Sol, encouraged by an invented story that the Málaga garrison would join him. Instead it surrounded and captured him.

In 1931, and again at the start of the Civil War five years later, left-wing citizens burned Málaga's churches and convents. The city held out against General Franco's Nationalists until 1937; when it finally fell, its refugees were bombed and shelled as they escaped up the coast road towards Almería.

MAIN SIGHTS

Málaga's most prominent landmark is the **Catedral A** (Calle Molina Lario; www.diocesismalaga.es/catedral; Mon–Fri 10am–6pm, Sat 10am–5pm, Sun for Mass). Built in fits and starts between 1528 and 1782, it is still unfinished, as one of its twin towers is missing – the other rises an impressive 100 metres (330 ft) above street level. From that, it gets its nickname, 'La Manquita', the One-Armed Lady. The highlight of the interior is the choir, completed in 1662 by the great Granada sculptor Pedro de Mena.

On the square in front of the Cathedral's western facade is the **Palacio Episcopal** (Tue–Sun 11am–9pm), now a venue for temporary art exhibitions.

Málaga's Plaza de Toros viewed from the Alcazaba.

La Manquita,
Málaga's Cathedral.

PICASSO MUSEUM

A short walk from the Cathedral, on Calle San Augustín, is the magnificent Buenavista Palace, built between 1516 and 1542 by Diego de Cazalla and housing the **Museo Picasso B** (www.museopicassomalaga.org; daily 10am–8pm July Aug, 10am–7pm Mar–June & Sept–Oct; 10am–6pm Nov–Feb), dedicated to Málaga's most famous son. Comprising 233 paintings, drawings, sculptures, ceramics and prints, spanning Picasso's entire career, the bulk of the collection was donated by Cristina and Bernard Ruiz-Picasso, Picasso's daughter-in-law and grandson. They range from works such as a portrait of his younger sister Lola, painted when he was just 15, to familiar Cubist works painted from 1910 onwards.

The family home on nearby Plaza de la Merced, where Picasso spent the first 10 years of his life, has been restored, and functions as the **Casa Natal** (www.fundacionpicasso.malaga.eu; daily 9.30am–8pm), primarily a study centre and reference library, but with a collection of family photographs, sketches and pots.

THE FORTIFICATIONS

Málaga's historical sights are mainly evident on the high ground at its eastern end, dominated by the **Alcazaba G** (Tue–Sun 9am–8pm, 9am–6pm in winter), and the Castillo de Gibralfaro above it. The route up to the Alcazaba passes through a maze of pretty gardens to the **Arco del Cristo** (Gateway of Christ) – where the Catholic Monarchs celebrated Mass following their conquest of the fortress in 1487 – and then to an old palace housing an archaeological museum. At the foot of the route is the **Teatro Romano** (Roman Theatre; Tue–Sat 10am–6pm, Sun 10am–4pm; free).

Connecting the Alcazaba with the **Castillo de Gibralfaro D** (daily 9am–8pm in summer, 9am–6pm in winter) formidable double walls with square turrets ascend the hill. Named from the Arabic Jebel al Faro (Lighthouse Hill), this immense structure was founded by Abd-al-Rahman I in the 8th century and enlarged in the 14th century. A rocky path climbs beside the wall to a height of 130 metres (425 ft), though you can also drive up here from behind

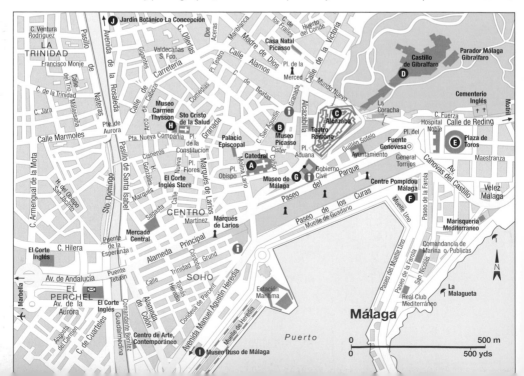

the hill (or catch bus 35). A *mirador* offers superb views over the harbour and down on to the Plaza de Toros (see page 136), but for a beer (or more) with your view stop off at the luxurious Parador de Málaga Gibralfaro.

OTHER SIGHTS

The city centre offers quite a few more sights. Between the **Plaza de Toros** (bullring) **E** and the seafront the area known as **La Malagueta** has good restaurants and bars. At the port, behind the Muelle Uno shopping mall, is the **Centre Pompidou Málaga F** (Pasaje Doctor Carillo Casaux; www.centre pompidou-malaga.eu; Wed–Mon 9.30am–8pm), a branch of the Centre Pompidou in Paris in a striking long, low building topped by a glass 'Rubik's Cube', housing a stunning collection of contemporary art. To the west, opposite the Paseo del Parque, the Palacio de la Aduana houses the **Museo de Málaga G** (Tue–Sun 9am–3.30pm, mid-June–mid-Sept; Tue–Sat 9am–8.30pm, Sun 9am–3.30pm mid-Sept–mid-June; free to EU citizens) with its impressive collections of Spanish art and archaeology. Continuing west, the triangular area between Alameda Principa and Avenida Manuel Agustín Heredía, now known as Soho, has in recent years been decorated with street art and is crammed with hip cafés, bars and boutiques.

North of here near the dry river bed of the Guadamedina, which divides the city, is the **Museo Carmen Thyssen H** (Calle Compañia; www.carmen thyssenmalaga.org; Tue–Sun 10am–8pm), housed in a renovated 16th-century palace and focuses on 19th-century Spanish and Andalusian art. Closer to the port, in Málaga's old wholesale market on Calle Alemania, is the **Centro de Arte Contemporáneo** (www.cac malaga.eu; Tue–Sun 10am–8pm; 10am–2pm & 5–9pm in summer; free). It has works by leading national and international artists. Continuing west, the **Museo Ruso de Málaga I** (Avenida de Sor Teresa Prat 15; www.coleccionmuseo ruso.es; Tue–Sun 9.30am–8pm), is a branch of the Russian State Museum in St Petersburg and displays Russian art from the 16th to the 20th century.

Calle Marques de Larios, Málaga's pedestrian shopping avenue.

⌕ THE GOOD-TIME COSTA

From package-holiday tourists to criminals and from super-rich oligarchs to reality TV stars – all life is found in the resorts of the Costa del Sol.

The year 1932 is regarded as a turning point in the making of the Costa del Sol. Legend has it a certain Carlota Alessandri bought a piece of barren hillside at Montemar, west of Torremolinos. Asked what she intended to plant there, she replied haughtily: "Plant? I shall plant tourists!'

After World War II, the Marquis of Najera, a Spanish nobleman, took up residence in Torremolinos. In his wake came well-to-do Spanish families, and European diplomats and colonial officials unwilling to adjust to a retirement devoid of constant sunshine. In the 1960s Torremolinos became a magnet for bohemians, including Hemingway and the American novelist James Michener, who based his book *The Drifters* on characters plucked from the Costa del Sol's lotus-eaters.

While Torremolinos throbbed with life on the fringe, further down the coast the Spanish nobleman Ricardo Soriano, the Marquis of Ivanrey, was inviting his

Torremolinos before the onslaught of mass tourism, 1959.

wealthy friends to the village of Marbella. The Marquis's nephew, Prince Alfonso von Hohenlohe of Liechtenstein, was so impressed that he bought a decaying farmhouse on the outskirts of the fishing village for £2,000 (US$3,000), turned it into a hotel and named it the Marbella Club. Visitors included King Leopold of the Belgians, the Duke and Duchess of Windsor, Gina Lollobrigida, Sophia Loren and Frank Sinatra.

Inevitably, the rest of the world refused to be left out of the fun, and so between Torremolinos and Marbella a string of bucket-and-spade resorts sprang up. Increasing numbers of these holidaymakers decided that the Costa del Sol was to be their playground too, with many staying on to set up bars and restaurants.

More money flooded in during the 1970s, when the 1973 oil crisis and Middle East turmoil persuaded many rich Arabs to seek safer havens for their riches. The late King Fahd himself (then Prince), together with 60 relatives and minions, set up one of his many homes in a multi-million-dollar palace complete with mosque and heliport.

More recent celebrities on the Costa have included local boy Antonio Banderas, who owns a house in Los Monteros just outside Marbella; Simon Cowell, who has a home in the Sierra Blanca area of Marbella, Vladimir Putin, and Julio Iglesias, who has a house near Coín. Jennifer López attracts plenty of attention during her frequent visits to Marbella, and Prince Andrew, a keen golfer, frequents Sotogrande's Valderrama course.

There has also been a dark side to the money-fuelled hedonism. If it was Arab and British money that cemented the Costa del Sol as an international investment centre, it was the Costa del Sol's proximity to the cannabis plantations in Morocco's Rif Mountains just across the Straits of Gibraltar, and the absence of an extradition treaty between Spain and Britain, that helped the coast gain the dubious title of the Costa del Crime. The fortunes generated by drug trafficking have seen the growth of a sophisticated extension of the European underworld. A booming local economy and the ease with which a foreign face goes undetected aid the crooks, while the hostility of nearby Gibraltar to the local Spanish authorities proves a stumbling block to solving many crimes and gathering evidence.

On the northern outskirts of Málaga (off the Antequera road 4 km/2.5 miles from town), the **Jardín Botánico La Concepción** ❶ (www.laconcepcion.malaga.eu; Tue–Sun Apr–Sept 9.30am–7.30pm, Oct–Mar 9:30–4.30pm) is a pleasant place in which to while away a few hours. A tropical garden with lakes and waterfalls, it was created in the mid-19th century by a local aristocratic family.

The city buzzes in August when the Feria de Málaga sees locals and tourists dancing to live flamenco and knocking back sherry.

WEST OF MÁLAGA

From the start, **Torremolinos** ❷ epitomised the best and the worst of mass tourism on the Costa, and it is no different today. The town is busy and cosmopolitan (though in no sense sophisticated) and not particularly attractive, apart from the surviving kernel of the old town. That said, the 8 km (5 miles) of fine beaches, even if somewhat overcrowded, are a great attraction.

From its main drag, the pedestrianised **Calle Miguel**, a series of steps winds down to the attractive **Paseo Marítimo**, where just to the west the rocky promontory of the **Castillo de Santa Clara** divides the Bajondillo and Carihuela parts of town. La Carihuela, to the west around the headland, used to be a small fishing village, and even today fishermen in their brightly coloured, flat-bottomed boats catch the sardines that you see skewered and grilled at the many beachside *chiringuitos* lining the promenade.

The seafront continues west to **Benalmádena Costa** ❸, one of several gleaming-white marina villages. At first glance it seems like an extension of Torremolinos, but although it has its fair share of bars and restaurants it is nowhere near as brash. Three Moorish watchtowers and the neo-Moorish Castillo El Bil-Bil, built in the 1930s, are focal points along the beach, and the large Torrequebrada complex houses one of the Costa del Sol's biggest casinos. Its other half, **Benalmádena Pueblo**, located inland high above the sea, is much more unspoilt, and home to a surprisingly good museum of Pre-Columbian American art (www.benalmadena.com/museo; Tue–Sat 9.30am–1.30pm and 5–7pm, 6–8pm in summer, Sun 10am–2pm; free). Also in the village is Europe's largest Buddhist stupa (www.stupabenalmadena.org; Tue–Sat 10am–2pm, 4–7.30pm, Sun 10am–2.30pm, 3.30–7.30pm; free) next door to which is the Mariposario (www.mariposariadebenalmadena.com; daily 10am–7.30pm), which has more than 1,500 butterflies from all over the world.

Rather more typical attractions of the Torremolinos/Benalmádena area include Benalmádena's **Selwo Marina** (www.selwomarina.es), which has a dolphinarium and a 'penguinarium on ice', and **Teleférico Benalmádena** (www.telefericobenalmadena.com), operating spectacular cable-car rides over the area, as well as falconry displays. In a similar vein are **Tivoli World** (www.tivoli

Torremolinos beachfront.

costadelsol.com), the largest amusement park on the coast, with more than 40 rides; **Sea Life** (www.visitsealife.com/benalmadena) at Puerto Marina, and **Crocodile Park** (www.cocodrilospark.com), with hands-on displays in Torremolinos.

FUENGIROLA

A few kilometres further west along the coast, although the gap gets smaller every year as the towns expand, is **Fuengirola** ❹, which has been extremely popular with the British – as the numerous bars offering full English breakfasts, fish and chips, pints of beer and giant TVs screening British premier-league football matches testify. The best of the hotels are found on the very long **Paseo Marítimo** that stretches all the way down to Sohail Castle on the hill above the Río Fuengirola. With views up and down the coast, the castle was originally built in 956, some 250 years after the Moorish conquest of Spain, by Abd-al-Rahman III, the best-known of the Umayyad caliphs. Fuengirola grew up under its protection.

Even after the Christian conquest of Granada it survived for a few years, and was not finally captured and levelled until 1497. The present castle was built in 1730 to hamper trade with Gibraltar, which the British had occupied in 1704. Eighty years later, in 1810, it was connected with one of the more shameful (from a British point of view) episodes of the Peninsular War. A British expedition of 800 men under General Blayney landed here and advanced on Mijas, but found the country too difficult and retreated to the castle. Here Blayney disposed his troops 'with the utmost contempt of military rules' and as a result was forced to surrender to 150 Polish troops who were fighting for the French.

MIJAS

The mountain village of **Mijas** ❺, 8 km (5 miles) above Fuengirola, markets itself as a typical *pueblo,* but actually has more in common with the coast than with inland Spain. Its shops sell sheepskin jackets, local pottery and the usual souvenirs; you can even take

Benalmádena cable car.

a *burro* taxi (donkey taxi), much to the chagrin of animal welfare campaigners. Mijas also has Spain's only square *plaza de toros*, though for the most part the bullfights held here are for the consumption of foreign visitors and not comparable to what you would see in Málaga or other more serious plazas.

Despite all this, the village does have some appeal. The air is fresher up here, and there are fine views down to the coast. With its clean white houses and green shutters, this village is a good example of the Spanish genius for giving even tourist traps a certain enchantment. The **Centro de Arte Contemporáneo de Mijas** (CAC; www.cacmijas.info; Tue–Sun 10am–6pm) has a fine selection of works by modern artists including ceramics by Picasso.

Of the attractions in this area, the **Parque Acuático Mijas** (www.aquamijas.com), next to the busy A7 road on the outskirts of Fuengirola, has a full array of water amusements, and the **Hipódromo** racecourse, which also doubles as an arena for the El Cartujano Andaluz horse show (Thu at 6pm; www.elcartujano.com).

MARBELLA

The next resort of any size is **Marbella** ❻, long associated with wealthy celebrities and aristocrats. This is reflected in the plethora of five-star hotels on the beach front, including the Marbella Club, established by Prince Alfonso von Hohenlohe in 1953 and the acorn from which Marbella's exclusive reputation grew. The town's main thoroughfare, Avenida Ramon y Cajal, is usually jammed with traffic, but just north of its centre an old town survives. At its heart is the lovely **Plaza de los Naranjos**, planted with orange trees and overlooked by the 16th-century Casa del Corregidor, one of the town's few old buildings and home to the tourist office. On a hot summer night this plaza, set from side to side with dining tables, becomes one vast open-air restaurant. Housed in a beautiful former hospital, the **Museo del Grabado Español Contemporáneo** (Calle Hospital Bazán; www.mgec.es; Tue–Fri 9am–7pm; Mon & Sat 9am–2pm) specialises in the work of modern Spanish painters and has works by Picasso, Dalí and Miró.

Café life in Mijas.

Although Marbella has its own marina, few visitors will be able to resist a visit to **Puerto Banús** ❼ just west of town (the best way of getting there is on the little ferry that travels between the marinas), where the jetties are fringed with palm trees, and the neo Andalusian style architecture is pristine white. The main attraction is the many large yachts and the opportunities for celebrity-spotting. On the way there or back by car, stop off at **Museo Ralli** (www.rallimuseums. com; Tue–Sat 10am–3pm; free), which has an excellent collection of works by contemporary big-name European and Latin American artists.

Unlike the resorts further east, this part of the Costa del Sol is both cosmopolitan and sophisticated. Wherever you go you will see designer boutiques, international banks, huge estate agents, luxury-car dealers and gourmet restaurants.

THE HINTERLAND

There are numerous little villages in the hills behind Marbella, some of which were once genuine mountain *pueblos*, but almost all of them have been gentrified, and many are inundated by British retirees. **Benahavís**, about 10 km (6 miles) inland from Marbella, past the exclusive Atalya Golf Club, is a good example of this – more than half of its population is foreign, and it is self consciously pristine and quaint.

For a more Spanish experience, consider a half-day drive into the Sierra Bermeja, stopping for lunch in the Refugio de Juanar (www.juanar.com), 19 km (12 miles) from Marbella. Take the C337 off the coastal N340, twisting into the hills through fir and eucalyptus trees, with views of the coast to the rear. After 12 km (7 miles), past the village of **Ojén**, a signposted side road on the left leads to the Refugio, a parador until the Spanish government sold it to the workers for the symbolic sum of one peseta.

A pleasantly simple place, the hotel is where General de Gaulle chose to finish his memoirs. It has a good restaurant (barbecues on the terrace on summer weekends), and lunch here can be followed by a 2.5-km (1.5-mile)

Puerto Banús, the Costa's most exclusive marina.

stroll to the *mirador* overlooking the sierra and the coast, or a more strenuous hike through the forest following signposted trails to Ojén or **Istán**.

WEST OF MARBELLA

It was to **San Pedro de Alcántara** ❽ that the early British and American expatriates escaped when Marbella expanded out of recognition. A few kilometres west of Puerta Banús, the original village stands more than a kilometre from the sea, and thus retains a degree of Spanish character. North of here the bendy but beautiful 376 heads north to Ronda.

Estepona ❾, the most westerly of the Costa's swollen fishing villages (25 km/15.5 miles from Marbella), now a largish town, has avoided too many high-rises, and retains an old quarter of narrow streets and bars, while its long esplanade has a certain elegance. It also has some historical interest. Phoenician, then Roman – the remains of Salduba aqueduct are nearby – it was fortified by the Moors and then the Christians when they retook the town in 1456. It also has one of the little round watchtowers built when Barbary pirates plagued the coast in the 16th century.

The area around Estepona is developing fast and there are numerous attractions for children. The biggest of these is nearby **Selwo Aventura** (www.selwo.es), a safari park offering close-up views of some 2,000 mammals from every continent. Tours can be made on foot or in four-wheel drive trucks. Added attractions include the largest walk-through aviary in Europe, camel rides, plus activities such as archery. It's even possible to spend the night in a Masai hut.

For a more Spanish experience, Estepona is a good springboard for exploring the white towns of Caceres and Gaucín, which can be visited on an easy day circuit (see page 123).

The least changed section of the Costa del Sol lies closest to Gibraltar in the province of Cádiz, where the main highway runs a few kilometres inland. Where the road returns to the coast, near the mouth of the Río Guadiaro, you'll find the plush marina-resort of **Puerto Sotogrande**, along with the

Ojén is famous for aguardiente, a fierce anise spirit.

Grilled sardines for sale on the beach at Estepona.

exclusive Valderrama golf course. In the early evening the marina bars offer lovely views of the sun setting over Gibraltar. From here it is an easy run of some 50 km (30 miles) back to Marbella.

EAST OF MÁLAGA

This section of the Costa del Sol is quite different from its western counterpart. In general, the mountains recede further from the sea – at least until Nerja – and the resorts here are neither as large and crowded as Torremolinos and Fuengirola nor as sophisticated as Marbella and Puerto Banús. Though not undeveloped, the east is much quieter. A motorway runs far inland, taking much of the traffic away from what was formerly a slow and overcrowded coastal road.

From Málaga city centre the road initially passes some good city beaches, each offering a large choice of *chiringuito* restaurants, and after an ugly cement works **Rincón de la Victoria** comes into sight with tall blocks of flats lining an otherwise attractive shallow bay.

INLAND DIVERSION

At **Torre de Benagalbón**, just past Rincón, a road heads inland, climbing past the emerald-green fairways of yet another golf course to the tiny villages of Benaque and Macharaviaya. They first appear far below the road, tentacles of white houses set against the grey peaks of the Sierra de Tejeda. Immediately below, on the valley sides, are their vineyards.

Macharaviaya ⑩ is the smaller and more charming of the two, with cobbled streets and a huge dilapidated church, hinting at the village's former importance. In fact, in the 18th century Macharaviaya had a monopoly on the manufacture of playing cards. Its factory even supplied the Americas. In the church's crypt are memorials to the industry's founders, the Gálvez family, powerful Spanish colonialists who extended Spanish influence up the west coast of America as far as San Francisco Bay. Alas for Macharaviaya, the Gálvez family eventually petered out, its monopoly lapsed and the factory closed.

The road to Macharaviaya.

Benaque ⓫, slightly larger, is at the end of a road to nowhere, the village that time forgot and a world away from the Costa del Sol. It was the birthplace of poet Salvador Rueda and there is a small museum dedicated to him.

BACK ON THE COAST

After Torre de Benagalbón, the small community of **Benajarafe** sits across from the long, open **Playa de Chilches**. Just past there is the medium-sized resort of **Torre del Mar**, which has an attractive marina. After that, sporadic development interrupts the coastal plain and its fields of sugar cane, as do pockets of plastic agriculture (see page 216) encroaching from the provinces of Granada and Almería.

COVES AND CAVES AT NERJA

The main resort on the eastern side of the coast, **Nerja ⓬**, 56 km (34 miles) east of Málaga, has seen spectacular growth in recent years. It has not all been well controlled, but it remains an attractive town, backed by the Sierra de Tejeda and with a series of pretty, sandy coves nearby.

Follow signs to the so-called Balcón de Europa (the Balcony of Europe), a marble-paved projection above a headland, set with palms and decorated with a couple of cannons recovered from the sea. Alfonso XII gave it this name in 1885, and indeed there is nothing ahead but the Mediterranean, with Africa somewhere beyond the horizon. Tucked below the balcony to the east is a small sandy cove with fishing boats and a popular *chiringuito* called 'El Papagayo', while, beyond, the coast curves away in a big crescent of cliffs backed by mountains.

Maro, 3 km (2 miles) round this curving bay, has its own balcony, a palm walk above surrounding market gardens, with fine views east. Unmissable from the coast road is the **Puente del Águila**, a four-tiered aqueduct built in the 19th century to transport water from a local spring to the San Joaquín sugar factory.

Turn away from the coast for Nerja's other attraction. Here, in 1959, five young boys went on a bat-hunting expedition, felt warm air coming from a crack in the rocks and stumbled upon the **Cuevas de Nerja** (Nerja Caves; www.thenerjacaves.com; daily July–Aug 9am–5.30pm, Sept–June 9am–3pm). Every day, busloads of foreign visitors pour into Nerja to see these astonishing underground caverns, one of which has been fitted out as an auditorium and hosts the Festival Internacional de Música y Danza each June.

Artefacts from the caves, including the skeleton of an adult female, can be seen in the **Museo de Nerja** (Plaza de España; daily July–Aug 10am–8pm; Sept–June 10am–2pm, 4–6.30pm; free on Mon for EU citizens).

Beyond Maro, the Sierra de Tejeda drops sharply down to the sea, and the Costa del Sol gives way to the Costa Tropical of Granada province (see page 200). Here, steep, stony hillsides protect small rocky coves, and if you manage to climb down you can still bathe alone, quite possibly beside a farmer's avocado plantation.

The 19th-century Puente del Águila.

The impressive Cuevas de Nerja were inhabited 30,000 years ago.

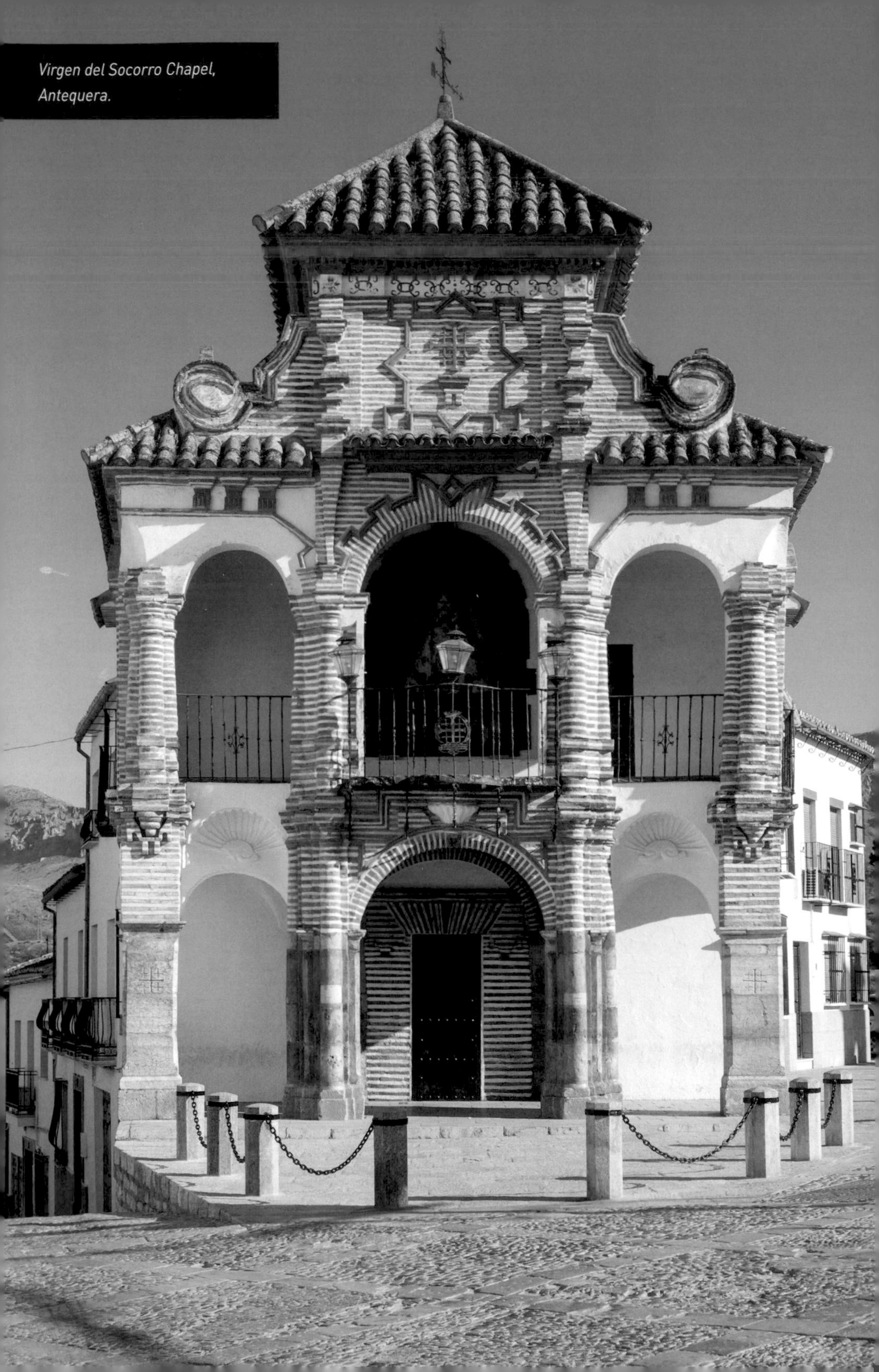

Virgen del Socorro Chapel, Antequera.

ANTEQUERA AND LA AXARQUIA

The highlights of the uplands behind Málaga
include one of Andalucía's most venerable
towns, ancient dolmens and perched villages.

Behind the hedonistic, high-rise resorts of the Costa del Sol, the province of Málaga quickly reverts to a procession of deeply rural mountain chains, with only the occasional north–south river valley facilitating communications. The peaks are at their highest and bleakest around Ronda (see page 131), west of which the landscape becomes tamer. While for the most part the scenery is unexceptional, there are areas of beauty to discover, most notably the belt of hills that makes up the Axarquia. To the north the uplands give way to plains which are surveyed by the venerable town of Antequera.

ANCIENT ANTEQUERA

Towns don't come much more ancient than **Antequera** ⓭, which stands at a strategic crossroads between the cardinal points of Córdoba, Málaga, Seville and Granada. It was old before the Romans arrived, and although the title they gave it, *Antikaria*, rings suggestively of antiquity, it was simply the name of a pre-existing Iberian settlement.

Modern Antequera is the service and shopping hub of the northern part of Málaga province. Suburban sprawl quickly yields to a centre of narrow streets leading to an immaculately preserved core of historic buildings. Rising out of the mass of white houses are many belfries: Antequera claims to

have more churches in proportion to its population than anywhere else in Spain.

The natural place to begin sightseeing is the **Plaza San Sebastián**, on which stands a 16th-century church of the same name with a baroque-Mudéjar tower and a Renaissance facade, an example of the town's architectural richness. Behind the tourist office, a straight street, **Calle Zapateros**, leads uphill away from the noise and traffic, around a dog-leg to the monumental gateway of the **Arco de los Gigantes** (Giants' Arch), dedicated

⊙ Main Attractions

Antequera and its
  dolmens
El Torcal
Fuente de Piedra
Caminito del Rey
Cómpeta
Ruta del Mudéjar

Map on page 140

Ibex in El Torcal.

⊙ Tip

El Torcal offers three marked walking routes: the *ruta verde* (green route, 1.5 km/1 mile), a fairly gentle 45-minute walk, the *ruta amarilla* (yellow route, 3 km/2 miles), which takes about two hours and the *ruta naranja* (orange route; 3.7 km/2.5 miles), which starts in the lower car park and ends in the higher one.

in 1585 to Felipe II. Through the arch you step into the **Plaza Santa María**, overlooked by the Renaissance church of **Real Colegiata de Santa María la Mayor** (Mon & Wed–Sun 10am–6pm, Tue 2–6pm; charge includes entry to the Alcazaba, free Tue). One side of the square looks over the Roman ruins of the **Termas Romanas** (Roman Baths), and access to the Muslim fortress of the **Alcazaba** (same opening times and charge as Santa María la Mayor) is also off the square. At the top of the Alcazaba, standing proud above the city, is the keep to which a belfry was added in the 16th century.

On the way downhill from this complex of monuments is the **Museo de la Ciudad de Antequera** (Tue–Fri 10am–2pm & 4.30–6.30pm, Sat 9.30am–2pm & 4.30–6.30pm, Sun 9.30am–2pm; free Sun), housed in the Baroque **Palacio de Nájera**. Although it has eight galleries of art and ecclesiastical silverware, most visitors are drawn to the archaeology section and to one piece in particular, the **Efebo de Antequera**. This 1.5-metre (5-ft) high bronze figure

of a youth has been described as the most beautiful Roman find in Spain, even without the glass eyes that once filled its hollow sockets. It was cast in the 1st century AD and probably served as a lamp or candle holder.

ANTEQUERA'S DOLMENS

In Antequera's suburbs, on the way out towards Granada, are three massive prehistoric dolmens – a Unesco World Heritage Site since 2016. Two of these, the **Dolmen de Menga** and the **Dolmen de Viera** (Tue–Sat 9–8pm, Sun 9am–3pm; free), stand together in a park created around them. Menga is the oldest, dating from 2500 BC, and also the most impressive: an assembly of 31 stones, the largest weighing 180 tonnes. Its construction testifies to an advanced Copper Age civilisation capable of mobilising, coordinating and feeding a sizeable labour force working to a shared purpose.

The third dolmen, **Romeral** (same opening times), stands alone in a surprisingly peaceful location behind a small industrial estate. Dating from

Inside the Dolmen del Romeral.

around 1800 BC, it is the most recent, but it is also the most interesting as it demonstrates use of architectural concepts. A long tunnel of finely laid stones, roofed by great slabs, leads into a perfectly round, domed chamber at the heart of the dolmen, 5 metres (17ft) in diameter and almost 4 metres (13ft) high, created by concentric courses of stones.

HIKES AND FLAMINGOS

In the hills behind Antequera is one of Andalucía's foremost beauty spots, **El Torcal ⓬**, reached by the C3310 towards Villanueva de la Concepción, which passes above the town, giving views of the rooftops, church towers and Alcazaba rising out of them. On the other side of the pass of La Boca del Asno ('The Ass's Mouth'), there is a turning to El Torcal at the top of the sierra. A visitor centre (tel: 952-243 324; www.torcaldeantequera.com; daily Apr–Oct 10am–7pm; Nov–Mar 10am–5pm), café and car park are at the base. From here there is an easy walk to a viewpoint or three marked hiking routes (see margin) through the distinctive rock formations. The towering limestone outcrops eroded by wind and rain into abstract sculptures not unlike piles of sandwiches have fanciful names such as El Cara Perro, El Sombrero, El Tornillo, La Tortuga.

Don't set off too late in the day, as it is easy to get disorientated in the labyrinth of rocks, depressions, corridors, crevices, cliffs and ledges.

There is another distinctive rock east out of Antequera, towards Granada, the **Peña de los Enamorados** ('Lovers' Leap'), named after the legend of a Christian boy and Muslim girl who, forbidden to marry, threw themselves off the top. Beyond the rock is **Archidona ⓭**, a sloping white town above olive groves, with medieval walls and an octagonal main square.

The plains north of Antequera don't look very promising, but they hide one place of interest, the salty lagoon outside the town of **Fuente de Piedra ⓰**. This is the largest natural lake in Andalucía and it is famous for its colony of flamingos, although you will be lucky to see any without high-powered binoculars as the lake expands and shrinks with the weather and can be distant from the road around it. There is a visitor centre (tel: 952-712 554; www.visitasfuentepiedra.es; daily Apr–Sept 10am–2pm, 5–7pm; Oct–Mar 10am–2pm, 4–6pm) with a lookout point on a rise 1 km (0.6 miles) from the town.

MOUNTAINS OF MÁLAGA

There are two routes between Málaga city and Antequera. The obvious and quickest is the motorway down the Guadalmedina valley, skirting the side of the **Montes de Málaga ⓱**. Although declared a *parque natural*, the landscape here is largely man-made, as these hills were planted with pine forests to prevent flooding in Málaga city. There are views of the coast and city from various points along the C345

The distinctive limestone outcrops of El Torcal.

road, which also takes you past the visitor centre at Lagar de Torrijos.

From Roman times until the 1870s, these hills were important for their vineyards. Málaga's strong, sweet wine made from moscatel and Pedro Ximénez grape varieties was known all over Europe. Then disaster struck. In just a few years the vines here, as in much of the rest of Europe, were destroyed by the phylloxera bug; but while other areas were replanted with resistant stock, Málaga's vineyards never fully recovered, perhaps because the taste for sweet wines was already diminishing. Wine is still made in Málaga, both in the Montes de Málaga and the Axarquia, but in much smaller quantities.

LAKES AND WATERFALLS

The alternative route to the coast is by way of the Guadalhorce valley and **Alora** ⑱, a sloping white town of narrow streets beneath a restored castle with a church beside it. Just up the valley from here is what should be Andalucía's principal beauty spot, the **Desfiladero de los Gaitanes** or

Walkers on the Caminito del Rey.

Garganta del Chorro ⑲, a tall, thin gorge of rock barely wide enough for the river Guadalhorce to slip through.

In 1921 King Alfonso XIII came to open a dam built at the head of the gorge holding back the three uninspiring reservoirs upstream which comprise 'Málaga's Lake District'. To impress him, a catwalk of concrete and iron, the **Caminito del Rey** (tel: 902 787 325; www.caminitodelrey.info; Tue–Sun 9.30am–5pm; reserve well in advance), was built on the rock face along the gorge with a bridge spanning the chasm. This vertiginous marvel of engineering, however, was allowed to fall into disrepair over the years, before undergoing a €5.5million restoration and reopening in 2015. Allow about four hours to do the walk and it's not for those without a head for heights. Almost as impressive is the railway line from Málaga that crosses a girder bridge and plunges into a tunnel beside the Caminito del Rey. The gorge, railway, the walkway and a tall sliver of waterfall can be viewed from the Complejo Turistico La Garganta (www.la garganta.com), in a restored old mill.

Heading towards Ardales from the gorge, the road passes through a nature reserve of large smooth rocks in scattered pine woods. A signposted turning off this road leads to the abandoned village of **Bobastro**, where a Mozarabic community – Christians living under Muslim rule – cut a church out of the rock. The forms of its horseshoe arches can still be seen.

SPA TOWNS

South and west from the Guadalhorce valley there is little of interest along the meandering B roads except scattered towns trying to revive their fortunes. On a hillside near Ardales is **Carratraca** ⑳, a small spa town on a steep hillside which today gives no hint of the success of its sulphur springs in the 19th century, when it attracted the celebrities of the time, including Byron, Dumas and Empress Eugénie of France, and incorporated three casinos. The neo-classical-style baths have been renovated and turned into a luxury spa hotel, Villa Padierna, where the emphasis is on the serious treatment of angina, asthma and other respiratory diseases.

There is another reincarnated 19th-century hydro at **Tolox** ㉑ (www.balneariodetolox.es; May–Oct), a long drive to the west, on the edge of the wild, underpopulated karst mountains of the eastern Sierra de Ronda. It goes by the uninspiring name of the Balneario de Fuente Amargosa ('Bitter Fountain'). Facilities are dated but the waters are beneficial in the treatment of respiratory diseases and kidney stones. Past visitors have included various famous bullfighters and Primo de Rivera.

LA AXARQUIA

If you want pretty countryside within reach of the coast, save your time for the **Axarquia**, the district extending back from the coast between Rincón de la Victoria and Nerja (see page 151) as far as the peaks of the Sierra de Almijara.

The roads into and around the Axarquia are, in the main, narrow, winding, steep and sometimes badly surfaced, but the scenery is worth the discomfort.

The district's official capital is **Vélez-Málaga**, an industrial town not worth the trouble of exploring, although it does have two churches converted from mosques and the remains of a castle if you can find your way up to it. Better, though, to stay on the road up the valley, which avoids the town centre. Soon after you leave the outskirts of Vélez-Málaga you will see the tantalisingly sited **Comares** ㉒, which balances on the top of a rocky mountain peak. A steep winding road takes you up to it from the valley floor, green with citrus and tropical-fruit trees, through slopes dotted with olive trees. There are few points of interest in the town except a badly eroded stack of stone (all that is left of the castle), which stands outside the cemetery. The charm of a visit is mostly in the panoramic views, but the town has genuine atmosphere and a 'Muslim Route' of blue-and-white ceramic footprints inlaid in the streets

Ceramic mural depicting musicians and flamenco dancers, Comares.

High-perched Comares.

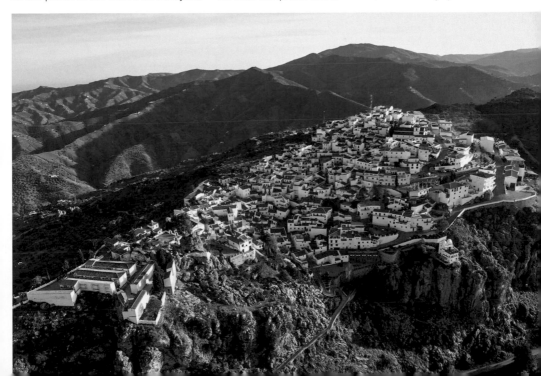

and alleyways leads you on a pleasant walk around the town.

COLOURFUL CÓMPETA

For the most picturesque part of the Axarquia head west from Vélez-Málaga towards the de facto capital of the region, **Cómpeta** . The patchwork of fertile hills around it is surprisingly populous, with modern villas and old *cortijos* all the way up the slopes to the summits. The terraced hillsides are planted with a great variety of crops, including oranges, subtropical fruit trees, olive trees, almonds and small vineyards. A typical feature of the older farmhouses is a *pasero*, an inclined rectangular enclosure for drying grapes into raisins.

When, after all the curves, you finally reach Cómpeta it can come as a surprise, not only for its size but for the composition of its population – this is a popular area for foreign house-buyers, and the main square is dominated by estate agents. Apart from that, Cómpeta is an attractive place, a dense labyrinth of streets and steps and houses built on various levels, picturesque and tastefully colourful in almost every corner. It may pull in the tourists and the foreign home-buyers, but Cómpeta remains a wine town (making sweet Málaga wine) and its main fiesta, on 15 August, is the Night of Wine, dedicated to wine-pressing.

Salamandra (Calle Rampa, 3; tel: 952-553 493; www.malaga-aventura.es) offers a wide range of activities in the area including hiking, cycling, caving, and 4x4 guided tours.

MOSQUES AND MINARETS

Of the several designated tourist routes around the Axarquia, the most worthwhile is the Ruta del Mudéjar, linking villages that still bear distinct traces of their Muslim past. The nearest of them to Cómpeta is **Archez**, where the church tower is a perfect 15th-century brick minaret. Outside the village (take the top road) is a delightful surprise from modernity, an extraordinary fantasy residence made up of three hobbit-like igloos with psychedelic decoration set in a stepped vineyard garden. Built by four artists working to the principles of Gaudí and Hundertwasser, it is private property but can be admired over the wall.

Salares, tucked into a valley at one remove from the rest of the Axarquia, is arguably the most unspoilt village in these hills. Its church tower is a 13th-century minaret. At the bottom of the village an Arab bridge crosses a verdant little valley planted with orange trees. A 5-km (3-mile) walk (allow up to three hours) departs from the far end of the bridge from the village.

There is still the prettiest and best-preserved and presented of all the towns, **Frigiliana** ㉔, to go. Being near the coast, particularly the popular resort of Nerja (see page 151), it receives lots of visitors but avoids being spoilt. Despite new buildings going up, the town centre retains a perfect cluster of stepped streets.

Competa.

The day draws to a close in Frigiliana.

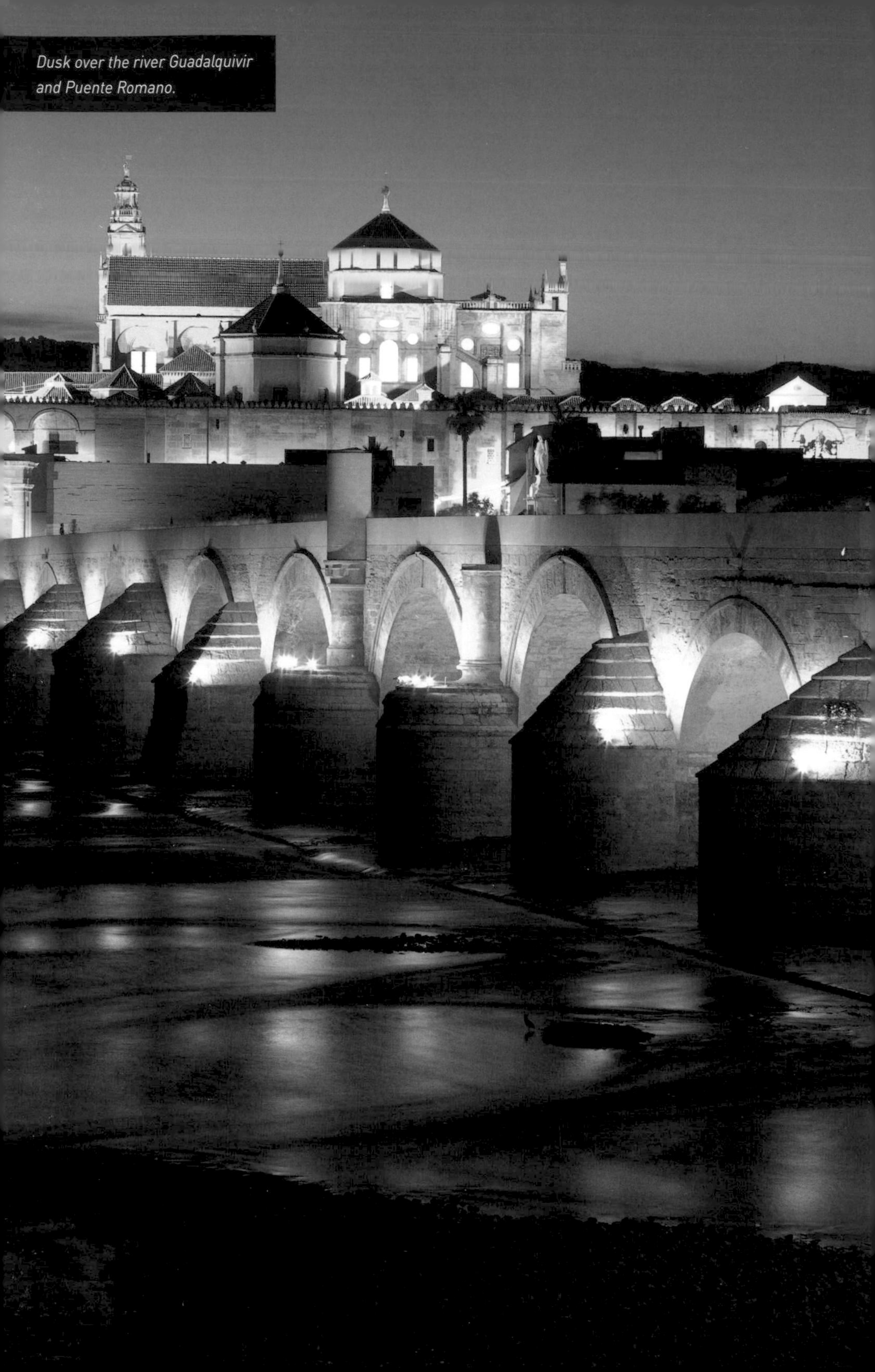

Dusk over the river Guadalquivir and Puente Romano.

CÓRDOBA

Córdoba is a labyrinth of winding alleyways and Moorish patios. Its supreme monument is La Mezquita, its fabulous Mosque.

The furthest north of Andalucía's great Moorish cities and not easily accessible on a day trip from the Costa del Sol, **Córdoba ❶** receives significantly fewer visitors than Granada and Seville. Partly for that reason, but also due to its particular charm – the gracious old town spreads around its extraordinary Mosque on a bend in the River Guadalquivir – it is often the city that people who do take the trouble to visit end up liking best.

It is possible to visit Córdoba for the day from Seville (a 25-minute journey on the Seville–Madrid AVE train) but it is well worth staying a night or two and perhaps also taking in Medina Azahara (see page 169).

THE CITY'S HISTORY

Córdoba is one of the oldest cities in Spain; its historic centre is a Unesco World Heritage site. In 206 BC it was invaded by the Romans, who later made it the capital of the Roman province of Further Spain. In 572, after nearly eight centuries of Roman rule, the Visigoths took control of the city.

In 711 it fell to the Moors, and in 756 Abd-al-Rahman I, Amir of the Umayyad dynasty, established it as an independent emirate ruling most of the Iberian Peninsula.

Abd-al-Rahman III raised the city to the status of Caliphate in 929 and

ushered in a golden age. Considered to be one of the cultural capitals of the world, second in wealth and culture only to Constantinople, the city was a respected centre of science and art. It had the first street lighting in Europe and a library containing over 400,000 volumes. Estimates of the population at that time range from 500,000 to one million.

This prosperity came to an abrupt end with the rebellion of Muhammad II al-Mahdi in 1009, a development that led to the disintegration of the

◎ Main Attractions

La Mezquita
Puente Romano
Alcázar de los Reyes
 Cristianos
Patios
La Judería
Museo Arqueológico
Palacio de Viana
Medina Azahara
Montilla wineries
Priego de Córdoba

Maps on pages 162, 164, 169

The superb pillared interior of La Mezquita.

⊙ **Quote**

Carlos V initiated the construction of the Christian cathedral inside the Mosque. Later, however, he appeared to regret the decision, saying, 'Had I known what this was, you would not have done it, for what you are building here can be found anywhere; but what you have destroyed exists nowhere.'

The gilded dome above the Mosque's mihrab.

Caliphate and triggered a long decline in the city's fortunes.

By the time Córdoba was reconquered in 1236 by Fernando III, the city was in ruins. During the ensuing years it was repopulated by people from northern Spain. In 1382 Alfonso XI ordered the construction of the Alcazar, which became the residence of Queen Isabel towards the end of the 15th century.

MONUMENT TO THE MOORS

Córdoba's most important monument, the **Mosque A**, La Mezquita (www. mezquita-catedraldecordoba.es; Mon–Sat Mar–Oct 10am–7pm, Nov–Feb 10am–6pm, Sun 8.30–11.30am, 3–6pm, Mar–Oct until 7pm; night-time guided tours are available; free Mon–Sat 8.30am–9.30am), is the oldest building in day-to-day use in the Western world. Its dominant feature is the 54-metre bell-tower, which has its origins in the 10th-century minaret; there are great views from the top.

Construction of the Mosque over the site of a Visigothic cathedral began in 786 at the order of Abd-al-Rahman I. The initial design was for an open courtyard (sahn) for ablutions, now known as the Patio de los Naranjos (orange trees), and a covered area that could accommodate as many as 10,000 worshippers. Three expansions later – by Abd-al-Rahman II in 833, under al-Hakam II in 926, and finally by al-Mansur, who was chief minister of Hisham II, in 978 – it was completed.

The architectural style evolved with each addition, reaching the greatest splendour and technical mastery in what came to be known as the caliphal style of architecture during the Caliphate of al-Hakam. Features to note are great skylighted domes for extra interior light, and an ingenious engineering system comprising clustered pillars bearing intersecting lobed arches to support the domes.

After Fernando III reconquered Córdoba in 1236, small Christian chapels were added in 1258 and 1260. Nearly three centuries later, in 1523, during the reign of Carlos V, the Christian cathedral was built in the centre of the Mosque. Whether inadvertent or

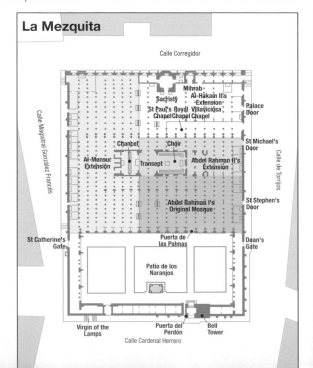

not, the incongruous mix of architecture and culture combines to produce a place of utter fascination. Inside are hundreds of columns – 856 to be exact – most supporting double-horseshoe arches. The different-coloured columns, fashioned from various types of stone, present a constantly mesmerising interplay of architecture and light.

TOURING THE MOSQUE

Walking through the original Mosque of Abd-al-Rahman I, you reach the Mosque's first extension, added by Abd-al-Rahman II in 833 (a slight ramp in the floor is evidence of the extension). To the left is the rear of the cathedral's *coro* (choir). Further on is the vaulted ceiling of an aborted church, planned in the 15th century. To the left you will see the domed Capilla de Villaviciosa, where the old Mosque's mihrab (indicating the direction of Mecca) would have been. Through a cutaway you can see the Capilla Real next door, redecorated in the 14th century in Mudéjar stucco. This was the mosque's *maqsura* (royal enclosure).

Continuing straight ahead, you enter al-Hakam's extension. He extended the southern wall to the river and built an opulent new mihrab (seen through the railings), decorated with dazzling mosaics and a stunning star-ribbed dome that was subsequently copied throughout Spain. The bejewelled side rooms formed Hakam's *maqsura*.

The third extension of the Mezquita by al-Mansur is functional rather than aesthetically pleasing. It widened the prayer hall and courtyard to accommodate Córdoba's growing population.

Construction of the cathedral within the Mosque required the removal of 60 of the original columns and some of the most beautiful stucco work. The contrast in styles is a jolt to the senses. In the cathedral, human images – taboo in Islamic art and architecture – abound in paint, stone and wood, particularly in the massive paintings of Christ and the saints.

The cathedral is of Gothic design with later additions in plateresque and baroque styles. Especially noteworthy are the mahogany choir stalls, carved by the Andalusian sculptor Pedro Duque Cornejo and depicting the lives of Jesus and the Virgin Mary in life-like detail. The magnificent golden altarpiece contains 36 tableaux of the *Life of Christ*.

The **Cathedral Museum** (Tesoro Catedralicio) contains religious art from the 15th to 20th centuries. Among its treasures is a stunning monstrance weighing over 164 kg (440 lbs) and fashioned from solid silver by the renowned goldsmith Enrique Arfe.

THE TOWN

Across from the Mosque (on Calle Torrijos), in a 16th-century former chapel is the **Palacio de Congresos**, a convention hall (closed for restoration until at least 2018). From here it is a few steps to the river, crossed by the **Puente Romano ⑧** (Roman Bridge), a good place to come at sunset for views over the old town. On the bridge is one of many images of Córdoba's patron

Admiring the exhibits inside La Mezquita.

saint, the Archangel Raphael, candles burning at his feet. In the river bottom, overgrown with rushes where ducks paddle, are the remains of three Arabic watermills, the **Molinos Arabes**.

On the far side of the bridge is the **Torre de la Calahorra** C (www.torrede calahorra.es; May–Sept daily 10am–2pm, 4.30–8.30pm; Oct–Apr daily 10am–6pm), a 14th-century watchtower which houses a museum depicting the glories of al-Andalus with wax figures and a 50-minute diorama, with audio-guides in several languages.

Back on the north bank of the river, a few blocks downriver from the Mosque is the **Alcázar de los Reyes Cristianos** D (Mon–Fri 8.30am–8.45pm, mid-June–mid-Sept until 3pm, Sat 8.30am–4.30pm, Sun 8.30am–2.30pm), a palace built by Alfonso XI in the 14th century, over the site of previous Visigoth and Moorish fortresses. For many years it was the home of the Catholic Monarchs, who received Columbus and planned the reconquest of Granada here. Following the fall of Granada in 1492, the

palace was used by the Court of Inquisition, and then functioned as a civil jail and military prison.

Inside, the highlight of the palace is the **Hall of the Mosaics**, featuring Roman mosaics and a Roman stone sarcophagus dating from the 2nd or 3rd century AD. Outside, you will note that four towers guard the walls, and the tops of those that are open to visitors provide an excellent platform from which to take photographs of La Mezquita. The extensive gardens are a peaceful place, the design of which includes a series of rectangular ponds similar to, but not as stunning as, those at the Generalife in Granada. There is a son et lumière show (Tue–Sun) which requires a different ticket but includes entry to the Alcázar and gardens. Nearby, on Campo Santos Mártires, is the Baños del Alcázar Califal (same hours as Alcázar), the palace's 10th-century baths.

PRETTY PATIOS

Monumental Córdoba is golden, but its *barrios* or neighbourhoods are

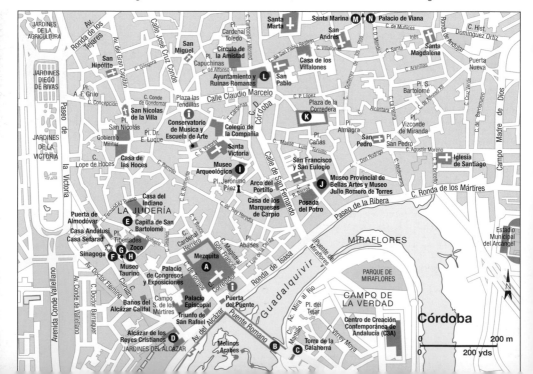

usually pristine white, kept lime-washed by house-proud owners. The city's old quarter, a compact warren of whitewashed houses, winding alleys and flower-filled patios, spreads out around the Mosque. It is best visited on foot, as many of the streets are hardly more than narrow alleyways. The houses generally present a blank facade to the street, broken only by an entryway closed by a *cancela*, wrought-iron gate. Through this gate is glimpsed a patio, shaded by a palm, furnished with ferns, perfumed with jasmine, air-conditioned by a bubbling fountain.

Whether the intimate heart of private homes or elegant courtyards of great buildings, the patio was developed as a survival technique – a cool oasis in the long hot summers. Fine examples can be seen in Calle San Basilio and around Plaza de la Magdalena in the district of Santa Marina. Córdoba celebrates its courtyards during the first half of May, when many private patios are opened to the public, and now on Unesco's Intangible

Cultural Heritage list. You can find out more about them at the interpretation centre at Calle Trueque 4 (daily 10.30am–2pm, 6–10pm; free).

THE JUDERÍA

The area northwest of the Mosque is Córdoba's medieval Jewish quarter, **La Judería** Ⓔ, entered through the **Puerta de Almodóvar**, one of the city's ancient gates.

If Córdoba is known for the splendour of its 10th-century achievements in art, architecture and science, a part of its glory is attributed to the Sephardim community, the Spanish Jews who settled here during the time of the Roman emperors, when they were allowed the same rights as other inhabitants of Baetica, Roman Spain.

Under the Visigoths Jews were persecuted so severely that they welcomed the Muslim invaders. In exchange, they enjoyed long periods of peaceful coexistence, and a flowering of Sephardim culture during which many achieved rare heights in diplomacy, medicine, commerce and crafts.

The whitewashed houses in Calleja de las Flores are decked with pots of geraniums, making it the most photographed street in Córdoba.

Alcázar de los Reyes Cristianos.

Casa de Sefarad courtyard.

Torahs in the Casa de Sefarad.

Sepharad simply means Spain in Hebrew. More than 500 years after King Fernando and Queen Isabel expelled the Jews from Spain in 1492, some Jews of Spanish descent still speak an archaic Spanish dialect. Were Columbus to come back to life today, he would find it easier to converse with the Sephardic Jews in, say, Istanbul than with modern *Madrileños*.

Córdoba's **Sinagoga** ⓕ (Tue–Sat 9am–8pm, mid-June–mid-Sept 9am–3pm, Sun 9am–3pm; free to EU visitors) is one of only three medieval synagogues remaining in Spain, where once there were hundreds (the other two are in Toledo). Córdoba itself had 26 synagogues between the 10th and 15th centuries. This survivor, built in 1315, is entered through a patio off the narrow Calle Judíos. Segments of Hebraic inscriptions and family history remain on the walls. The upper gallery, where women were seated, and the niche where the Torah was kept are still intact. Just up the street is the **Casa de Sefarad** (Calle Judíos; www.casasefarad.es; daily 11am–7pm),

a fascinating museum focusing on the life of Spanish Jews. And a little further on is the **Casa Andalusí** (Calle Judíos 12; https://lacasaandalusi.es; daily 10am–7.30pm), a very pretty 12th-century house with Islamic decoration and an exhibition on paper making.

Many Córdoban Sephardim achieved high status, either at the Muslim court or within the Jewish community. One was Maimonides, one of the greatest philosophers of Jewish history. A rabbi and Talmudic scholar with an Aristotelian bent, Maimonides was born in Córdoba in 1135. By this time, fanatic Berber sects, the Almohads, had changed the political landscape, initiating a period of unrest and repression. To escape the repression, Maimonides's family fled to Morocco, and he eventually settled in Egypt. But Córdoba still claims him as a native son.

Near the Synagogue, in the **Plaza Tiberiades**, under the bower of an enormous jasmine vine, is a statue of Maimonides. He presides over the tiny square with kindly dignity, his slipper rubbed shiny by thousands of

passers-by, possibly hoping some of his great wisdom might rub off on them.

BULLFIGHTING MEMORABILIA

In the plaza named after Maimonides is a different sort of monument. Opening off a beautiful patio, in the house said to have belonged to Maimonides's family is the municipal **Museo Taurino** ⑥ (Bullfighting Museum; Mon–Fri 8.30am–8.45pm, mid-June–mid-Sept until 3pm, Sat 8.30am–4.30pm, Sun 8.30am–2.30pm). This is one of the most comprehensive of its genre in Spain, and the normal quota of bulls' heads is complemented by some splendid suits of light (trajes de luces), posters (carteles), a large library, and permanent exhibitions dedicated to the local toreros Lagartijo, Machaquito, Guerrita and Manolete. The last, who dominated Spanish bullfighting in the 1940s, was eventually killed by a bull in the Plaza de Toros of Linares on 28 August, 1947.

Behind the museum, again on Calle Judíos, is the **Zoco Municipal** ⑪, a cluster of craft workshops around a central courtyard. Here artisans work in both traditional and modern styles, in silver filigree (for which Córdoba has long been famous), leather, wood and ceramics.

EAST OF THE MOSQUE

The area of the old town northeast of the mosque is also full of attractive little streets and plazas. Take Calle Encarnación and then Calle Horno del Cristo to reach Plaza de Jerónimo Páez, where the **Museo Arqueológico** ❶ (Archaeological Museum; Tue–Sat mid-June–mid-Sept 9am–3pm, mid-Sept–mid-June 9am–8pm, Sun 9am–3pm year round; free to EU visitors), housed in a fine Renaissance palace, has good displays of artefacts from the Bronze Age through Roman and Moorish times. In the basement, a walkway takes visitors through the ruins of a Roman theatre.

The other highlight of the old town east of the Mosque is the **Plaza del**

Potro (an easy walk from the mosque along the interesting Luis de Cerda and Lucano streets), which is mentioned in Cervantes's *Don Quixote*. It is named after a small statue of a colt on the 16th-century fountain in the centre of the square. The 13th-century inn on one side of the plaza, where Cervantes once stayed, houses the **Centro Flamenco Fosforito** (www.centroflamencofosforito. cordoba.es; Tue–Fri 8.30am–7.30pm, mid-June–mid-Sept 8.30am–3pm, Sat & Sun 8.30am–2.30pm; free), an excellent museum tracing the history of flamenco, where there are also regular live performances.

On the other side of the square is the 15th-century Hospital de la Caridad (Charity Hospital), home to two small but noteworthy, museums. The **Museo de Bellas Artes** ❶ (Fine Arts Museum; Tue–Sat mid-June–mid-Sept 9am–3pm, mid-Sept–mid-June 9am–8pm, Sun 9am–3pm year round; free to EU visitors) is entered through a courtyard, elegantly tiled on one side. The collection, largely based on works of art from disentailed

Shopping for souvenirs in the Judería.

Eat

Córdoba has a lively custom of the *tapeo*, stopping at one or several *tabernas*, neighbourhood bars for tapas. Good *tabernas* in the old quarter are Guzmán (Calle de los Judíos, 7) and Sociedad de Plateros (Calle María Auxiliadora, 25). Dishes to look out for are *salmorejo* (thick soup made from tomatoes and bread) and *rabo de toro* (bull tail stew).

monasteries and convents, is wide-ranging: a haunting head of Christ, dating from 1389; several paintings by the local master of baroque, Antonio del Castillo Saavedra (1616–68); Pedro Duque Cornejo's clay sketches for his carving of the Ascension in Córdoba Cathedral; works by the Seville artist Juan de Valdés; a wonderful painting by Joaquín Sorolla of a woman with downcast eyes and a red hat, and a whole section devoted to Córdoban sculptor Mateo Inurria, including a life-size sculpture of the Roman philosopher Seneca the Younger, another native Córdoban, looking wise and wizened.

In addition, just across a delightful patio enhanced by a fountain and busts, is the ever-popular **Julio Romero de Torres Museum** (Mon–Fri 8.30am–8.45pm, mid-June–mid-Sept until 3pm, Sat 8.30am–4.30pm, Sun 8.30am–2.30pm), devoted to the works of a well-known local painter who specialised in mildly erotic portraits of sultry Andalusian women. The museum contains over 50 works donated by the artist's family.

PLAZA DE LA CORREDERA

A little to the north of here is the **Plaza de la Corredera K**, from this direction accessed through the main entrance in the south facade (its other entrances and exits are known as the High and Low arches). This impressive plaza is rectangular in shape and consists of a lower colonnaded level and three upper floors, embellished with galleries and balconies supported by semicircular arches. Built by the Magistrate Corregidor Ronquillo Briceno in the late 17th century, the building is Castilian in style and the only one of its kind in Andalucía. It has been used for bullfights and public executions.

In 1896 the central area was converted into a covered market – the roof was removed during the 1950s. These days it hosts a general market on Monday to Saturday, a flea market *(rastro)* on Sunday morning, and shoppers can treasure-hunt in any number of second-hand shops under the arcades.

A few blocks up from this plaza, on Calle Capitulares, is a curious architectural landmark, Córdoba's

Painting for sale at the Plaza de la Corredera Sunday flea market.

Ayuntamiento ❶ (Town Hall), built in the late 1980s in a modern style, but incorporating the ruins of a Roman amphitheatre in its foundations. Beside it rise the columns of a Roman temple. Just across from the Town Hall is the church of **San Pablo**, a Romanesque building fronted with spiral columns.

BULLS AND CONVENTS

Continuing north along Alfaros brings you to **La Marina**, another interesting neighbourhood, named for the beautiful Gothic church of **Santa Marina ⓜ**. This is the *barrio* of bullfighters, hence the extravagant homage to Manolete in front of the church. Around the corner from here, in the **Convent of Santa Isabel**, the Clarisa nuns keep up an old Andalusian tradition of making almond-based biscuits to sell to the public.

Near Santa Marina (along Calle Morales) is the **Palacio de Viana ⓝ** (Tue–Sat 10am–7pm, Sun 10am–3pm), a 15th-century palace which belonged to the Marquis of Viana. Finding it difficult to maintain such a large establishment, the family advertised the palace for sale in a French newspaper. It was acquired in 1980 by a local savings and loan bank, the Caja Provincial de Ahorros de Córdoba, and converted into a museum. A year later it was declared a historic and artistic monument of national character. Its most unusual feature is the incorporation of 12 entirely different patios. On entering the first patio, note that the corner column has been deliberately omitted to facilitate the entrance of horse-drawn carriages. The 38 rooms and galleries inside the house are crammed with antique furniture, tapestries, porcelain, etc, and include an extensive library.

IN THE HILLS

No visit to Córdoba is complete without a visit to **Medina Azahara ❷** (www. medinaazahara.org; Tue–Sat mid-June–mid-Sept 9am–3.30pm, Apr–mid-June 9am–8.30pm, mid-Sept–Dec 9am–6.30pm, Jan–Mar 9am–5.30pm, Sun 9am–3.30pm year round; free to EU visitors), the city-palace of Abd-al-Rahman III, in the foothills of the Sierra Morena, just 8 km (5 miles) west

Statue of the great Jewish philosopher Maimonides in the Plaza Tiberiades.

of Córdoba. If you do not have your own transport, note that special buses for Medina Azahara leave from Córdoba at least twice a day (book in advance at the tourist office).

The palace, reputedly built in honour of Abd al Rahman III's favourite concubine, the Syrian-born Al-Zahra, the Flower, was famous for its size and splendour. Its construction was said to have involved 10,000–12,000 workmen, and materials were brought from Constantinople as well as North Africa.

Life inside the palace was full of pomp and ceremony and was luxurious in the extreme, as witnessed by the mystic Ibn-al-Arabi. To impress an embassy of Christians from the north of Spain, the Caliph 'had mats unrolled for a distance of 5 km (3 miles) from the gates of Córdoba to the entrance of the palace, and a double rank of soldiers stationed along the route, their naked swords meeting at the tips like the rafters of a roof'.

Inside the palace, 'the Caliph had the ground covered with brocades. At regular intervals he placed dignitaries whom they took for kings, for they were seated on splendid chairs and arrayed in brocades and silk. Each time the ambassadors saw one of these dignitaries they prostrated themselves before him, imagining him to be the Caliph, whereupon they were told, "Raise your heads! This is but a slave of his slaves!" At last they entered a courtyard strewn with sand. At the centre was the Caliph. His clothes were coarse and short: what he was wearing was not worth four dirhams. He was seated on the ground, his head bent; in front of him was a Koran, a sword and fire. "Behold the ruler," the ambassadors were told'.

Despite its grandeur, the palace had a short life. After the breakup of the Caliphate of Córdoba early in the 11th century, it was utilised by various factions, then sacked. Many of the materials were used on constructions in Seville and other places and, over the next 900 years, it was allowed to fall into disrepair.

It was not until 1910 that the arduous work of excavation began. This work continues today and a new museum,

The Upper Basilica at Medina Azahara.

complete with finds from the site, takes visitors on a tour of the palace's origins to its demise.

THE SIERRA MORENA

Continuing west, the Córdoba to Seville river road (C431) passes through a rich agricultural region of fruit and citrus orchards, wheat, sugar beets and cotton. After the autumn cotton harvest, fluffs of cotton border the road like snowdrifts.

At **Almodóvar del Río**, on a hill dominating the river valley, is a picture-book castle (www.castillodealmodovar. com; Apr–Sept Mon–Fri 11am–2.30pm, 4–8pm, Sat & Sun 11am–8pm; Oct–Mar Mon–Fri 11am–2.30pm, 4–7pm, Sat & Sun 11am–7pm), built by the Moors and later embellished. Halfway between Córdoba and Seville, on the Guadalquivir river, is **Palma del Río ❸**, famed for its citrus groves and as the birthplace of the popular bullfighter, El Cordobés. The 15th-century **Monasterio de San Francisco** was a springboard for missionaries bound for the New World, such as Fray Junipero Serra, who established California's missions.

The monastery has been converted into a small hotel and restaurant where, in season, the menu features venison and boar from the nearby **Sierra Morena**.

WINE AND OIL

South of the capital (main road to Málaga, N331) is Córdoba's wine region, centred on the towns of **Montilla ❹** and **Moriles**, where wine has been made since the 8th century BC. Comparisons with sherry are inevitable, for Montilla wines are produced by the *solera* system of blending in the same way as the more widely marketed Jerez wines. These days, a light, young white wine, rather similar to the Vinho Verde from northern Portugal, is being produced around here.

The oldest winery is **Bodegas Alvear** in Montilla (tel: 957-652 939; www.alvear. es; tours Mon–Sat at 12.30pm). Other wineries offering guided tours include Bodegas Cruz Conde (www.bodegascruz conde.es; Mon–Sat at noon) and Pérez Barquero (www.perezbarquero.com). The region celebrates its wine festival in the last week of August.

The castle at Almodóvar del Río.

Bodegas Alvear cellar.

Other towns in the region worth a visit are **La Rambla** ❺, with more than 50 ceramic workshops; **Cabra** ❻, with the 13th-century sanctuary of the Virgin of the Sierra; and **Lucena** ❼, which was a totally Jewish town in the caliphal epoch, specialising in trade and crafts. Lucena is still a centre for copper, brass and bronze workshops. Outside the town are many furniture factories where newlyweds from all over Andalucía come to furnish their homes at factory prices.

Adjoining the vineyards is Córdoba's olive-oil region, centred on **Baena** ❽ (off the main road to Granada), dominated by its Moorish fortress and surrounded by olive-covered hills.

Beyond Baena the terrain becomes craggier, with villages such as **Luque**, built against a grey rock, and **Zuheros**, with its Moorish castle, Museo Arqueológico (Tue–Fri 10am– 2pm, 5–7pm in summer, 4–6pm in winter, Sat–Sun times vary; admission charge includes visit to the castle) and maze of narrow streets. High above the village is the interesting

A rare male white-headed duck.

prehistoric **Cueva de los Murciélagos** (Cave of Bats; tel: 957-694 545 from 10am–1.30pm Tue–Fri to reserve a place on an available tour Tue–Sun), which has some interesting rock formations and Neolithic art; finds from the cave are on display in the Archaeology Museum (see above).

PRIEGO DE CÓRDOBA

The jewel of the province is the town of **Priego de Córdoba** ❾ situated on a bluff above the Río Salado, a saltwater river.

Known as the capital of 18th-century Andalusian baroque architecture, Priego has several beautiful churches in this style, notably the **Parroquia de la Asunción** (Tue–Sat 11am–1.30pm, Sun 11–11.30am, 1–1.30pm), with a white-and-gold dome in the Sagrario chapel. The **Fuente del Rey** is a monumental baroque fountain with 139 spouts. Locals say that when the water level is high enough to cover the private parts of Neptune's statue, there will be sufficient water for the crops.

During the 18th century, Priego's thriving silk industry brought prosperity to the town. The fine buildings, including a number of noble mansions with handsome wrought-iron balconies and window grilles, date from that time. The old quarter of town, where passageways are no more than an arm's breadth, dates from Moorish times. Here, neighbours keep up the curious custom of carrying an image of a favourite saint, complete with tiny altar in a carry-case, from house to house. A complex schedule allows each family to keep it for one day.

South from Priego, almost to the Málaga and Granada borders, is Córdoba's lake region, stretching from **Iznájar** and along the Río Genil's tributaries. Here, numerous species of wildlife can be found, including some that are threatened with extinction. Among the rarer examples is one of Europe's last colonies of white-headed ducks.

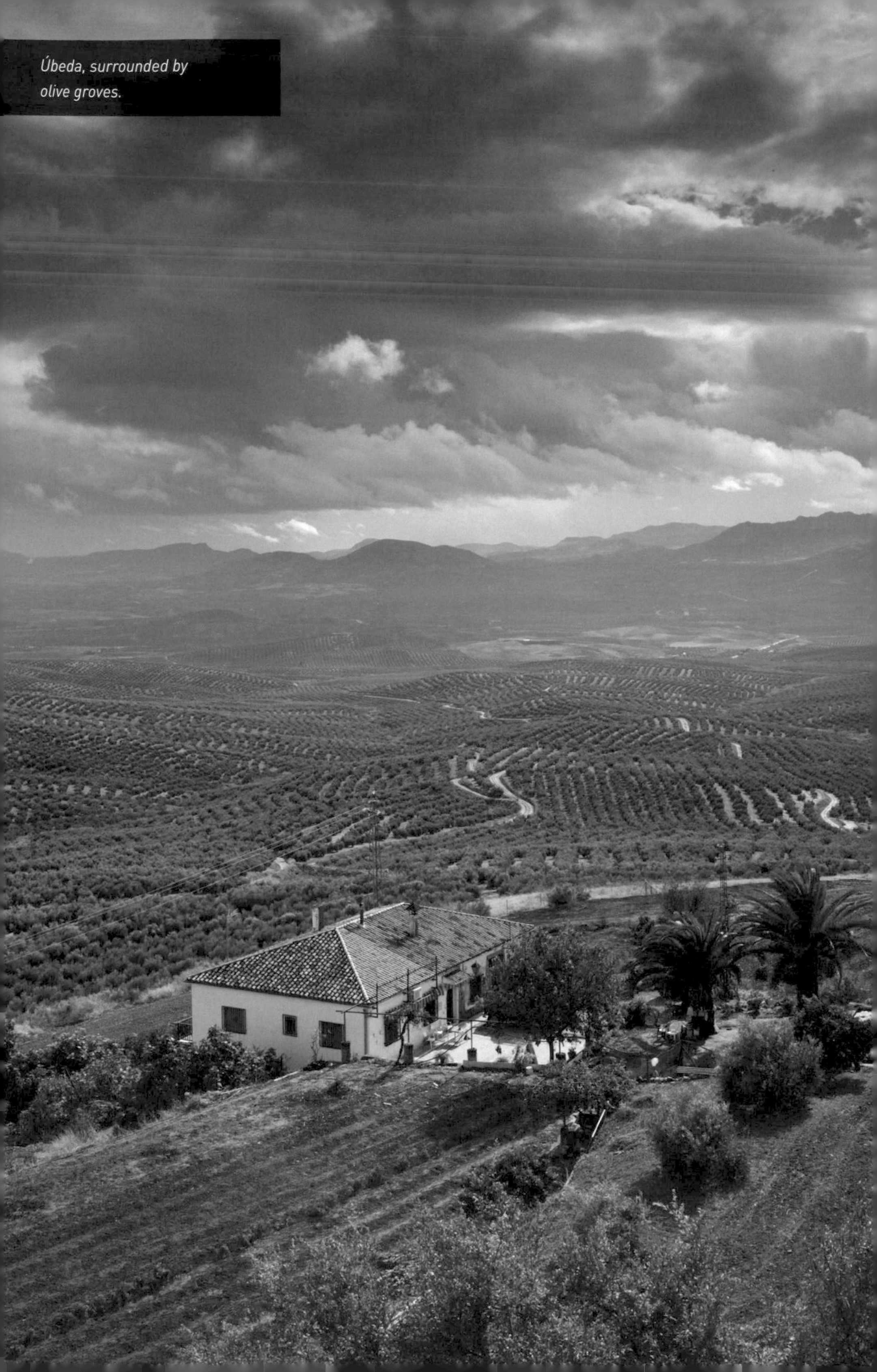

Úbeda, surrounded by olive groves.

JAÉN AND ITS PROVINCE

Mountain nature reserves, towns filled with Renaissance architecture and olive oil in abundance are the main attractions of this province.

A massive, undulating sea of 40 million olive trees, Jaén province is often thought of as a place to hurry through rather than somewhere worth stopping to explore. Named *Giyen* ('caravan route') by the Arabs who conquered it in 712, throughout history it has been trudged across by armies, saints and traders on their way between central Spain and the great cities of Andalucía.

If any of these travellers of old did halt here, it was to fight a battle. In 208 BC the Romans defeated the Carthaginians at the battle of Baecula, a key step in the Romanisation of Spain. At Navas de Tolosa, in 1212, a coalition of Christian monarchs from northern Spain scored their first decisive victory in their reconquest of the Peninsula against the Muslim 'occupiers'. For a long time in the late Middle Ages, Jaén was the contested frontier between the Moorish Kingdom of Granada and the Christian Kingdom of Castile, leaving it with a legacy of more castles per square kilometre than any other region of Europe.

Jaén became a war zone again in the 19th century when, at the battle of Bailén on 19 July 1808, a Spanish victory against French forces meant that the tide began to turn against Napoleon in the Peninsular War.

All armies gone, Jaén remains a region of transit with different kinds

of trade caravans – trains and lorries – rolling across its plains and hills. But Jaén is worth devoting time to. There is more here than transport corridors and interminable lines of smoky green-grey olive trees marching over the hills in defiance of the contours, and the locals well know it. '*A quien Dios quiso bien, casa le dio en Jaén*', they say: 'Whomever God wished well, He gave a house in Jaén'. If nothing else – and there is much else – the province has all those castles to admire, but it also has Spain's largest nature

Main Attractions

Baeza
Úbeda
Jaén
Desfiladero de
  Despeñaperros
Parque Natural de la
  Sierra de Cazorla,
  Segura y las Villas
Vía Verde del Aceite

Map on page 176

Úbeda nightlife.

reserve and two exquisite Renaissance towns which are by far the best places to begin a visit.

BEAUTIFUL BAEZA

The astounding richness of both Baeza and Úbeda gives the lie to books that suggest that there is little of architectural interest in Andalucía outside the great Moorish cities. Their splendid honey-coloured palaces, churches and civic buildings, dating largely from the wealthy 15th to 17th centuries, have a cherished rather than lived-in air, as if history had left them frozen in their glory days.

Despite their similarities, each is different from the other. **Baeza ❶** – the sight of which at dusk prompted the poet Federico García Lorca to remark: '*Borrachera espléndida de romanticismo!*' ('What a glut of romanticism!') – is the smaller of the two. Its historic centre is so compact that you could walk around it in half an hour, although it deserves a far more leisurely visit.

The natural starting point for a stroll is the little square off the bottom of the large and unharmonious Plaza de la Constitución, the **Plaza del Pópulo**, also called the Plaza de los Leones after the lion fountain in the middle of the square, built using stone from the ruined Roman town of Cástulo. At the head of this square is the **Casa del Pópulo**, containing the tourist information office and beside it two monumental gateways, the **Puerta de Jaén** and the **Arco de Villalar**.

The other handsome Renaissance building on the square, the **Antigua Carnicería**, was built as Baeza's slaughterhouse or butcher's shop.

If you head uphill from here and bear left you will soon reach the **Cathedral** (Mon–Fri 10.30am–2pm, 4–6pm, Sat 10.30am–6pm, Sun 10;30am–5pm), remodelled in the 16th century but including some of its earlier Gothic elements. Its main door looks down onto a quiet cobbled square surrounding a quaint triumphal arch of a fountain, the **Fuente de Santa María**. The former Seminario de San Felipe Neri opposite the Cathedral (on the lower side of the square) is adorned with the

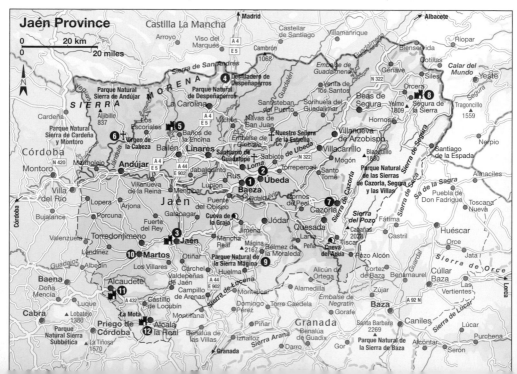

fading red calligraphic *vitores* dating from between 1668 and 1720: graffiti by former students of the school in praise of someone or something of their fancy.

Downhill to the right of the seminary is Baeza's finest building, the **Palacio de Jabalquinto** (patio only: Mon–Fri 9am–2pm; free), which has a decorative Isabelline facade framed by two pillars and topped by a gallery of arches. At the bottom of the slope you emerge on the Paseo de la Constitución. Across this and one street back is the **Ayuntamiento** (Town Hall), once used as an old prison, which has ornate window surrounds on its upper floor.

ELEGANT ÚBEDA

A stone's throw from Baeza, on an adjacent hill, is **Úbeda ❷**, where a group of monumental palaces and churches forms the core of a modern town. The ensemble is largely the work of the architect Andrés de Vandelvira, a native of Castilla–La Mancha, under the patronage of two noblemen,

Francisco de los Cobos and his nephew Juan Vázquez de Molina, both powerful and ambitious secretaries to the emperor of Spain.

With one exception, all the buildings worth seeing are contained within the area circumscribed by the old city walls, of which only fragments remain. The centrepiece of this network of small streets of museum-like calm is the **Plaza de Vázquez de Molina**, an open-plan public space planted with clipped hedges and ornamental trees. At one end of it stands the domed chapel Sacra Capilla **El Salvador** (www.fundacionmedinaceli.org; Mon–Sat 9.30am–2.30pm, 4–6pm, Sun 11.15am–3pm, 4–7pm), commissioned by Francisco de los Cobos as a family pantheon with an extravagant interior. The north side of the square is formed by two other imposing buildings, the former Dean of Málaga's residence, converted into a parador, which has a delightful patio and the **Palacio Vázquez de Molina** (Mon–Fri 8am–3pm, 5–9pm, Sat 9am–2pm; free), by Vandelvira,

⊙ Shop

Before leaving Úbeda be sure to buy some of the town's famous emerald green pottery, made using ancient techniques, which you will find in the Barrio San Millán. The award-winning Tito family's workshop (Plaza del Ayuntamiento 12; www.alfareriatito.com; daily 9am–8pm) has a 14th-century kiln and a small museum.

Baeza's Plaza del Pópolo.

OIL WEALTH

From its Roman origins and mule-driven stone presses to modern methods and superior quality, Andalucía's most famous product merits its nickname of 'liquid gold'.

The Romans planted olive trees across what are now Jaén, Córdoba and Seville above the Río Guadalquivir. After milling, the oil was transported down-river to the sea, to be shipped to Rome. Later, the Moors extended the cultivation of the olive across much of the Peninsula. They called it *az-zait*, 'juice of the olive'. From this derives the Spanish *aceite*, the generic word for oil. The tree in Spanish is *olivo*, from the Latin, but the fruit, *aceituna*, is from the Arabic.

These days, when harvesting the olives a vibrating machine is used to shake the trees, and plastic crates rather than baskets are used to collect the fallen olives; a tractor rather than a mule hauls the olives to the mill; and great stainless-steel vats have replaced the clay amphorae of yore. At the mill, the olives are thoroughly washed, then crushed to release the oil. The oil is extracted by purely mechanical means and, unlike other vegetable oils,

The olive harvest in Jaén.

can be consumed without further refining and purification.

Modern methods have brought a dramatic improvement in the finished product. The old fashioned *almazaras* may have presented a romantic image, with their mule-driven stone presses, but the process was slow, the olives often bruised and rotted in the sun while awaiting their turn, and the oil was more often than not rancid and highly acidic. Today's continuous presses and temperature controls ensure a much higher and consistent quality.

The oil is filtered into a series of settling tanks. The oil rises to the top and is drawn off, while the sediment and water content settle to the bottom. The resulting product is pure virgin olive oil, first pressing.

The quality of that oil depends on several factors, such as variety of olive, soil and climate, but, most importantly, how the olives were picked, transported, stored and milled. The best oil, labelled 'extra virgin' or 'fine virgin', comes from olives which are picked ripe and milled immediately. Its colour can vary from pale gold to amber to greenish-yellow, depending on the type of olive. It is usually completely clear after filtration. New oil has a slight bitterness, appreciated by many people, which disappears with a few months' maturation. Two, even three pressings can be made from the same olive pulp.

The product is used extensively in Andalucía. In a typical village home the housewife serves the midday meal. The fish, croquettes, pork and potatoes are all fried in olive oil. The salad is dressed with olive oil. For breakfast, toasted slabs of bread are lavishly drizzled with olive oil.

Everything from glowing complexions (before commercial moisturisers, Spanish women used olive oil and water whipped together) to strong hearts and good digestion have been attributed to olive oil. To encourage production of the highest-quality oil, a control board authorises a few select *denominación de origen* labels, or 'guarantee of origin', for virgin oils.

There are 29 such DOs, 12 of them in Andalucía: the sierras of Magina, Segura and Cazorla in Jaen; the Sierra de Cádiz; Priego de Córdoba; Baena, Lucena and Montoro-Adamuz (also in Córdoba); Poniente de Granada; Montes de Granada; Antequera (Málaga) and Estepa in Seville province.

now the Town Hall. On the other side of the square are the **Antiguo Pósito** (the Old Granary) and, set back a little, **Santa María de los Reales Alcázares** (open daily but times vary). This last is the third largest church in the province after the cathedrals of Jaén and Baeza, and is essentially 13th-century incorporating part of an old mosque and fortress and with a conspicuous Renaissance facade.

Wander away from the square to the east or west and you quickly pass through the city walls and are faced with an endless vista of olive trees. You can find out about the local olive oil industry at the well-executed **Centro de Interpretación Olivar y Aceite** (Corredera San Francisco 32; www.centrodeolivaryaceite.com; June–Sept Tue–Sat 10am–1pm, 6–9pm, Sun 10am–1pm; Oct–May Tue–Sat 11am–2pm, 5–8pm, Sun 11am–2pm) in the north of the town. On the way to the west exit take a detour and stop off at the **Casa Museo Arte Andalusí** (Calle Navarez, 11; tel: 953-754 014; daily 11.30am–2pm, 5–8pm), a private

museum housed in a 16th-century palace, which as well as containing an interesting collection of the owner's antiques from Spain and Morocco.

To the north, there are other buildings to discover, notably the **Palacio Vela de los Cobos** (behind the Town Hall; guided tours only), which has a gallery of arches along its top floor ending with a white marble column in one corner, and the **Casa de las Torres**, an early 16th-century mansion with a Plateresque facade framed by two towers. If you crave relief from the smugness of the Renaissance, you will find it in the Iglesia de San Pablo, a 13th-century church with a Gothic southern door and a Romanesque west door. In the square outside, there is a monument to St John of the Cross who died in Úbeda in 1591. A short walk east is a **museum** (Calle del Carmen 13; www.sanjuandelacruzubeda.com; Tue–Sun 11am–1pm, 5–7pm) dedicated to the saint.

Continuing north, the **Sinagoga del Agua** (Calle Roque Rojas 2; tel: 953-758 150; daily, guided tours only) is a

Easter procession in Úbeda.

synagogue and rabbi's house dating from (at least) the 14th century. These important remains were only discovered in 2006 when a local businessman bought and began renovating adjoining buildings to turn into shops and flats.

The one building of renown which stands outside the line of the old city walls is the **Hospital de Santiago** (daily 10am–2pm, 5–9pm; free), next to the bullring. It is considered to be the masterpiece of the mature Vandelvira for its facade, patio and, above all, arcaded staircase.

Up on a hilltop not far from Úbeda is a town which gets fewer visitors than it deserves. **Sabiote** has Arab ramparts and a Moorish castle treated to a Renaissance facelift by Vandelvira. Several of the town's noble mansions have carved portals and coats of arms.

PROVINCIAL CENTRE

After such concentrated architectural beauty, the city of **Jaén ❸**, perched halfway up a hillside with its back to the sierras, can come as an anticlimax,

especially as it is often clogged by traffic. All the monuments are in the old part of the city, at the top, and if you arrive by car it's best to park downhill and brace yourself for the hike up steep streets towards the **Cathedral** (Mon–Fri 10am–2pm, 4–8pm, Sat 10am–2pm, 4–7pm, Sun 10am–noon, 4–7pm), a Renaissance work of the 16th and 17th centuries. In the Capilla Mayor is a singular relic, one of three cloths in Christendom claimed to be indelibly stamped with the face of Jesus Christ after being used by Veronica to wipe the sweat from his face as he went towards his crucifixion.

From one corner of the Cathedral, Calle Maestra Martínez de Molina leads past the tourist information office and around the contours into the prettiest corner of the city, San Juan. On the discreet square of Plaza Santa Luisa de Marillac is the **Palacio de Villardompardo** (Tue–Sat 9am–10pm, Sun 9am–3pm; free to EU visitors), a 16th-century mansion built by Fernando de Torres y Portugal, Count of Villardompardo and Viceroy of Peru,

Courtyard in the Hospital de Santiago, Úbeda.

now a folk museum with a collection of naïve art, of more depth, literally, than at first meets the eye. It lies on top of a complete suite of Arab baths (**Baños Arabes**), the largest and arguably best-restored example in Spain, their chambers divided by horseshoe arches and lit by star-shaped skylights. The baths were built in the 11th century, but after the Christian reconquest of the city turned into a tannery.

The city has other fine buildings to see, but if time is short you may just want to drive up the hillside beyond the busy streets above the Cathedral to the **Castillo de Santa Catalina** (July–Sept Mon–Sat 10am–2pm, 5–9pm, Sun 10am–3pm; Oct–June Mon–Sat 10am–6pm, Sun 10am–3pm), a crumbling Arab castle which offers spectacular views. In the 1960s it was extended by building a 'castle-style' parador next to it – the perfect place to stop for a refreshing drink.

INTO THE HILLS

Having seen what the towns have to offer, it is time to head for the mountains. Jaén has a greater extension of protected wildlife areas than any other province in Spain, including four designated *parques naturales*. Two of these protect chunks of the large, empty Sierra Morena to the north. The most accessible of them is the gorge-pass of the **Desfiladero de Despeñaperros** ❹, which funnels the motorway and mainline railway between Madrid and the plains of La Mancha and the cities of Andalucía. The last town on the motorway before the frontier with Castilla-La Mancha is **La Carolina**, a 'new town' laid out by order of Carlos III in 1767 as a lead-mining community, and populated with immigrants from Central Europe. Much more ancient is the enormous 10th-century castle overlooking the plains from **Baños de la Encina** ❺, as if waiting for one last army to come and lay siege to it.

The other *parque natural* in Jaén's stretch of the Sierra Morena is to the north of the Iberio-Roman town of Andújar and encompasses within its borders one of Andalucía's most

⊙ **Tip**

If you're around at the start of June, head to El Yelmo for the Festival Internacional del Aire (www.fiaelyelmo.com), a three-day festival of paragliding. In July, Cazorla hosts a three-day blues festival, Blues-cazorla (www.bluescazorla.com), which attracts well-known international acts like Wilko Johnson and Imelda May to the town.

Baños de la Encina's 10th-century castle.

popular shrines. It takes a 33-km (20-mile) drive from the main road along winding roads to get to the **Santuario de la Virgen de la Cabeza** . Every April half a million pilgrims make the trip on foot, horseback or by car to pay homage to the diminutive statue of the Virgin contained therein. Outside the church stands an elegy to the idealism and futile sacrifice of war: a simple stone tablet which tells how Capitán Cortés, leading 250 rebel troops and a handful of local villagers, defended the sanctuary against eight months of Republican onslaught during the first year of the Civil War.

SPAIN'S LARGEST RESERVE

There are even more appealing mountains in the east. The forested limestone ridges and deep, steep valleys of the **Parque Natural de las Sierras de Cazorla, Segura y las Villas** comprise Spain's largest nature-and-game reserve and take up almost one-fifth of the province of Jaén. The new 479-km (297-mile) GR247 footpath passes through the park in 21 stages. Apart

A new footpath winds its way through the Parque Natural de las Sierras de Cazorla, Segura y las Villas.

from its importance in terms of wildlife preservation – the reserve has a rich population of eagles and vultures amongst other birds, and its endemic species of plant include a singular carnivorous species – it has symbolic significance, as it is here that Andalucía's principal river, the Guadalquivir, rises. To begin with, this modest stream is forced north by the mountains into the reservoir of Embalse del Tranco, but as soon as it finds a way through the Sierra de Cazorla it sets off westwards, along the base of the Sierra Morena, picking up speed as it passes through Córdoba and Seville, finally emptying into the Atlantic. Another important river, the Segura, also rises within the reserve, but flows the other way, to the Mediterranean.

The nature reserve has a visitor centre (tel: 953-713 017; daily 10am–2pm, 5–8pm in summer, 4–7pm in winter), but it is a long way inside the park's boundaries. The best point of access is **Cazorla** , which clings to a steep slope under a rocky ridge and looks out onto an endless view of olive trees. It centres on the Plaza de la Corredera, with its fine town hall, but another good square is the Plaza de Santa María, which has lively terrace cafés in summer.

The road into the reserve from Cazorla passes under the Templar castle of **La Iruela** before leading over the Puerto de las Palomas pass to bring you winding down to a cross-roads, the Empalme del Valle. The only thing to do here is turn up the valley northeast, unless you want to visit the parador – a modern luxury hotel in a stunning setting – or go in search of the source of the Guadalquivir (a round trip of almost 40 km/25 miles from the crossroads).

The valley road takes you to the Torre del Vinagre visitor centre (details above), which has displays on the sierras' geography and wildlife, as well as an adjacent botanic garden. A hunting museum is a reminder of the days when wildlife was to be hunted rather than given protection: General Franco bagged a record-breaking deer in Cazorla in 1959.

After the visitor centre, the road continues north and runs beside the reservoir. From here a scenic route follows the gorge of the Guadalquivir towards Iznatoraf, but if you have the time it is worth continuing to the end of the lake into a more open, much less wooded landscape. This is surveyed by **Segura de la Sierra 8**, an important town under Muslim rule, from which times it retains a castle with impressive views. In the 16th century, as Spain's empire was expanding, Segura made a fortune by cutting down the trees around it and shipping the timber down the Guadalquivir to build ships. Today, the town lives from its olive oil, for which it enjoys a *denominación de origen*.

GR 247 waymarker.

FACES IN THE FLOOR

The remaining *parque natural* covers a compact massif reaching to 2,165 metres (7,103ft) between Jaén city and Cazorla, the **Sierra Mágina**, where olive trees cover the lower slopes and then give way to scrub vegetation and crags. The prettiest parts are to the north and the south: the area around Albánchez

de Mágina and Torres is worth driving through, and there are good views from the Huelma to Cambil road.

The name Mágina is thought to mean 'magic' or 'mysterious', and it is fitting that it should be the location for one of the best-known paranormal enigmas of Spain. On the eastern slopes of the sierra is **Bélmez de la Moraleda** ❾, an undistinguished little town which would receive no visitors at all were it not for a phenomenon which has been occurring since 1971. Since then a multitude of ghostly, monochrome faces have been appearing in the concrete floor of a house supposedly to the bafflement of scientists – although it only seems to be paranormal enthusiasts who care either way.

You can see this for yourself by following the signs to the 'Casa de las Caras' (or the 'Nueva Casa de las Caras' – because another house has been experiencing similar receptivity in a concrete floor). Both houses are advertised as being open weekends only, but if you visit on a whim at other times you may be lucky and find someone who will let you see the faces in return for a tip.

THREE CASTLES

The southeast corner of Jaén province is agricultural, but three olive-processing towns built around castles are worth a visit. The first two form part of a 55-km (33-mile long) cycle way (also used by hikers), the **Vía Verde del Aceite** (The Olive Oil Green Way) from Jaén city along a disused railway line which passes through two illuminated tunnels. **Martos** ❿ is considered the epicentre of world olive-oil production although it is not a *denominación de origen* – such distinction is reserved for the better oils produced on the sierras to the east.

Alcaudete ⓫, a dusty town above a sea of olive trees, has a castle built by the Knights of Calatrava in the 13th and 14th centuries. At **Alcalá la Real** ⓬, meanwhile, in the far south, the abbey church of Santa María la Mayor was built on the site of the former mosque in the Moorish fortress of La Mota after the Renconquest, and its presence there creates a strangely postmodern effect.

Jaén province is carpeted with olive groves.

Alcaudete castle.

The beautifully landscaped Patio
de la Acequia in the Generalife.

GRANADA

The last city to fall to the Reconquest, Granada's Alhambra is the most impressive medieval Moorish palace in the world.

Legend has it that, when the Moors were finally ousted from the Kingdom of Granada in 1492, their defeated king, Boabdil, could not contain his tears as he looked back at the magnificent city his ancestors had forged over nearly seven centuries and which he had been obliged to surrender. The site of this legendary moment of sadness is a pass in the hills 13 km (8 miles) south of Granada. It is called El Suspiro del Moro, the Moor's Sigh.

These days the view from this spot is less impressive, as the foreground is dominated by the sprawl of Granada's modern suburbs, which seem determined to fill the fertile farming plain (the *vega*) with housing estates and shopping centres. To get a truer appreciation of the old city of **Granada** ① it is better to begin with a view from a vantage point closer in.

The **Mirador de San Cristóbal** Ⓐ, on the road which winds up and out of Granada in the direction of Murcia (No. 7 bus from the city centre), provides the best view of all, and is an excellent starting point for the newcomer to Granada. Across the valley of the Darro river, the Moorish fortress-palace of the Alhambra seems to grow out of the burnt sienna rock and the dark-green vegetation, asymmetrically in harmony with the natural landscape. Behind it are the snow-capped peaks

Shopping in the Albaicín.

of the Sierra Nevada, at one's feet the old quarter of the Albaicín.

HUB OF THE OLD CITY

When Granada became an independent Moorish kingdom at the beginning of the 11th century, the royal court was in the **Albaicín** Ⓑ, and not transferred to the Alhambra opposite until 250 years later. Today, with its network of steep erratic streets, steps and alleyways, it is still easy to imagine what the Albaicín must have been like when it was the hub of Moorish Granada with its 30 mosques,

Maps on pages 188, 190, 198

Tip

Don't leave the Albaicín without taking a stroll along Calderería Nueva (turn east off Calle Elvira), which feels more like North African than Spain. It's famous for its *teterías* (tea rooms), where mint tea and sweet, sticky pastries are on the menu as well as vegetarian food.

its potters and weavers, and its women fetching water from the *aljibes* (public water tanks), still used as recently as the 1960s. Today, the Albaicín is a desirable place to live and an atmospheric place in which to stroll, even if it keeps most of its secrets behind the tall walls of its typical house-patio complexes, known as *cármenes*. You can see inside one at the **Centro Cultural Max Moreau** (Camino Neuvo de San Nicolás 12; Tue–Sat 10am–1.30pm, 5–7pm, 4–6pm in summer; free), the former home of a Belgian painter.

The best place to begin a walking tour of the Albaicín is along the **Carrera del Darro**, the little river valley separating the Albaicín and Alhambra hills, which starts just north of Plaza Nueva. Several old properties along this route have been converted into interesting hotels. At No. 31 are the 11th-century Arab baths, **El Bañuelo** ⒞ (daily May–mid-Sept 10am–2.30pm, 5–8.30; mid-Sept–Apr 10am–5pm; free Sun). Entered through a leafy patio, the baths are perfectly restored with sunlight playing through the stars and octagons pierced through the roof. Turn left at any point along here to zigzag up through the Albaicín, where the smells of jasmine, of damp, of heat or of cooking take over from car fumes, where the sound of burbling water is common, and where mules are occasionally still used to carry bricks and bags of cement. Little trace of Islamic architecture remains, as churches and convents – several enclosed orders still function here – rapidly supplanted the mosques after the reconquest of Granada. One survivor is the **Palacio de Dar al-Horra** (Queen's House; same times as El Bañuelo; free Sun), on the other side of the Albaicín, built for King Boabdil's mother in the mid-15th century. It is behind the convent of **Santa Isabel la Real**, also a former Moorish palace.

THE HOLY HILL

Up the hill north of the Albaicín is **Sacromonte** ⒟, literally the 'Holy Hill'. This was once a well-known cave quarter inhabited by a strong gypsy community, but these days only a handful of caves still offer *zambras*, gypsy fiestas

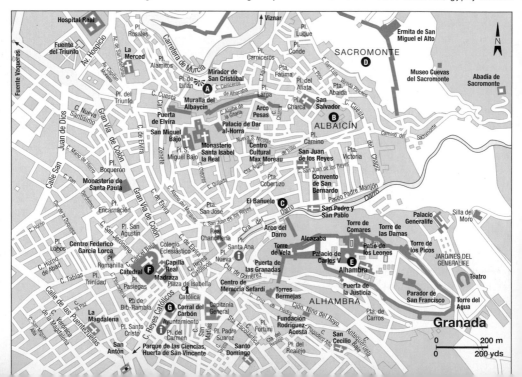

Granada

0   200 m
0   200 yds

of flamenco music and dance. You can find out what cave life is/was like at the **Museo Cuevas del Sacromonte** (Barranco de los Negros; www.sacromonte granada.com; mid-Mar–mid-Oct 10am–8pm; mid-Oct–mid-Mar 10am–6pm), an ethnographic museum where they also occasionally host flamenco concerts. Past the caves is the **Abadía de Sacromonte** (Mon–Sat 10am–1pm, 4.30–6.30pm in summer, 5–7pm in winter), a late 15th-century abbey founded on the site where the remains of four Christian martyrs were discovered, including the patron saint of Granada, San Cecilio. It has five fascinating subterranean chapels.

THE ALHAMBRA

Everything else in Granada, however, is merely a foretaste for the one building everyone comes to the city to see, the **Alhambra E** (see page 191). No other monument in Spain has exerted such fascination over travellers and historians over the centuries, or inspired so many poets, composers, painters and writers.

That the palace-fortress, its gardens and the summer residence, the Generalife, can still be termed 'the best-preserved medieval Arab palace in the world' is nothing short of a miracle given the Alhambra's history after the defeat of Boabdil. An earthquake in 1522 and an explosion in 1590 caused significant damage. During the Peninsular War, Napoleonic troops used the Alhambra as a garrison and destroyed part of its ramparts. Further destruction was undertaken in 1626 by Carlos I (known as Emperor Charles V outside Spain), who decided to build a palace in the confines of the Alhambra in a style of jarring incongruity. Then, 50 years later, the palace's mosque was knocked down to make way for the Church of Santa María.

It was largely thanks to the 'discovery' of the Alhambra by 19th-century writers and artists that the monument was at last recognised as unique. Mérimée, Chateaubriand, Gustave Doré and Victor Hugo were all profoundly influenced by their stay in Granada, while Washington Irving (see page 195), Théophile Gautier and Richard Ford enjoyed the

Along the picturesque Carrera del Darro.

extraordinary privilege of lodging within the Alhambra itself, in the quarters where Carlos I spent his honeymoon.

In 1870 the Alhambra was declared a national monument and restoration began, although the first efforts were geared more to creating the ideal image of a fairy-tale castle as envisioned by the romantics of the day than a faithful recreation of the building. It wasn't until the 1920s that a measure of historical rigour was applied to the restoration, a painstaking process that continues to this day, carried out by a permanent staff of architects and craftsmen.

FORM AND FUNCTION

The Alhambra is made up of three principal parts: the Royal Palace, the Alcazaba or fortress, and the Medina, where up to 2,000 members of the royal household lived but which today is mainly given over to gardens. Further up the slope stands a fourth part of the complex, the summer palace of the rulers of Granada, the Generalife.

The Alhambra largely dates from the 14th century, but it is better thought of as an accumulation of buildings over time. When in 1238 Muhammad Ben Nasr founded the Nasrid dynasty that was to rule Granada until 1492, he held court in a castle where today's Alcazaba stands. It wasn't until his descendant Yusuf I became king 100 years later that building on the new palace began. The reign of this Nasrid king, and that of his son Muhammad V, which together lasted from 1333 to 1391, saw the construction of all the most important elements of the royal palace as we know them today.

The core of the Alhambra is the Royal Palace (the Casa Real or Palacios Nazaries), a fantasy of delicate arches, intricate carving and trickling fountains. Unlike the self-confident grandeur of the Mosque in Córdoba, or the restrained elegance of the Almohads' Giralda in Seville, the Alhambra has an almost ephemeral quality, and, indeed, the carved patterns and inscriptions on plaster which are the most striking decorative feature were regarded as no more permanent than today's wallpaper; successive rulers would remove the work of their predecessors and

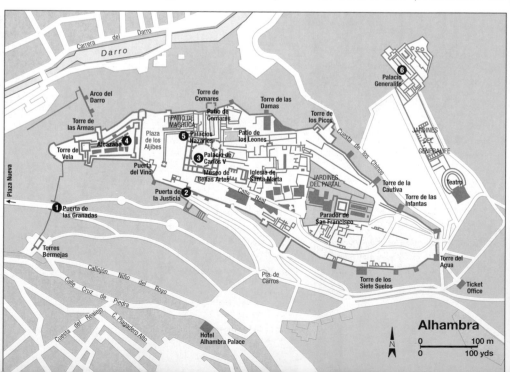

Alhambra

have it replaced with inscriptions more to their liking.

Built with clay bricks, mortar and wood, the whole palace is the architectural expression of a civilisation in its twilight years, when the once formidable military might of Muslim Spain had been replaced by the intense, if relatively brief, cultural flowering of Nasrid Granada.

The intrigues that unfolded in the rooms of the Royal Palace, pitting the sultan Mulay Hassan and his favourite concubine, the Christian-born Zoraya, against his wife Aixa and their luckless son Boabdil, would spark a civil war and precipitate Granada's eventual downfall.

APPROACHING ON FOOT

If your legs and lungs are up to it, it is well worth starting out from the **Plaza Nueva**, at the foot of the Alhambra hill in central Granada, and walking up the shaded Cuesta de Gomérez and through the **Puerta de las Granadas ❶** (Gate of the Pomegranates), built on Carlos I's orders in 1536. It is decorated with three pomegranates,

symbol of the city (the Spanish word for pomegranate is *granada*, although the city's name has a different origin; it comes from the name given to the city by its sizeable Jewish population during Visigoth days, Garnatha).

As you approach the Alhambra, on the left-hand side you'll see the impressive **Puerta de la Justicia ❷** (Gate of Justice or Bib Xaria), one of the main entrances to the palace, on which are engraved the Islamic symbols of a hand and a key. As every tour guide will tell you, the Moorish legend insisted that Christian visitors would never enter this gate until the hand reached down to grasp the key.

Visitors arriving by coach or car follow a ring road, which avoids the city centre. They join pedestrians in the queue outside the ticket office, at the bottom of the car park.

THE PALACIO DE CARLOS V

Once inside the complex, you can stroll along the garden pathway, through the former medina, the surrounding town, following the signs to 'Palacios

View from the Alcazaba.

Nazaries', until you reach the imposing **Palacio de Carlos V** . Although glaringly out of place among the Nasrid architecture, this is one of the most outstanding examples of Renaissance architecture in Spain, with its unique circle within a square layout.

Off the central courtyard is the **Museo de la Alhambra** (Apr–mid-Oct Wed–Sat 8.30am–8pm, 8.30am–6pm mid-Oct–Mar, Tue and Sun 8.30am–2.30pm; free), which has well-arranged exhibits of Spanish Islamic art. Upstairs is Granada's **Museo de Bellas Artes** (Museum of Fine Art; Tue–Sat mid-June–mid-Sept 9am–3pm, mid-Mar–mid-June & mid-Sept–mid-Oct 9am–8pm, mid-Oct–mid-Mar 9am–6pm, Sun 9am–3pm; free to EU citizens).

THE ALCAZABA

Leaving the palace, you reach the **Plaza de los Aljibes**. This square commands the first of many magnificent views over the Albaicín and Sacromonte. If you have half an hour to spare before your allotted time in the Royal Palace, this is the best time to tour the **Alcazaba** (if

you visit later, its stark military aspect will come as an anticlimax after the splendour of the Nasrid Palaces). The massive fortress juts out like the prow of a ship on the Alhambra hill.

Make your way across the **Plaza de Armas** (which has a small snack bar selling beers, sandwiches and soft drinks), where you can view the foundations of the soldiers' domestic quarters, and climb up to the **Torre de Vela**. Isabel had a bell installed in this tower after the fall of Granada to symbolise the Christian triumph (bells are banned under Islam).

One last stop before the Nasrid palaces is the illuminating **Sala de Presentación**, in a Moorish *aljibe* (water cistern) under the Palace of Carlos, an introduction to the Alhambra covering both its history and the techniques and materials used in its construction.

THE NASRID PALACES

The **Royal Palace** (Palacios Nazaries), the highlight of the visit, comprises three distinct parts, leading from the most public areas to the most private

The Alhambra, seen from the Albaicín.

quarters, ending up with a visit to the baths or *hammam*. Inside the entrance to the palace is the *mexuar*, where citizens of Granada were received and justice was meted out; from here, you enter the *serail*, where official, diplomatic life took place; and finally, the *harem*, the monarch's private quarters.

The *mexuar* is the least well preserved part of the palace, having been converted into a chapel shortly after the expulsion of the Moorish court and also damaged by the 1590 explosion. At the end of the main room is an oratory with a glimpse of the intricate geometrical motifs so prolific elsewhere.

From here a small courtyard (Patio del Mexuar) leads to the **Cuarto Dorado** (Golden Room), where the sultan's visitors were received. The entrance to the *serail*, through the left-hand door at the end of the patio, follows a zigzag route, thus protecting its access. Within this part of the palace diplomatic life was intense, especially in the latter half of the 14th century when the power of the Moors in Spain was draining away. Central to

this part of the Alhambra is the **Patio de Comares** (also called Patio de los Arrayanes/Courtyard of the Myrtles), which, with the reflection of the buildings in the water of the pool, is an outstanding example of the symmetry of Islamic art. Critics refer to this as 'the Parthenon of Arab art in Spain'.

At one end of this patio is the **Torre de Comares**, in the ground floor of which is the majestic **Salón de Embajadores** (Ambassadors' Hall), perhaps the room which leaves the most lasting impression on visitors. The domed ceiling, representing the firmament, is inlaid with cedar and reaches a height of over 15 metres (50 ft). The sultan used to sit with his back to the light, facing entering visitors, thus keeping an advantage over them.

From the Patio de Comares you pass into the *harem*, accessed from the **Patio de los Leones** (Patio of the Lions). The domestic quarters of the sultan, his wives and the sultan's mother (a key figure in Moorish court life) lead off this central courtyard – the **Sala de los Reyes** (Hall of the

The Patio de los Arrayanes (Patio of the Myrtles) is a lesson in symmetry.

Some of the 12 lions comprising the central fountain of the Patio de los Leones.

Detail in the Salon de las Dos Hermanas.

The magnificent Patio de la Acequia in the Generalife.

Kings); the **Sala de los Abencerrajes** (Hall of the Abencerrajes) and the **Sala de las Dos Hermanas** (Hall of the Two Sisters).

Amid the overwhelming richness of the *harem* as a whole, several architectural and decorative features are distinctive. First there is the anti-earthquake device, a lead plate inserted at the top of the 124 white-marble pillars. Next, the 12 lions themselves, surrounding the central fountain: according to one theory, the lions represent the Twelve Tribes of Israel, and the two marked with an equilateral triangle on the forehead symbolise the Chosen Tribes.

The paintings on leather in the Sala de los Reyes, where human figures appear, were probably done by Castilian artists who sought refuge in Granada from the reign of terror of Pedro the Cruel. Look for the traces of 'blood' in the fountain in the Sala de los Abencerrajes, 'proof' of the veracity of the legend which tells of how 36 members of the Abencerraje family (Boabdil's family's rival clan) were beheaded

one by one as they entered – a sultan's revenge for his mistress's infidelity.

Exit the patio via the Sala de las Dos Hermanas, with its cupola said to be decorated with more than 5,000 cavities, to reach the **Baño de Comares** (Royal Baths), titled chambers with star-spangled domed roofs. From here you can wander down to the area where the 19th-century American author Washington Irving lived in 'delicious thraldom' while writing his best-seller *Tales of the Alhambra* (see box).

THE GENERALIFE

The itinerary continues through an open garden area, flanked by the **Palacio del Partal** (the oldest part of the complex) and unrestored parts of the exterior walls, as you head for the Nasrids' summer palace, the **Generalife ⑥**, whose gardens are perhaps the most magnificent in Spain. The sound of running water is particularly soothing for anyone who has had enough of heat and monuments, although it is questionable whether the Italianate layout of the present gardens owes

anything to the Moors, who were more interested in roses, aromatic herbs and fruit and vegetables than in trimmed cypress hedges.

The gardens and adjoining palace are all that remain of what was once a much larger estate. The likeliest explanation for the name Generalife is that it derives from the Arabic *Gennet al-Arif* ('architect's garden'). The River Darro was diverted 18 km (11 miles) to feed this oasis of fountains and waterfalls. Only a part of the old summer palace remains, including the **Patio de la Acequia**, with its long and narrow central pond flanked by water spouts, and the **Patio de los Cipreses** (Courtyard of the Cypresses). Despite the name, there is only one cypress tree here now, the dead trunk of a venerable tree that was supposedly witness to the illicit encounters between Zoraya, the sultan's concubine, and her Abencerraje lover, a liaison that led to the massacre of the Abencerraje family in the Sala de los Abencerrajes. Ascending from here is the **Escalera de Agua**, a stairway whose banisters hold channels of rushing water.

ALHAMBRA HOTELS

Before descending to the city, there are two hotels on the Alhambra hill worth visiting for different reasons. Nudging up to the Alhambra itself is the 15th-century **Monasterio de San Francisco**, now one of the most desirable hotels in the state-run parador chain. A room here needs to be booked in advance and does not come cheap, but you can always stroll in to the public areas and enjoy a drink or lunch on the terrace, which has views of the Generalife in the distance.

The **Hotel Alhambra Palace** (www.h-alhambrapalace.es), meanwhile, is a kitsch imitation of its namesake, and was built in 1910 when Granada was enjoying an economic boom thanks to its sugar industry. It has a hanging terrace with a superb view over part of the city and beyond to the *vega*, which in 1829 the American writer Washington Irving described as 'a blooming wilderness of grove and garden and teeming

Snapping away in the gardens.

⊘ ALHAMBRA TALES

Washington Irving, more than anyone else, helped put Granada on the map, with his *Tales of the Alhambra*, written following a visit in 1829 when the American author was travelling through Spain as a diplomat. Although the monument had been maintained by the Spanish rulers following the Reconquest, the Bourbon dynasty that acceded to the Spanish throne in the early 18th century was less attached to it, and it fell into disrepair.

By the time Irving arrived and set up headquarters in the Alhambra, the palace had become home to a colourful bunch of squatters. Ironically, it is thanks to the fact it was inhabited that the monument survived, even if it was the worse for wear, rather than being dismantled and carted away piecemeal for building materials.

Irving's fanciful tales of lovesick princesses and hidden Moorish treasure captivated the imagination of bourgeois society when the book was first published in 1832, and the many visitors who followed in the author's wake to see for themselves this magical place soon made the authorities aware that it was a major attraction that needed to be preserved. It's now a Unesco World Heritage Site (along with the Albaicín) and one of the most visited attractions in Spain.

orchard', but is now disappearing under housing estates.

BARRIO REALEJO

On the south side of the Alhambra is the atmospheric Realejo district, which was home to the city's Jews from the 8th century until their expulsion by the Catholic Monarchs. The **Centro de la Memoria Sefardí** (Placeta Berrocal 5; www.museosefardide-granada.es; Mon–Fri & Sun 10am–2pm, 5–8pm, 4–8pm in winter), in a pretty, traditional house, has an informative exhibition on the life and times of these Sephardic Jews; the owners occasionally organise guided tours of the district and put on cultural events. About 10mins' walk to the east is the **Fundación Rodríguez-Acosta** (Callejón Nino del Royo 8; www.fundacionrodri-guezacosta.com; daily mid-Mar–mid-Oct 10am–6.30pm, mid-Oct–mid-Mar 10am–4.30pm), a carmen built in 1914 by modernist artist José-Maria Rodríguez-Acosta in a range of styles; the art collection, library and gardens are well worth a look.

THE CITY CENTRE

Most of Granada's other sights lie in the narrow streets of the city centre and the best way to visit them is on foot. Rising out of the hubbub is the **Cathedral** ⓕ (Mon–Sat 10am–6.30pm, Sun 3–6pm; free Sun), built on the site of the main mosque of Granada and considered one of the most important examples of Renaissance architecture in Spain. The warm, honey-coloured exterior, however, contrasts with the austere interior. Next to the Cathedral, accessed from Calle Oficios, which runs alongside the east side of the Cathedral, is the much more appealing **Capilla Real** (Royal Chapel; www.capillarealgranada.com; Mon–Sat 10.15am–6.30pm, Sun 11am–6.30pm), the mausoleum of the so-called 'Catholic Monarchs', Fernando and Isabel. The black-lead coffins of this famously pious and pro-active double act are on public display in the crypt, along with those of their luckless daughter, remembered by history as Juana the Mad, and her philandering husband, Felipe the Fair. Above the family vault,

The honey-coloured Cathedral blends perfectly with its surroundings.

the chapel has superb iron grillework and a lavish baroque altarpiece. The sacristy, on the way out, houses an exquisite collection of primitive Flemish paintings.

Across the street from the chapel is the **Madraza** (daily 10am–8pm), the Arab university founded in the 14th century by Yusuf I, of which only the oratory remains from the original building (across the patio on the left); its intricate Arabic decoration was covered over for centuries, only to be rediscovered under a layer of plaster in 1893.

Next to the Madraza, pass through the Alcaicería, a warren of souvenir shops designed to resemble an Arab souk, to reach central Granada's main traffic artery, the Calle de los Reyes de Católicos, which intersects with the Gran Vía de Colón at Plaza de Isabel La Católica, dominated by a statue of Queen Isabel receiving Columbus.

Across Reyes Católicos is the attractive **Corral del Carbón** (daily 9am–8pm; free) **G**, built as an inn in the 14th century but later used as a theatre and coal depot (hence the *carbón* part of its name), and now houses government offices.

One of the best squares for cafés is the lively **Plaza de Bib-Rambla**, immediately south of the Cathedral. It is a popular place to come in the early evening for a beer or aperitif before going shopping. The adjacent streets are a rich source of restaurants, though most don't open until 9pm or later.

GRANADA'S FAMOUS SON

Granada's most famous son is the poet and playwright Federico García Lorca, who was shot dead by Franco's Nationalists at Viznar, north of the city, on 19 August 1936, during the first weeks of the Spanish Civil War. He was born in **Fuentevaqueros ❷**, 17 km (10 miles) northwest of Granada, where the house where he was born has become a museum, the **Museo Casa-Natal Federico García Lorca** (www.patronatogarcialorca.org; guided visits Tue–Sat July–Sept 10am–2pm; Apr–June 10am–1pm, 5–8pm; Oct–Mar 10am–1pm, 4–5pm; Sun 10am–2pm year round).

Plaza de Bib-Rambla is a popular meeting place.

Zambra in full swing at the cave setting of El Templo del Flamenco, in the Gitano (Gypsy) area of Sacromonte.

In the south east of Granada, a 15-minute walk from Puerta Real, is the summer home of the Lorca family, **Huerta de San Vicente** (www.huertadesanvicente.com; Calle Virgen Blanca; guided visits Tue–Sun June–mid-Sept 9am–3pm, mid-Sept–May 9.30am–5pm; free Wed), where Federico wrote most of his major works. A new cultural centre, **Centro Federico García Lorca** (www.centrofedericogarcialorca.es), now stands in Plaza de la Romanilla, west of the cathedral.

EAST OF GRANADA

East of Granada, the motorway towards Almería and Murcia leaves the *vega* behind to cross the wooded Sierra de Huétor. Over the other side of the Puerto de la Mora pass (1,390 metres/4,560 ft) it drops down into an ancient lake bed in the middle of which sits **Guadix ❸**.

Although this city has a monumental centre radiating from the cathedral beneath the restored 11th-century fortress of the alcazaba, what visitors come here to see is the southern

suburb, the **Barriada de las Cuevas**, a cluster of bluntly pointed mud hills pockmarked by hundreds of inhabited caves in various states of conservation and restoration, ranging from hovels to luxury homes.

Around 3,000 people out of a population of just over 20,000 live underground, almost all of them by choice rather than out of necessity (as was historically the case). Caves maintain their temperature at around 18°C (64°F) year-round because of the insulating properties of the clay into which they are dug. They are therefore said to be comfortably cool in summer and correspondingly warm in winter. The only drawback is the lack of natural light. Several caves around Guadix have been turned into cave hotels. There are caves in almost all the villages around Guadix, notably **Purullena**, which is also well known for its ceramics industry.

In Guadix, the natural centre of the cave quarter is the bright white church of the **Iglesia Nuestra Señora de Gracia** on **Plaza del Padre Poveda**, which has a cave chapel on the far side of the

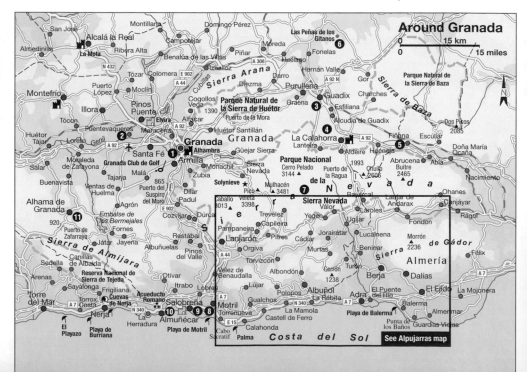

nave. Opposite the church is a municipal cave museum, the **Centro de Interpretación Cuevas de Guadix** (Mon–Sat 10am–2pm, 4–6pm, Sun 10am–2pm), which illustrates life in a cave a century or so ago. The scrape marks of the adzes used to dig it can be seen in the ceiling, proving that it hasn't been restored using modern materials as many other caves have.

For an overview of Guadix, you need to make for the balcony at the quarter's highest point, behind the Colegio Padre Poveda. It takes some finding, but the walk there offers a chance to see a variety of cave houses close up. The view is surreal: half-houses stuck haphazardly to banks of clay which sprout white chimneys seemingly at random.

On the outskirts of Guadix, the motorway from Granada forks sending a southern branch heading into Almería past the Renaissance fortress of **La Calahorra** ❹ (tel: 958-677 098; Wed 10am–1pm, 4–6pm) and, just over the provincial border, **Fiñana** ❺, which has a 12th- to 13th-century Almohad mosque thinly disguised as a chapel

– if it is closed you can see all there is to see by peering through a small glass window in the door.

The northern branch of the motorway makes for Murcia, but an inconspicuous turn-off from it leads towards **Gorafe** and the lip of a canyon where 180 prehistoric dolmens, known as **Las Peñas de los Gitanos** ❻ (Ctra de Ilora km 5, tel: 628-305 337), are open to visitors by appointment.

SNOWY MOUNTAINS

North–south communications in the province of Granada are restricted by the **Sierra Nevada** ❼, the second-highest mountain range in Europe after the Alps. Its peaks are the highest in the Iberian Peninsula: Mulhacén 3,479 metres (11,414 ft) and La Veleta 3,398 metres (11,149 ft). National park status protects the rare vegetation of the mountains: the highest zones are frosty desert where only lichens grow, but lower down the tundra is inhabited by indigenous plant species of wolfsbane, violet, camomile, narcissus, thistle and saxifrage.

The unusual city of Guadix, with its cave houses.

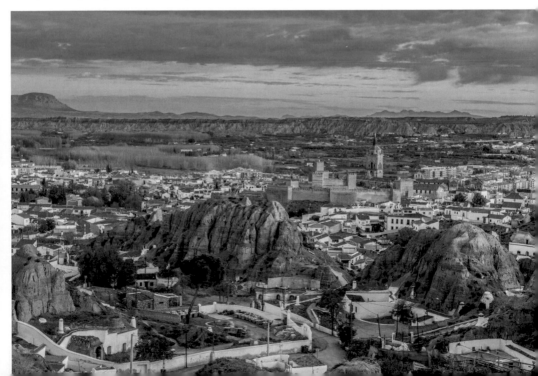

Synonymous with the mountain range is the southernmost ski resort in Europe (www.sierranevada.es), and also one of the continent's highest, with pistes descending from up to 3,300 metres (10,827 ft). Only 32 km (20 miles) southeast of Granada, it has reliable snow cover from December until April, and sometimes as late as May. Being largely above the tree line, it is not scenically spectacular, and its two stations – **Pradollano** at 2,100 metres (6,890 ft) and **Borreguiles** at 2,645 metres (8,677 ft) – aren't likely to win any beauty contests. But it makes up for that with the brilliant sunshine of its southern European climate and the proximity of Granada and the coast.

It's not too difficult to go even higher. An unsurfaced road – claimed to be the highest road in Europe – crosses the range from the ski resort to Capileira in the Alpujarras (see page 208), but it can only be used by authorised vehicles. In summer, the national park offers a minibus shuttle from its **Hoya de la Mora** visitor centre (tel: 671-564 407) above the Pradollano ski station,

almost to within reach of the summit of La Veleta. The ascent takes about three hours, and you can either return with the bus or walk down.

THE COSTA TROPICAL

From the heights of the Sierra Nevada, skiers and walkers look down upon Granada's Mediterranean coast, a world away from the rest of the province. This short, indented strip of shore is now officially called the 'Costa Tropical' because of its abundant subtropical orchards growing bananas, mangoes, avocados and other fruit. A succession of mountainous headlands, Granada's coast is now as built up as the Costa del Sol.

The main town of the Costa Tropical is the port of **Motril ❽**, but it has little to lure tourists except a museum explaining the once-important sugar industry. In places you can still see plantations of sugar cane as a reminder of the past industry. Neighbouring **Salobreña ❾**, the most attractive town on this strip of coast, where the bright white houses of the old town pile around a tall rock that culminates

On the slopes of Pradollano.

in a well-kept Moorish **castle** (daily 10am–2pm, 5.30–9pm in summer, 4–6 pm in winter). Beside the sugar canes on the coastal plain below the town is a small, family-oriented resort.

Almuñécar ⑩, next along the coast, is an ancient town which has surrendered itself to tourism – its Velilla beach is a prime example of insensitive, short-term planning, but it does have historic monuments to show off. Chief of these is the ruined castle on a low hill overlooking the Parque del Majuelo, where there are the remains of a Roman fish-salting factory which once exported its products across the empire. Roman Almueñécar (Sexi) was fed by a 7-km (4.5-mile) long series of aqueducts: with the aid of directions from the tourist office, the line of these can be followed up the lush valley towards Jete.

A few more curves around the coast road bring you to the small resort of **La Herradura**, which has an attractive beach between two headlands, Cerro Gordo and the Punta de la Mona. Beneath the latter is a beautiful cove beside the pleasure boat harbour of Marina del Este. La Herradura is well-known for its watersports, especially diving and windsurfing.

INTO HOT WATER

Granada province has one more town worth seeing, although being lost in the middle of unpopulated farmland en route to Vélez-Málaga from the coast, it demands a special effort to reach. **Alhama de Granada ⑪** nudges up to the edge of an attractive gorge (overlooked by a balcony behind the Iglesia del Carmen), but its attraction lies in the spa hotel down a mini-gorge of its own below the town. The waiting room for guest-patients using the baths, and the source of the thermal waters, is a 12th-century Moorish chamber built of horseshoe arches.

The complex can only be visited during the afternoon (daily 2–4pm). If you need somewhere to pass the time while waiting for it to open, you can join the bathers in the river outside the hotel, where a series of improvised pools is fed by a steady stream of surplus thermal water.

⊙ Tip

For a luxurious modern version of a traditional Arab hammam, visit Aljibe Baños Arabes, San Miguel Alto 41, tel: 958-522 867, www.aljibesanmiguel.es. Sessions, where you bathe in hot and cold pools, start at 10am, noon, 2pm, 4pm, 6pm, 8pm and 10pm daily and last for 1hr 30mins. Massages and other body treatments are also available.

The gorge near Alhama de Granada.

THEY CAME, THEY SAW, THEY PLANTED

From intimate patios to the magnificent gardens of the Alhambra, Andalucía is a magnet for gardeners from all over the world.

Fertile soil and abundant sunshine make Andalucía a gardener's paradise, and the region is home to some outstanding gardens, including Seville's María Luisa Park and the gardens of the Generalife in the Alhambra.

For the Muslims, gardens were intimate places appealing to all the senses. Aromatic plants such as mint and basil were key elements, along with the soothing sound of running water. Moorish homes were arranged around interior courtyards that provided a scented refuge from the heat.

After the Moors departed, the reigning style was the Italian garden of the Renaissance, designed to impress with symmetrical layout, manicured aspect, statues and fountains. The Generalife gardens we see now owe more to this style than to the Moorish.

COLOURFUL IMPORTS

Each subsequent wave of settlers brought with them their preferred plants. The Phoenicians, Greeks and Romans introduced olive trees, date palms and vines. The Muslims brought orange trees and a great many herbs and flowers native to Asia. Explorations of new continents added to this botanical wealth. Geraniums came from southern Africa, mimosas from Australia, wisteria from Asia and bougainvillea from South America.

The Generalife in Granada belonged to the Moorish summer palace, but its present layout displays Italian rather than Moorish influences.

Geraniums are often considered the quintessential Andalusian pot plant, brightening many a white wall. Yet, like so many of Andalucía's plants, they originated from elsewhere, in this case South Africa.

A statue in the Jardín de los Leones in Seville's María Luisa Park. Lions are a recurring motif in Andalucía, whether in the mysterious Patio of the Lions in the Alhambra or the conquering lion of Castile, which crops up everywhere.

Running along the calle Cairuán, next to a cascading series of ponds and water channels, lies a stretch of the city walls which surrounded the Medina in Córdoba.

The wonder of water

Using their considerable engineering skills, the Romans were the first to harness Andalucía's water resources. Their canals and aqueducts turned the region into the breadbasket of the empire, and they built baths over several natural springs. But it was the Muslims who, adapting and improving on the Roman irrigation system, regarded water as an aesthetic element as well. Fountains, pools and elaborate channels, such as the 'water stairway' in the Generalife gardens of the Alhambra, cooled the air and filled it with soothing sound. Water had a symbolic significance for the Muslims. Gardens were divided into four sections separated by channels of water representing the four Rivers of Life.

Taking a leaf out of the Moors' gardening book, Christian landscapers also used water for dramatic effect, especially with exquisite fountains, such as in the Palacio de Viana in Córdoba, a sumptuous 15th-century palace noted for its gardens incorporating 12 different patios.

tiled fountain in María Luisa Park's Plaza de América, eville. Donated to the city by Duchess Marie Louise of rléans in 1893, the park contains many delightful features.

hough designed several centuries later, the El Partal ardens in the Alhambra successfully unite some of the ldest sections of the Nasrid Palace.

One of the 12 tranquil courtyards in the Palacio de Viana in Córdoba.

Las Alpujarras is a pretty area of steep hillsides and deep valleys.

THE ALPUJARRAS

Over the Sierra Nevada from Granada are the deep, leafy valleys
of the Alpujarras, one of Spain's most charming corners.

Once a poor, remote and self-contained world of its own, the gigantic mountainsides and plunging valleys of **Las Alpujarras** first became known to the world in the 1950s because of a book written by Gerald Brenan, an English intellectual, who had taken refuge there from civilisation 30 years before. In recent decades his example has been followed by innumerable other migrants from northern Europe with a variety of similar motives – urban escapees, downsizers, alternative lifestyle-seekers, artists, neo-pastoralists, nature-lovers – and the Alpujarras fame has been given a fillip by another book by a refugee Englishman, called Chris Stewart, whose best-selling *Driving over Lemons* is an autobiographical account of his life as sometime smallholder and sheep-shearer in the area.

Many of the native inhabitants, meanwhile, have been migrating the other way, towards the comforts of the city. Despite improvements in communications between the Alpujarras with the outside world, young men and women are not anxious to take on subsistence hill farming in the mould of previous generations.

MEMORIES OF THE MOORS

It's easy to get the impression the newcomers are gatecrashing a way of life that has been going on for ever, but population-replacement is nothing new in the Alpujarras, and tradition is not as deep-rooted as it first might seem. When the Kingdom of Granada fell to Christian forces in 1492, its Muslim inhabitants were driven into the Alpujarras with the promise that they would be able to carry on their lives here as before. After a brief period of toleration, however, they were forced to choose between baptism or exile. Most chose the former, becoming *Moriscos*, nominal Christian, who discreetly maintained their Muslim traditions.

⊙ Main Attractions
Lanjarón
Trevélez
Yegen
Valór

Map on page 206

Typical houses in the village of Pampaneira.

But when a series of decrees sought to ban their traditional costume, their use of Arabic and even their bathing ritual, the Moriscos of the Alpujarras revolted. The rebellion was bloodily crushed, the Moriscos driven into exile and the Alpujarras resettled with yet another wave of immigrants, this time from northwest Spain – indeed, several of the villages of the Alpujarras have Galician names.

Despite this historic handover of religion and culture, the Alpujarras retain a strong air of Arab influence, and it is this which makes them so attractive. Although many hill terraces have fallen into disrepair and become overgrown, they are still fed by the same ingenious system of irrigation channels appearing out of nowhere and slipping silently out of sight among the chestnut trees as they distribute the meltwaters of the Sierra Nevada according to a strict rationale. The occasional mulberry tree is a reminder of the Moriscos' once-important silk industry – the mulberry leaves being the food plant of the silkworm.

VILLAGE ARCHITECTURE

Above all, the lingering influence of the departed Muslims is evident in the architecture of the villages, which has its closest echo in the Atlas Mountains of Morocco. The houses are built onto each, as if at random – a confused agglomeration of boxes, one box rising above another, and so on to the top', as Gerald Brenan saw them.

This creates higgledy-piggledy street patterns of shaded, narrow lanes and alleys widening and constricting again for no apparent reason, and often stepped or ribbed to prevent pedestrians and pack-mules slipping on a frosty day. Smaller villages will have only one road in and out; in other directions they peter out into intriguing-looking paths which wander past disused threshing floors.

Traditionally, the houses of the Alpujarras were built using the materials available close to home, and those that have not been modernised with brick, aluminium and double-glazed windows still blend harmoniously into the landscape. Older houses usually consist of

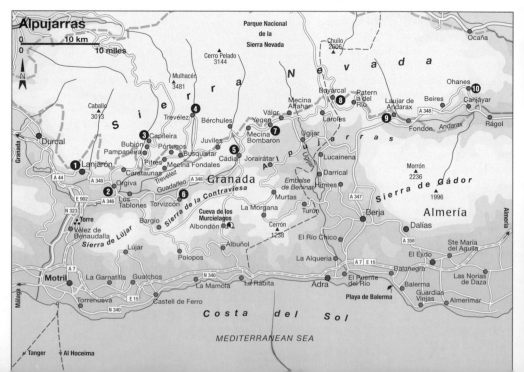

two storeys: the upper one for human habitation, the ground floor for livestock and farming equipment. The flat roof, supported by chestnut beams and spread with *launa,* an impermeable gravel of decomposed slate, served as a place for hanging out the washing, the line being attached to the tall, white chimney.

A CIRCUIT OF THE ALPUJARRAS

A circuit of the Alpujarras looks fairly short on the map, but the roads are steep and winding, so progress is slow. You will need a full day to tour the area, and at least one overnight stay if you want to enjoy some walking (see box).

The point of access coming from Granada is the spa of **Lanjarón ❶**, which has turned its spring water into one Spain's most popular bottled brands. It is also a serious health spa with extensive facilities. Its one monument – the ruins of a Moorish castle on a rock adrift from the rest of Lanjarón – can be seen from the ring-road around the bottom of town.

From here, the road descends into **Órgiva ❷**, the main shopping and service town of the western Alpujarras, and again there is no intrinsic charm making it worth a stop. Best to turn left at the crossroads before you enter the town, and take the main road through the Alpujarras towards Trevélez and Pitres.

From this point the road climbs inexorably, passing by two typical Alpujarran villages, Carataunas and Soportújar. Beyond them you reach a pass from which a narrow road takes off to the left. It may be the last thing you expect to find, but 7 km (4.5 miles) along this side road and up a dirt track is a Buddhist meditation and retreat centre, **O Sel Ling** (www.oseling.com; tel: 958-343 134; daily June–Sept 5–7.30pm, Oct–May 3.30–6pm). In 1986, the fifth son of two of the pioneers of O Sel Ling made international headlines when he was declared to be the new embodiment of the late Lama Yeshe – one of very few Westerners to be acknowledged by Tibetan Buddhism to be a reincarnated spiritual master.

> ### ◎ Tip
> Pony-trekking is exhilarating way of exploring the Alpujarras. Look out for signs at the side of the road or ask at the local tourist office about riding schools in the area. Caballo Blanco Trekking (tel: 627-794 891; www.caballoblanco trekking.com) in Lanjarón offers lessons, two or four-hour treks and holidays in English.

Happy hikers on the Lanjarón river trail.

◎ WALKING COUNTRY

To really experience the Alpujarras fully you need to stop the car and take to the footpaths and mule tracks – usually centuries old and sometimes stone-paved – that wind around the terraces, connecting the villages and hamlets. Such paths are not always signposted or clearly marked on maps, but at least there is usually abundant shade and water available en route while you sit down and think which way to go. Spring and early summer are exceptionally pretty times for being outdoors here because of the abundant wild flowers.

If you want to be safe and do some serious walking there are several long-distance paths through the Alpujarras – the GR7 (or E4, the so-called 'Mediterranean Arc' running from Greece to Tarifa) crosses the southern flank of the Sierra Nevada in seven daily stages, and the GR142 will take you around the whole area in 13 days. The GR140 crosses the Almerian Alpujarras while the GR240 loops around the Sierra Nevada. You can get information and also book a guided hike, as well as several other outdoor activities, at Nevadensis (Plaza de la Libertad 19; www.nevadensis.com) in Pampaneira. Despite the gradients, the Alpujarras are good cycling country too.

Even if you don't want to walk too far, you can find much of interest in and around the villages.

Where

There are a couple of interesting rural life museums in the area. Next to the church in Bubión, there's the Casa Alpujarreña (Sun–Mon & Wed–Thu 11am–2pm, Fri & Sat 11am–2pm, 5–7pm) and in Capileira the Casa Museo de Pedro Antonio de Alarcón (Calle Mentidero; Tue–Sun 11.30am–2.30pm).

Hillside Pampaneira.

POQUEIRA AND TREVÉLEZ

Continuing on from here, the main road suddenly rounds a corner and enters the deep ravine of the **Barranco de Poqueira**, the most scenic and most visited part of the Alpujarras. It contains three villages spaced out on the south-facing hillside. The first (the lowest of the three) is **Pampaneira**, at the entrance to which a sign welcomes you with an invitation to stop and live here. Assuming you don't do that, you can enjoy a view of the flat, gravel-spread roofs and hobbitish chimneys as you pass above the village.

As the road climbs out of the valley, there is a detour to the left leading to the two higher villages of **Bubión** and **Capileira** ❸, the latter perhaps the best-kept and most typical of all those in the Alpujarras. Although the road continues past Capileira and over the top of the Sierra Nevada, descending past the ski resort on the other side (see page 199), it is closed to traffic. You can, however, take a minibus from the **Sierra Nevada**

National Park visitor centre above Capileira to the higher slopes.

The main road through the Alpujarras continues beyond the Bubión and Capileira turn-off and across the Barranco de la Sangre ('Valley of Blood'), named after a battle that was fought here during the Morisco rebellion.

Down the slope are two pretty villages to explore, **Mecina Fondales** and **Ferreirola**. The road passes through the towns of **Pitres**, **Pórtugos** (just after which there is a spring flowing with rusty-coloured, iron-rich water) and **Busquistar**, before swinging into a large, almost uninhabited valley at the head of which, on the lower slopes of Mt Mulhacén, stands **Trevélez** ❹. The highest village in Spain, sited at 1,476 m (4,843 ft), it puts its altitude to good use for the dry-curing of hams known throughout Andalucía. But don't expect to see any pigs here. The pork shoulders are imported from elsewhere to hang in the curing cellars at the bottom of the village, where they acquire their distinctive flavour and the privilege of being called Jamón de

Trevélez. Although the lower part of this village seems like one big tourist shop, the two upper parts *(barrios)* are attractive.

SIERRA DE LA CONTRAVIESA

Shortly after Trevélez, the road passes above what looks like another typical Alpujarran village but is actually a hotel modelled to look like one, complete with a dummy church tower. Round the next corner and the best scenery, the prettiest villages and most of the tourists have been left behind. You can make a round trip back to Órgiva by turning right after Juviles and Bérchules and heading downhill to the undistinguished **Cádiar** ❺, on the valley floor. From here, take the road towards the coast and turn off onto the minor road that follows the ridge of the Sierra de la Contraviesa through high-altitude vineyards before descending to the small town of **Torvizcón** ❻, where fruity red wines (known as 'Costa' wine) are made to be drunk unbottled, still young. Along the valley from here is Órgiva.

YEGEN

If, on the other hand, you are determined to travel through the Alpujarras all the way to Almería – or if you have an interest in literary connections – keep to the high road after Bérchules. Most of the villages in the eastern Alpujarras have lost their charm to the cult of indiscriminate home improvement using modern materials. One such village, however, stands out from the rest because of its reputation – although it would be easy to drive through it without realising that it is known to Hispanophiles everywhere.

It was to **Yegen** ❼ that the young Gerald Brenan made his way, along with his considerable book collection, to get some reading done after two years' active service on the Western Front during World War I. Disappointingly, Brenan's adopted village has all but forgotten him. Few of the locals will tell you with any confidence where he lived, even though the house is not at all tricky to find. Privately owned and not open to visitors, it is just below the square in which stands a reproduction

⊙ Shop

Trevélez is famous for its air-dried ham and you can buy some, along with other local products, at La Ruta de Trevélez (Pisto del Barrio Medio 19; www.jamonescanogonzalez. com). In Pampaneira, artisan Abuela Ili Chcolates (Plaza de la Libertad 1; www.abuelailichocolates. com) makes delicious bars in a wide range of flavours; they also have shops in Capileira, Lanjarón and Granada.

Trevélez is known for its serrano ham.

of the Alhambra's Patio de los Leones. A plaque on the wall recalls the man who put this otherwise nondescript town on the international map.

Brenan's account of the periods he spent in Yegen between 1920 and 1934, *South from Granada* became a classic travel book. While in Yegen he was visited by some of his literary friends from Britain, including Virginia Woolf and Lytton Strachey, who found that too much olive oil caused him indigestion and muleback riding exacerbated his piles.

During his time in Yegen, Brenan fathered an illegitimate child by a village girl, but rather than settle down with her, he married an American poetess. After periods back in Britain, he eventually settled permanently in southern Spain, and died near Málaga.

MORISCOS AND MOORS

After Yegen, the road climbs through the last settlements of Granada province, including **Válor**. This was the birthplace of Don Fernando de Córdoba y Válor, a nobleman descended from the caliphs of Córdoba. On 24 December 1568 he reclaimed his ancestral Muslim religion under the name of Ibn Umayya (or Aben Humeya), and was crowned 'King of Córdoba and Granada' by his fellow Moriscos, who were by now in open revolt against the repression ordered by Felipe II in Madrid. Less than a year later, in October 1569, Ibn Umayya was assassinated, almost certainly by his own followers but the revolt went on without him for almost two more years.

By coincidence rather than because of all this, in mid-September Válor celebrates the most well-known of the Alpujarras' many festivals of Moros y Cristianos (Moors and Christians) – ritualised mock battles and negotiations in which the Muslims at first gain the upper hand but are finally 'persuaded' to convert to Christianity. Although it nominally celebrates the Christians' final ascendancy in Spain's wars of religion, like similar fiestas elsewhere, it is really no more than an excuse for the populace to dress up and have fun.

Bayarcal, on the rocky border between Granada and Almería provinces.

Beyond **Laroles**, which has a fine 16th-century domed bell-tower, is the provincial border between Granada and Almería. **Bayarcal** ❽ is the first village on the other side. It stands above a rocky valley and below the Puerto de la Ragua, a pass across the Sierra Nevada and a popular spot for cross-country skiing.

THE ALMERIAN ALPUJARRAS

From here the road drops down into the tamer, drier landscapes of the Almerian Alpujarras to enter the sprawling **Laujar de Andarax** ❾, which was the last toehold in Spain of Boabdil 'the Unlucky', ex-ruler of Muslim Granada before he was forced into permanent exile in Africa. Although the modern town is something of a mess, serving as a destination for school trips and excursions by city-dwellers, it does have a handsome Mudéjar church in the centre, and a town hall built of three levels of brick arches standing on the main square.

Beyond Laujar is a succession of low-altitude Alpujarran towns of which **Fondón**, the first, is the most interesting. Here the Morisco rebellion was ostensibly brought to an end in 1570 by a peace supposedly signed between Don Juan de Austria, half-brother and emissary of Felipe II, and Ibn Umayya's successor, his cousin Abén Aboo. The latter, however, went on fighting, moving from cave to cave until he was assassinated in March 1571. The Moriscos were finally expelled from Spain in 1609.

Already, there are signs of the arid landscapes so characteristic of Almería, even if they are spruced up here and there by the occasional vineyard or citrus orchard. The remaining towns and villages are of only passing interest, but one of them is worth making a detour to see. Halfway up a great mountain slope, and on the road to nowhere, is **Ohanes** ❿, known for its sweet table grapes, its small centre a pleasant complex of narrow streets and whitewashed houses – in all, a suitable souvenir of the best of the Alpujarras.

Colourful cotton rugs are some of the rustic crafts on sale in the Alpujarras.

Tabernas – the region's uncanny resemblance to the American West made it a popular film location for spaghetti westerns.

ALMERÍA AND ITS PROVINCE

Spain's southeastern province is a region of stark desert landscapes concealing some surprising beauty spots and providing unconventional science lessons.

Almería is Mediterranean Spain in the raw; a land governed by the sun, and home of Europe's only desert. The attractions here may not at first be obvious, but they are surprisingly numerous, however often you have to endure drab, dusty kilometres through what the British travel writer Rose Macaulay called the 'burnt, cactus-sharp, breathless sprawl of hills' between them.

Such a tough terrain takes a little more effort to explore than the other provinces of Andalucía, and the joy of touring here lies not in long scenic drives – although there are some stretches of untamed, lonely grandeur to enjoy – but in stumbling upon unexpected oases of interest. The best of these are an education in the enjoyable sense of the word, and a tour around Almería could almost be seen as a do-it-yourself geography-and-science field trip.

FALL AND RISE

Of all the provinces of Spain, Almería has arguably had the most historical ups and downs. In the Copper Age it had the most advanced civilisation in Western Europe, but its next period of glory wasn't until after the arrival of the Muslims in Spain, when the Caliph of al-Andalus founded the port of Almería as one of his principal lifelines with the east to trade on equal terms with the famous Alexandria. Even when the Caliphate disintegrated,

Beachlife, Parque Natural Cabo de Gata-Nijar.

Almería kept its head held up as one of the *taífas*, or splinter kingdoms, into which Spain was divided.

But the Christian Reconquest of Spain at the end of the 15th century heralded a change in the times. The new rulers turned their gaze westward to the riches available across the Atlantic, leaving Almería, still looking unfashionably east, to languish as a redundant limb of the empire. The province fell into obscurity and rural poverty – despite a brief recovery in the 19th century based on mining and the export of grapes – so

⊘ Main Attractions

Almería
Tabernas
Yesos de Sorbas
Cabo de Gata
Cueva de los Letreros

Map on page 214

much so that even the proudest inhabitants would reluctantly admit that there was some truth in its cruel nickname, '*el culo de España*' ('the backside of Spain'). The Civil War and post-war periods further exacerbated the decline, and countless migrants departed from Almería in search of work in northern Spain or abroad.

But then, in the 1970s, two economic miracles took hold, and in starkly contrasting ways Almería began to turn its biggest resource, sun power, into gold. While poor migrants were heading one way out of hardship, tourists started to head the other way for pleasure, and parts of Almería's coast began to develop as an overspill of the Costa del Sol.

More significantly, Almería's warm winter temperatures were found to be ideal for a peculiar system of agriculture which could meet the needs of growing consumerism in northern Europe (see page 216).

It was largely this agricultural revolution which turned Almería's fortunes around: in a decade or so, the province went from being the poorest in

Andalucía to being one of the richest in Spain. But a heavy price was paid, and is still being paid, in the spoiling of the landscape – although to anyone who remembers the times when there was no work, or whose parents or grandparents were forced to emigrate, this is not an important consideration.

SHRINK-WRAPPED SHORELINE

Production figures suggest that the greenhouse boom has passed its peak and ceded to North Africa, where labour is cheaper than in Europe. But there are few signs of this in the so-called 'Costa del Plástico', more properly called the **Campo de Dalias**, which bulges out into the sea from the foothills of the Sierra de Gádor. When Gerald Brenan first passed by here in the 1920s, he complained of 'a delta of stone and rubble... it might have been the wilderness of Sinai', without a single house or tree. On his return in the 1950s, he found that underground springs had been tapped to irrigate fields of corn and fruit orchards.

It is hard to believe that this intensively

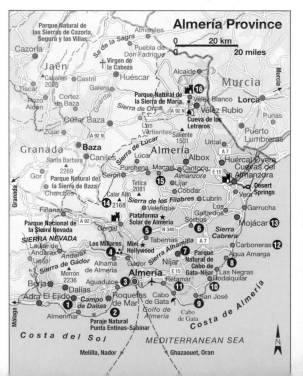

farmed, semi-industrialised strip of coastal plain was ever considered infertile. Presiding over its economic empire is **El Ejido** ❶, a town that mushroomed overnight from being unmarked on most maps to having the second-largest urban population in the province – and a bank for every 1,500 inhabitants.

On the coast, meanwhile, there is just space between the greenhouses for two high-rise resorts, **Aguadulce** and **Roquetas del Mar** ❷, and the smaller **Almerimar**, where you can take a break from the beach and learn about the methods of modern greenhouse farming from one of its leading exponents – Clisol (tel: 620-843 385; www.clisol.com).

THE PORT AND ITS PROTECTOR

The city of **Almería** ❸, over a small range of hills to the east, comes almost as a relief after the shrink-wrapped plains. It has grown since Brenan came upon it as 'a bucket of whitewash thrown down at the foot of a bare, greyish mountain', although its growth is still hemmed in by the steepness of the bone-dry slopes behind it and its sea views are obscured by the commercial and passenger port where a railway pier, the Cable Inglés, is an ugly remnant of the city's maritime history. If Almería gets little rain, it gets lots of sunshine, claiming to have more hours per annum (3,217 on average) than any city in Europe.

Looming proudly over the port and the huddle of flat-roofed houses which form the old part of town is the great fortress of the **Alcazaba** (Tue–Sat 9am–6pm, Sun 9am–3pm; free), built by Abd-al-Rahman III, first Caliph of al-Andalus, to protect the walled trading settlement that stretched from the castle walls to the sea. It's a short, easy climb from the old town to the gateway of the fortress, and once inside you continue climbing through three enclosures, the first being a garden, the last a Christian castle planted as an indestructible victory pennant on the highest point of the Muslim city.

ALMERÍA'S CATHEDRAL

Back down below in the city centre, which gradually smartens towards the broad, shady 19th-century **Paseo de Almería**,

Almería's Alcazaba looms large on the hilltop above the city.

PLASTIC AGRICULTURE

Almería's economy is booming thanks to intensive fruit and vegetable farming – but at what cost? Swathes of plastic covering the countryside and poor working conditions.

Until a few decades ago, the pattern of Andalucía's agriculture was dictated solely by tradition. Farmers grew the crops which their forebears had always grown, largely for their own or local consumption, using centuries-old methods.

Then, in the late 20th century, came improved communications with the rest of Spain and Europe, and the prospect of profits from the consumer economy. Now supermarket buyers in distant countries indirectly decide what is grown in large parts of Andalucía.

Nowhere is the trend more obvious than in Almería, which has led the way in a new style of get-rich-quick farming since the 1970s. Back then, the idea seemed nothing short of revolutionary to farmers used to a subsistence living. If winter temperatures could be kept above a particular, critical level, it was proposed, then delicate summer fruit and vegetable plants could

A greenhouse labourer in Pechina near Almería.

be forced to crop in December and January to feed the whims of northern European shoppers.

Whole swathes of the province consequently disappeared under plastic greenhouses whose purpose was to coddle the tomato or melon plants, giving them those few vital extra degrees of warmth above the outside temperature without the need for artificial heating. Not only was it apparent that Almería could beat the seasons: land cultivated under plastic proved to be at least five times more productive than the same land left exposed to the weather.

The result of the greenhouse miracle was spectacular. What was once Andalucía's poorest province became its wealthiest. The unofficial capital of the industry, El Ejido, rose from obscurity to a financial services centre almost overnight. Fortunes were made not only by enterprising smallholders and venture capitalists but also by a vast ancillary industry that was needed to supply polyethylene sheeting, pipes, wires, fertilisers – and cars and other luxury goods for the nouveaux riches to spend their money on.

Some of the greenhouses are run as hi-tech concerns with plants grown hydroponically and farmers dressed in white coats watching computer screens rather than the weather. Others are more conventional, low-key market gardens, providing employment for a family of four or five people who work hard from autumn to spring and rest during the summer, when midday temperatures under plastic would cause a human to faint.

But while money was being made, the landscape was being smothered. It is estimated that around 3 per cent of the surface of Almería is now farmed in this way. Across the whole of southern Spain, plastic covers land equivalent to an area the size of Ibiza.

Critics of the 'plastic farming' complain of the lack of planning, the strain on the watertable and the excessive use of chemicals – pests and diseases, too, flourish in frost-free winter gardens – and the pollution that their disposal causes. Most workers these days are immigrants from North Africa or Eastern Europe, who earn less than €40 per day, have no rights and have bought their employment contracts – which have to be repaid to their bosses. But as Spanish agriculture elsewhere has slipped into crisis, most people in Almería believe the gains far outweigh the costs.

there are few monuments worth the trouble of seeking out. The Plaza Vieja or Plaza de la Constitución is a pleasant assembly of buildings, however, and the 16th-century **Cathedral** (Mon–Sat 10am–6.30pm, Sun 1.30–6.30pm) is unavoidable because of its bulk – it was built with defence in mind against attacks by pirates and rebel Muslims. Its bulky golden exterior largely belies the graceful vaulting and superb wood carving of the choir inside, although on one outside wall is a delightful reminder of Almería's interest in all things solar: the Sol de Portocarrero, a carved personified sun named after the 16th-century bishop who commissioned it. In the side chapels you will find paintings by Ribera, Murillo and Alonso Cano.

At night the city centre comes alive as bars and cafés take over the narrow streets and alleys to the north east of the cathedral. Almería has a famous tradition of tapas; as in Granada, one comes included in the price of each glass of beer or wine.

ART AND HISTORY

To the south of the cathedral are two 'must visits' for lovers of the arts. The **Museo de la Guitarra Española** (Ronda Beato Diego Viaja; Tue–Sun 10.30am–1.30pm, also Fri & Sat 5–8pm) tells the history of the Spanish guitar via a good interactive exhibition, while the **Centro Andaluz de la Fotografía** (Calle Pinto Diaz Molina, 9; daily 11am–2pm, 5.30–9.30pm; free) showcases permanent and temporary exhibitions of the work of some of the world's leading photographers.

In the east of the city, the **Museo Arqueológico** (Ctra. de Ronda, 91; Tue–Sat 9am–8pm; Sun 9am–3pm; free) has a well-displayed collection of finds from Los Millares (see page 217) as well as Roman and Islamic relics, while in the north, the **Refugios de la Guerra Civil** (Plaza Manuel Pérez Garcia; tel: 950-268 696; guided tours in English and Spanish) are a network of underground tunnels which sheltered the

last Republicans in Andalucía during the Civil War. It's also worth checking out the **Centro de Interpretación Patrimonial** (Plaza de la Constitución; same times as Museo de la Guitarra Española; free), next to the tourist office, which traces the city's history and has roof terrace affording great views.

FROM COPPER TO CELLULOID

Until the building of the Alcazaba, the omphalos of Almería was a short way inland, in the corridor between the Sierra de Gádor and the Sierra Alhamila. The walled Copper Age settlement **Los Millares** ❹ (Wed–Sun 10am–2pm; free), between a gulley and the Río Andarax, near Santa Fe de Mondújar, could be said to be one of the prehistoric cradles of Europe, as it was occupied from around 2700 to 1800 BC by the first community in the western Mediterranean to work metals. Of particular archaeological importance is the necropolis, with a hundred collective tombs of which one has been restored.

The road beyond Los Millares, following the Río Andarax, leads into the fertile

Almería's fortified Cathedral was built in the 16th century, when Barbary pirates were terrorising the coast.

valleys of the Alpujarras (see page 205). Going in the opposite direction, around the back of the Sierra Alhamilla, you enter the desert of Tabernas. With so much of Almería being parched and uncultivated it is often hard to tell where the desert technically begins and ends (there are no sand dunes to spell it out), but the bald hills, badlands and dry ravines were close enough to the archetypal deserts of North America to draw the Italian film-maker Sergio Leone here to shoot his 'spaghetti westerns'.

Tabernas ⑤ probably never had much glamour as the low-budget Hollywood it likes to pretend it used to be, but three of the former western sets have been saved for posterity and are commercially run as tourist attractions in continuance of the western theme. The most developed of them is **Oasys Theme Park** (tel: 950-533 532; www. oasysparquetematico.com; daily Easter-Oct 10am–6pm, 10am–9pm July & Aug), to which a zoo, a cactus garden and swimming pool have been attached.

On the other side of Tabernas is something not of past but present and

future importance. The **Plataforma Solar de Almería** (tel: 950-387 990; www. psa.es; Mon–Fri 8.30am–4.30pm, reserve in advance for guided visits) is a longrunning project into the use of solar power as a source of unlimited energy. The first banks of reflectors concentrating the sun's rays onto a receiving dish at the top of a white tower were set up in the 1970s, but only recently has the technology become sufficiently effective to lead to Europe's first viable solar power station.

KARST LANDSCAPE

The desert scenery continues to the coast, but halfway there it is punctuated by a beauty spot sunk out of sight amid the threadbare hills. This is an area called the **Yesos de Sorbas**, an instance of karst scenery formed not by chalk, as is more common, but by gypsum. There is a visitor centre (tel: 950-364 563; opening times vary) to explain the features of gypsum karst at **Sorbas ⑥**, a town built above a gorge-cum-river meander. To see the karst landscapes you can either start a 38-km (24-mile) hike from the visitor centre or take the winding minor road to the hamlet of **Los Molinos del Río Aguas**, park there and walk up and down the valley of the Río Aguas – ask for a map at the Sorbas centre. Los Molinos is also home to Sunseed, a charity run by volunteers pioneering low-cost technologies for poor communities living in semi-arid environments in developing countries (www.sunseed.org.uk).

Caves are typical of karst scenery, and the **Cuevas de Sorbas** have been opened for visitors (tel: 950-364 704; www.cuevasdesorbas.com; by prior reservation only; appropriate shoes essential) who are willing to forgo concrete paths and electric lighting in favour of cave helmets and miners' lamps.

DESERT CAPE

On the east coast of Almería, the desert meets the sea in the bewitching

The Wild West at Oasys Theme Park.

landscapes of the **Parque Natural Cabo de Gata-Nijar** (www.degata.com). The town of **Níjar 7** is something of an incongruous ally in this nature reserve. It stands inland, above the motorway to Murcia, overlooking a valley of plastic greenhouses, and is only worth visiting for its craft shops and working potteries.

More because of its topography than conscientious planning restrictions, the coast from Agua Amarga to the cape *(cabo)* has not been spoilt by tourism. **Agua Amarga 8** is a small, pleasant resort with a sandy beach squeezed between two headlands. **San José 9**, to the south, is larger and more developed, but still in proportion to its surroundings. Between these two the coast is only sporadically accessible by surface road and there are empty beaches if you are prepared to walk to them.

Halfway along this stretch of coast is **Rodalquilar 10** and its disused gold mines, which had been worked to the point of unprofitability by the end of the 1960s. The nature reserve's head office is here together with an information office and a botanical garden.

The Cabo de Gata proper, one of the Iberian Peninsula's few volcanic landscapes, is best approached from San José. You can drive down a dirt track to two beautiful un-built-up beaches – **Playa de los Genoveses** and **Playa de Monsul**, setting for a scene in *Indiana Jones and the Last Crusade* – but thereafter you can only follow the track by foot as it continues around the cliffs to the cape.

To get to the cape by car, you have to approach it from the Almería side by way of the village of **San Miguel de Cabo de Gata 11**, beyond which a long flat road follows the beach and passes salt pans visited by flamingos before climbing steeply up to the lighthouse to meet the end of the track from San José.

CARTOON CAPERS

Going the other way from Agua Amarga it is a different story. After climbing over the headland encouragingly named Punta de los Muertos (Dead Men's Point) you plunge into a strip of modern mass tourism beginning with **Carboneras 12**, named after the old

Remote Playa del Monsul, Cabo de Gata.

ANCIENT CAVES

Given its undisputed charms, it's no surprise that man has been living in Southern Spain for thousands of years – leaving behind some fascinating evidence.

Twenty thousand years ago, human beings dipped their fingers in ochre and traced the outlines of fish and deer on cave walls in southern Spain. Today, evidence of these early cave-dwellers is still coming to light. Indeed, archaeologists have a difficult time keeping up with the past. Almost daily, a plough or a bulldozer uncovers traces of early human endeavour.

Finds that reach the hands of the archaeologists throw essential light on prehistoric man. One discovery occurred in the cave of the Boquete de Zafarraya, on the border of Málaga and Granada provinces, where investigators' torches revealed the large bones and lower jawbone of a Neanderthal man, possibly dating back 85,000 years. Other traces of Neanderthal occupation have turned up in caves at Piñar (Granada), Vera (Almería) and on the Rock of Gibraltar.

There are abundant indications that, as the last Ice Age receded (around 40,000 years ago, Cro-Magnon

Indalo inscriptions, Cueva de los Letreros.

man took up residence in Andalusian caves. Regarded as our direct ancestor, he was an artist, used tools and was skilled in hunting. Arrow and spear heads and other evidence of his presence have been found in the Almerian caves of Zájara at Vera, and Ambrosio at Vélez Blanco.

Evidence of religious rites is common. Near Vélez Blanco in Almería province, the Cueva de los Letreros shelters prehistoric inscriptions that include the Indalo, depicting a man holding an arc over his head. This symbol was long believed to ward off the 'evil eye' and it has been chosen by Almería's artists to represent the province.

One significant discovery occurred on 12 January 1959, when five boys playing on a hillside near the hamlet of Maro, in Málaga province, came across an immense grotto, now known as the Cueva de Nerja (see page 151). Investigators found evidence that it was inhabited at least 15,000 years ago, and that it had also been used as a burial chamber. Remains of shellfish and the bones of goats and rabbits have been found, as well as wall paintings depicting deer, horses and fishes. Drawings representing a female deity and red-painted pebbles indicated that religious rites had taken place.

Another fascinating cave to visit is La Pileta (see page 124) near Ronda, where limestone galleries scoured out millennia ago by an underground river provided shelter for man as long ago as the Upper Palaeolithic period, when he daubed the image of a stag's head on a wall. La Pileta was discovered in 1905 when José Bullón Lobato, whose family still owns the cave, was searching for *guano* (bird droppings) to fertilise his land. Seeing a large hole, he let himself down 30 metres (100 ft) by rope into a chamber. Penetrating further, he noted human remains and wall-paintings. Later exploration turned up human skeletons, silex (fused quartz), bones, stone tools and ceramics from the Neolithic period.

Some caves had been known about for centuries, but for one reason or another were not fully explored. This was the case with the Aracena cave in Huelva province, which was flooded until the early 20th century. When the water was pumped out, dazzling stalactites and stalagmites formations were revealed, now known as the Gruta de las Maravillas (Grotto of the Marvels).

charcoal-burning industry which thrived here until all the available trees had been cut down. This curious town combines a magnificent broad sandy beach with a cement works, desalination plant and power station whose chimney spoils the view for miles around.

A belt of steep hills to the north of Carboneras has so far inhibited the apartment blocks, hotels, shops and restaurants from becoming a continuous sprawl down the coast of Almería, but they resume once you descend to the coast south of Mojácar. The village of **Mojácar** ⑬, a cluster of white cubic buildings, is geographically and metaphorically raised above the excesses of the coast.

MARBLE MOUNTAINS

Of the several mountain ranges that stride west to east across Almería, the highest and most impressive is the Sierra de los Filabres, which for 60 km (37 miles) reduces the choice of north–south route to two roads. One of these crosses the chain from Tabernas to Macael, over a 1,247-metre (4,091-ft) pass, and serves a group of villages including the bellicose Líjar, which waged its own non-violent hundred years' war with France.

The other route, between Gérgal and Serón, goes even higher (1,970 metres/ 6,464 ft) and leads almost past the door of the Hispano-German observatory at **Calar Alto** ⑭ (2,168 metres/6,937 ft; www.caha.es; tel: 950-632 500; visits by appointment only). Both these roads lead down into the Almanzora valley, where everything seems to be coated in marble dust. Spain's marble industry has its headquarters at **Macael** ⑮, which supplied the stone for the Alhambra and the Mosque at Córdoba.

LOS VÉLEZ

In the far north of the province, across another mountain range, the Sierra de las Estancias, and the Murcia–Granada motorway, is the district of Los Vélez, dominated by a double act of towns,

Vélez Blanco and Vélez Rubio. The epithets 'White' and 'Blond' are thought to have been bestowed on them by the Muslims, who were referring to the colours of the local earth. By far the more interesting is **Vélez Blanco** ⑯, which has a 16th-century Renaissance castle (Wed–Sun 10am–2pm, 5–8pm in summer, 4–6pm in winter), still handsome even if it has been reduced to a shell by the removal of its grand patio to the Metropolitan Museum in New York.

Near the town is the Cueva de los Letreros (tel: 694-467 136; www.hazyenves. es; guided visits by appointment only; June–Aug Wed, Sat & Sun 7pm; Sept– May Wed & Sat 4.30pm, Sun noon). In this rock shelter, decorated by prehistoric artists, was found the drawing which has become the symbol of Almería, a stick figure of an ancestral god holding aloft a rainbow. He was christened the Indalo after St Indaletius, an apocryphal preacher supposedly dispatched by the Apostles to evangelise Almería in the 1st century AD, and is to be seen everywhere in the province, a sign of local pride and bringer of good luck.

Vélez Blanco's Renaissance castle.

SOUTHERN SPAIN
ANDALUCÍA & COSTA DEL SOL

TRAVEL TIPS

TRANSPORT

GETTING THERE

By Air

Southern Spain has frequent air links with the rest of Europe and North Africa and is within 2.5 hours' flying time of London. Most transatlantic flights operate via Madrid.

There are airports in Almería, Granada, Jerez de la Frontera and Seville, with Málaga being the main airport for the region. **Iberia** (UK tel: 0203 684 3774, US 1-800-772-4642; www.iberia.com) and **British Airways** (UK tel: 0344 493 0787; www.britishairways.com) offer the most comprehensive service.

In addition, several **budget airlines** operate flights from the UK to Southern Spain. **easyJet** (UK tel: 0330 365 5000; www.easyjet.com) flies to Málaga from several UK airports and to Granada, Seville and Almería from London Gatwick. Flybe (UK tel: 0371 700 2000; www.flybe.com) flies to Málaga from several UK airports. Jet 2 (UK tel: 0333 300 0404; www.jet2.com) flies to Almería and Málaga from several UK airports. **Monarch** (UK tel: 0333 003 0700; www.monarch.co.uk) flies to Almería from London Gatwick and Manchester and to Málaga from several UK airports. **Ryanair** (UK tel: 0871 246 0000; www.ryanair.com) flies to Almería, Jerez and Seville from London Stansted and to Málaga from several UK and Irish airports. Vueling has direct flights from Birmingham and Cardiff to Málaga (UK tel: 0905 078 1000; www.vueling.com). Large numbers of visitors also arrive by charter flights.

On arrival

Airport porters have set charges, often displayed, for handling baggage. Trolleys are available in bigger airports. For transport from the airport see *Airport Transfer* under Getting Around.

By Sea

Other than cruise liners, the only sea passage between the UK and Spain is from Plymouth to Santander and from Portsmouth to Bilbao and Santander, in northern Spain. The service is operated by **Brittany Ferries** (UK tel: 0330 159 7000; www.brittany-ferries.co.uk).

Acciona Trasmediterranea vessels, carrying passengers and vehicles, ply the routes between Almería, Málaga, Algeciras and Cádiz, ports on the African coast and on the Canary Islands (www.trasmediterranea.es). As do Baleària (www.balearia.com), FRS (www.frs.es) and Naviera Armas (www.navieraarmas.com).

There are frequent services across the Straits of Gibraltar, both by ferries and hydrofoils, from Algeciras to the Spanish enclave of Ceuta and/or Tangier in Morocco (a popular day-trip). A small number of hydrofoils also operate from Tarifa (just west of Algeciras).

By Rail

Rail travel to Spain from other European countries can be organised through **Voyages SNCF** (UK tel: 0844 848 5848; www.voyages-sncf.com), which offers a variety of saver passes for different periods of travel, as well as for senior citizens and under-25s.

AVE and Talgo

Rail services in Spain are operated by Renfe. It offers a range of different trains, the fastest of which is **AVE**. This high-speed rail service links Seville to Madrid in 2.5 hours (some trains also stop in Córdoba) and to Málaga in 2.5 hours. There are also AVE trains from Seville to Barcelona and Valencia and from Málaga to Barcelona.

The special AVE track is also used on other services, such as the Madrid–Málaga **Talgo**, which is also fast and very comfortable. AVE and Talgo services are best booked in advance.

Timetables and reservations are available through the Renfe website (www.renfe.com).

By Road

Road access to Andalucía has improved dramatically in recent years, as part of a massive expansion of the motorway system throughout Spain. It is now possible to drive on four-lane highways virtually all the way from the French border at La Junquera to Seville. For advice on driving in Andalucía see Getting Around.

An alternative for those travelling from Britain is the **ferry service** from Plymouth to Santander or from Portsmouth to Bilbao or Santander on the northern Spanish coast, then south via Madrid on the A4/AP4.

Four-lane *autovías* link Granada, Córdoba, Málaga, Seville, Cádiz and Huelva. The *Autovía de Andalucía*, running from Madrid to Córdoba and Seville, has slashed driving times, and the age-old bottleneck created by the Despeñaperros Pass, which cuts through the Sierra Morena, has been removed.

Entry from Portugal's southern coast – served by Faro airport – is quickest via the bridge across the Guadíana river at Ayamonte.

Driving requirements

When driving your own vehicle in Spain you must have third-party insurance (arrange European cover before leaving home), a valid EU or international driving licence with photocard, and the vehicle log book/registration document as well as proof of insurance. It is also sensible to get European breakdown cover, and you must carry a fluorescent warning triangle to set up on the road in case of accident or breakdown and a reflective jacket in the car's front compartment. Lead-free fuel is widely available. For speed limits, information on fines and seat belt requirements, see Getting Around.

When planning your trip, avoid peak holiday times. Easter and the first weekend in August (when many North African migrant workers travel home for their annual holidays) are particularly busy.

By Bus

Eurolines (UK tel: 08717 818177; www.eurolines.co.uk) operates a thrice-weekly **bus service** from the UK to Andalucía's main cities (Málaga, Seville, Granada, Algeciras, Almería, Marbella and Córdoba), taking around 30 hours plus depending on changes. There are daily services to the region from Barcelona and Madrid.

GETTING AROUND

Airport Transfer

If you take a bus into town from any of these airports, you will need to have small change, as drivers cannot change notes.

Almería

The airport is 9 km (5 miles) from the city. Bus No 22 (€1.05) leaves for the city centre from outside the arrivals terminal almost every hour from 7.10am–10.10pm. A taxi from the airport costs around €15.

Granada

Granada's airport is 17 km (10 miles) from the centre. A bus (€2.90) meets each flight arrival and the journey takes about 45 minutes. Taxis cost €27–34 (more to hotels within the grounds of the Alhambra).

Jerez

The airport is 8 km (4 miles) from the centre. Several buses link the airport with Jerez, Cádiz and other towns in the area. There is also a train line from the airport to Jerez (9mins) and Cádiz (57mins) and also to Seville (1hr). A taxi into Jerez costs €15–19.

Málaga

The airport is 8 km (4 miles) from the city centre. Bus No 75 (€3) leaves from the city bus stop outside the arrivals hall every half hour from 7am–midnight and the journey takes 15 minutes. Alternatively, the train station is a five-minute walk from the terminal: trains run every 20 minutes from 6.44am–12.54am to Málaga (€1.80) to the east and Fuengirola (€2.70) to the west (stops include Torremolinos and Benalmádena). A taxi from the airport to Málaga costs €17–19 depending on the time of day.

Seville

The airport is 8km (5 miles) from the centre, but the journey takes about half an hour. A bus from the Tussam company (€4) – look for the 'Aeropuerto de Sevilla' sign – leaves from outside the arrivals terminal to the centre about every 40 minutes from 4.30am–1.15am. A taxi from the airport to the centre costs €22–30.

Shuttle Service

A company called **Shuttle Direct** can organise a pick-up (shared or individual) from any of the airports: www.shuttledirect.com.

Public Transport

Inter-city buses

Regular bus services run between Andalucía's cities and towns. This is a cheap and generally comfortable way to travel (buses on longer journeys show films and have a toilet) and can be preferable to the train on some routes. For example, the journey between Seville and Granada (or Córdoba and Granada) is quicker and less expensive by bus than by train,

as the latter involves an inconvenient and time-consuming change. Tourist offices can provide bus and train timetables for comparison on key routes.

Bus stations and buying tickets

You can buy bus tickets immediately prior to travel, but arrive early for popular routes (such as Seville–Granada) or better still book the day before.

Bus stations usually have an information booth where staff will direct you to the bus company serving your route. In most cases this will be **Alsina Graells**: (tel: 902-422 242; www.alsa.es), the main company serving the inter-city routes in Southern Spain.

When taking a taxi to the bus station ask for the *Estación de Autobuses*. Note that Seville has two stations, Plaza de Armas (serving regional, national and European cities; www.autobusesplazadearmas.es) and El Prado de San Sebastián (near the Parque de María Luisa), serving the city and its outskirts.

City buses

Buses can be a good and inexpensive way of getting around the main cities. Diagrammatic plans of the various routes are posted at bus stops, making it easy to find your way around. Passengers pay on the bus (small change necessary).

In **Granada**, the Alhambra and Albaicín are served by special minibuses (prices are on a par with the normal bus service). You can pick up both services, which are frequent, from the Plaza Nueva, at the foot of the Alhambra Hill.

Seville and Málaga also have tram systems and one opened in Granada in 2017.

A tight squeeze for this tourist bus in Granada.

Open-top tourist buses

Seville, Granada, Málaga, Cádiz and Benalmádena have open-top hop-on, hop-off buses linking the main tourist sites. These offer a commentary on the sights you pass and can be a good way of seeing them if time is short. See www.city-sightseeing.com for details.

Trains

As a rule, Inter-city buses tend to be a better bet than trains when it comes to getting around Andalucía. The journey between Seville and Granada, for instance, often involves an inconvenient change at Bobadilla. That said, the AVE train is convenient (though relatively expensive) for travelling between Seville and Córdoba: it takes just 30 minutes.

Seat reservations are advisable on the high-speed AVE and the Talgo, where seats are allocated on purchase. It is also best to reserve seats if you are travelling at peak periods (Christmas, Easter, July–August, and at long weekends). You can book online on the Renfe website: www.renfe.com.

Children under 12 years of age travel at reduced cost.

Taxis

Taxis are readily available in the major centres and fares are officially controlled; in urban areas fares are by meter, outside towns fixed rates apply. It's a good idea to ask the driver how much it will cost to go to your destination before you set off.

Car Hire

To hire a car you will need to be over 21 (23 in some cases) and possess a valid EU (with photo; not the UK's old green paper version) or international driving licence. US and Canadian licences are also usually accepted.

Cars in Marbs.

Scores of car hire companies offer their services. International chains such as **Avis**, **Europcar** and **Hertz** have airport offices, and offer a collect and deliver service. Smaller local companies can be cheaper and will arrange to meet you on arrival if you book beforehand.

Avis (www.avis.es)
Almería: tel. 950-297 818
Granada: tel: 958-446 455
Jerez de la Frontera: tel: 956-150 005
Málaga: tel: 902 109 384
Seville: tel: 902-110 264
Europcar (www.europcar.es)
Almería: tel: 902-105 055
Granada: tel: 902-105 030
Jerez de la Frontera: tel: 902-105 055
Málaga: tel: 902-105 055
Seville: tel: 902-105 055
Hertz (www.hertz.es)
Almería: tel: 950-297 797
Granada: tel: 958-204 454
Jerez de la Frontera: tel: 956-903 306
Málaga: tel: 902-998 706
Seville: tel: 902-449 944

Advice for drivers

Driving in Spain is on the right. Traffic from the right has priority except on roundabouts or unless otherwise signalled.

The **speed limit** in built-up areas is 50 kmh (30 mph), on open roads 80 kmh (50 mph) to 100 kmh (62 mph), and 120 kmh (75 mph) on motorways.

Civil Guard motorcycle patrols, out in force on holiday weekends, brook no nonsense and can administer heavy, **on-the-spot fines** for driving offences (they will issue a receipt; keep this and present a copy to your car hire company). Radar traps are common. **Seat belts** are obligatory in the front and back seats of vehicles. Children under the age of 12 must not travel in the front seat.

☉ Distances

Almería to:
Córdoba 332 km (206 miles)
Granada 166 km (103 miles)
Seville 422 km (262 miles)
Málaga: 219 km (136 miles)
Málaga to:
Córdoba 187 km (116 miles)
Granada 129 km (80 miles)
Seville 219 km (136 miles)
Seville to:
Córdoba 166 km (103 miles)
Granada 256 km (159 miles)

Motorways

Southern Spain's motorways (autopista) have been extended and improved in recent years. The following stretches of motorways have tolls (peaje): the AP4 Seville–Cádiz and the AP7 Málaga–Gibraltar.

Tolls can be paid in cash or with a major credit card. It can be worth paying the extra to travel on a toll road, as they tend to be considerably quieter than other routes.

Motorcycles

Mopeds can be hired in main centres. They are ideal for short excursions, but make sure you are fully covered by insurance. Helmets are compulsory.

Cycling

Cycling is an idyllic way to enjoy the beauty of Andalucía's scenery, though intense heat makes it hard going in summer. The region has several vías verdes, cycling and hiking routes running along disused railway lines: there is one from the white town of Olvera to Puerta Serrano west of Algodonales; the Via Verde del Aceite, a 55-km (33-mile) cycle ride southwest from Jaén city; and three vías verdes in Huelva (a 49-km/30-mile route from Ayamonte to Gibraleón; a 36-km/22-mile route between San Juan del Puerto and Velverde del Camino; and a 17-km/10.5-mile route between Puerto de la Laja and Mina La Isabel). For more information visit www.viasverdes-ffe.com.

Bikes can be taken on most regional trains providing they are not in the way of other passengers.

Seville has a bike-sharing scheme called Sevici (www.sevici.es), which is a cheap (or free for the first 30 minutes) and eco-friendly way to explore the city.

A

Accommodation

Choosing a Hotel

Spain may no longer be the bargain it once was, but accommodation still offers good value. Hotels are officially rated from one to five stars. Well-known hotel chains include Barceló (tel: 902-101 001, www.barcelo.com), Iberostar (tel: 971-998 060, www.iberostar.com), Melia (tel: 912-764 747, www.melia.com) and NH Hotels (tel: 916-008 146, www.nh-hotels.com). Five-star establishments are in the luxury category with all the comforts one would expect in a first-class hotel. Bear in mind that the rating has more to do with the amenities offered than the quality of the service.

The ratings do not take into account charm or friendly atmosphere. Small, **family-run** places in the lower categories can be more comfortable than large soulless establishments with gilded fittings and marble halls. Try i-escape (tel: 0117 946 7072 (UK), www.i-escape.com), Little Hotels (tel: 0117 230 3500 (UK), www.littlehotels.co.uk) and Secret Places (tel: 902-430 310, www.secretplaces.com). Hotel prices are posted at the reception desk and behind your room door. IVA (value added tax) is added on top. There is a maximum and minimum price, but often the maximum rate is applied year round. Hotels in Seville are more expensive than the equivalent elsewhere in Andalucía, and a hefty premium is charged during Holy Week and the April Fair. There is no obligation to take breakfast or other meals, except at boarding houses. In any case, breakfast in smaller hotels often consists of little more than coffee, bread and jam, and better value can be obtained in the nearest bar.

If the **blue plaque** at an establishment's door carries the sign "**Hs**", this signifies that it is a *hostal*. These also have star ratings but offer fewer facilities and are worth seeking out if you are on a tight budget. "**HR**" and "**HsR**" signify *hotel residencia* and *hostal residencia*, meaning there is no restaurant or meal service.

At the bottom of the market are the *pensión* (boarding house), the *fonda* (inn) and *the casa de huéspedes* (guesthouse). These are small and spartan, but usually clean. They may not run to carpets and the beds may sag, but most are perfectly adequate considering the low price.

Paradors (www.parador.es) are state-run hotels. The service can be a little glum, but they are often located in unrivalled positions, sometimes in modern buildings but often in old castles, palaces and convents.

Thousands of apartments have been built in tourist areas and if you are planning to stay more than a few days it is worth renting one. Try www.airbnb.com, www.apartmentsspain.com, www.housetrip.com, www.ownersdirect.co.uk and www.holidaylettings.co.uk. In summer they are usually fully booked, but off-season it should be possible to negotiate a reasonable price.

For accommodation in rural areas try www.toprural.com and www.atlasrural.com. You will find motels off the main highways.

Prices: In a *pensión*, expect to pay about €40–50 for a double room. In one- and two-star *hostals*, prices range from €50–60. Hotel prices run roughly from €50 for a one-star establishment to €100–150 for a four-star. A double in a five-star hotel is usually in the €150–250 bracket. Paradors usually charge €100–180 for a double.

Note on addresses: s/n in an address signifies *sin número* (no number); ctra means *carretera* (highway). Hotel names are in bold print.

Admission Charges

Most sights charge less (often half price) for students under 26 and senior citizens over 65, but it is necessary to show valid ID (a passport in the case of over-65s). There are also reductions for many joint sights, for example the Alcázaba and Castillo de Gibralfaro in Málaga.

Some museums, especially the various fine arts museums and archaeological museums, are free for EU citizens; it isn't always necessary to provide proof. Tourist offices in the main cities tend to have special discount cards on sale, such as the 'Granada Card', which offer entry to the main attractions and several journeys on local transport.

It is increasingly necessary to book tickets for Granada's Alhambra in advance, though you must still allow plenty of time to pick them up on arrival, as the queues can be very long. For more information on this, see page 191.

B

Budgeting for your Trip

You can still drink and dine out for less than in the UK. Two people should budget using the rough guidelines below (though variables in meals and hotels can cause prices to rise considerably). Prices in Seville, Granada and on the Costa del Sol will be higher than in rural areas.

Double room per night in a three-star hotel: €40–80
Glass of beer or wine: €2
Simple lunch (per person): €10
Three-course dinner for two: €50
Car hire per week: €150 (book well in advance)
Admission charges: up to €30 per day
Bus ticket (urban): €1.50 (day, week

and monthly tickets available)
Miscellaneous (drinks, tips etc): €20
per day.

C

Children

Andalucía is very child-friendly destination with plenty of activities to entertain all members of the family year round. Children under 12 go free in many museums and there are often family tickets available for attractions. The Playa Senator Hotel Group (www.playasenator.com) is particularly family friendly and has special offers for single parents. Most large resort hotels offer babysitting and have children's clubs. Rosa Mari (tel: 620-753 865; www.rosamaribabysitting.com) offers a babysitting service on the Costa del Sol.

Climate

Andalucía's position at the southern edge of Europe gives it an excellent climate. Summers are hot and winters mild. However, there are considerable variations due to the size of the region, its mountainous character and the fact that it is bordered by both the Atlantic and Mediterranean. Summers can be extremely hot in the interior, with temperatures rising to 45°C (113°F) and higher in the provinces of Seville and Córdoba. Almería has an extremely arid, desert-like climate. Snow covers the Sierra Nevada from November to June, and frost is common in upland areas.

Weather in coastal areas is moderated by the sea and offshore breezes so that neither extremes

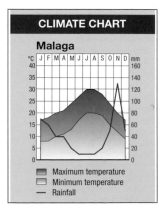

CLIMATE CHART

Malaga

- Maximum temperature
- Minimum temperature
- Rainfall

of heat nor cold are experienced, except for a few weeks at the height of summer. Strawberries ripen in Huelva and Málaga in early February, and tropical fruits can be grown along the Mediterranean without the aid of greenhouses. The levante wind has considerable influence, often blowing hard for several days on the Cádiz coast and creating a persistent cloud over Gibraltar. June to October are mainly dry, but punctuated by occasional downpours. Heavy rain in the winter months is usually interspersed with brilliant sunshine.

The best seasons to tour the region are spring and autumn, when there are no climatic extremes.

What to wear

Light clothing is fine for much of the year on the coast, with perhaps a light sweater or jacket for the occasional cool evening. In winter take a heavy sweater or fleece and raincoat or umbrella.

Although Andalusians like to dress elegantly, they do not demand the same of visitors. Informal dress is acceptable almost everywhere, although avoid anything too garish or too scanty when visiting cathedrals and religious sites, and men should not go bare-chested anywhere but the beach or poolside.

More formal clothing (jacket and tie for men) is usual in casinos and more elegant dining spots.

Crime and Safety

Thefts from tourists and their cars have become common in recent years. Taking common sense precautions (see below) should prevent your holiday being spoiled in this way.

Cities, particularly Málaga and Seville, are black spots. Never leave anything of value in your car. Don't leave cash or valuables unattended while you are swimming. When staying overnight, take all your baggage into the hotel. If possible, park your car in a garage or a guarded car park.

When driving into Seville, do not leave anything of value within sight of other motorists, motorcylists or pedestrians. There have been many cases of thieves smashing the windows of cars stationary at traffic lights, seizing handbags and cameras and then speeding off on a motorcycle.

When walking, hold on tightly to all bags. Avoid badly-lit back streets at night. Carry photocopies of your

passport and other documents and leave the originals in the hotel safe.

If you are confronted by thieves, do not resist, as they often carry knives. If robbed, remember that thieves usually want easily disposable cash and toss away the rest. Check the nearest gutters, rubbish containers and toilets for your belongings.

Police

Municipal police, who generally have limited powers and are mostly seen controlling traffic, wear blue uniforms and peaked caps. **National police** wear dark blue uniforms and caps. Both will assist you, but it is the national police who will take details of an offence and conduct any investigation. In smaller towns and rural areas, **Civil Guards** – in olive-green uniforms (but without the distinctive tricorn hat, which is only used for ceremonial purposes) – perform these duties. Few policemen speak anything but Spanish, but many national police stations (comisarías) now have report forms in several European languages to aid tourists.

Customs Regulations

Spanish customs officials are unlikely to hassle travellers unless they have reason to believe they are wrongdoers. They are particularly on the lookout for drug smugglers at such ports as Algeciras and Málaga.

EU nationals are not restricted in what they can import, but anybody moving products in commercial quantities may require appropriate licences.

Non-EU nationals can import the following items duty-free: 200 cigarettes or 50 cigars or 250 grammes of tobacco products, 1 litre of alcohol over 22 percent proof or 2 litres up to 22 percent, 4 litres of still wine, 16 litres of beer, other goods up to the value of €430 for air and sea travellers (€300 for other travellers).

D

Disabled Travellers

Spain is gradually making advances in improving facilities for disabled visitors. Many public buildings are now accessible and many hotels have rooms for wheelchair users.

Beaches: the official guide on Spanish beaches, with indication of suitability

Cerveza on tap in Granada.

for the disabled is available on line at: www.mapama.gob.es (click on 'Costas y Medio Marino' then 'servicios')
Train: RENFE usually provides wheelchairs at main city stations.
Taxi: ask for a 'eurotaxi' as these have usually been adapted for wheelchairs.
Parking: the UK's orange badge scheme is not recognised in Spain. However, holders of the EU document (blue, depicting a photograph of the authorised person) will be entitled to the same parking provisions as local residents.

Useful websites

www.accessibletravel.co.uk – holidays for disabled people.
www.disabledtravelers.com – US website that lists travel agents and tour operators specialising in disabled travel.
www.miusa.org – US site with info for disabled travellers.

Wheelchair hire

The following organisations can assist with wheelchair (and mobility scooter) hire.
Mobility Abroad
Tel UK: 0208 144 8674
www.mobilityabroad-costadelsol.com
Mobility Spain
Tel: 633 127 901
www.mobility-spain.com

Specialist organisations

ECOM (Federation of Spanish Private Organisations for the Disabled)
Gran Vía de las Cortes
Catalanas, 562 principal 2a Barcelona.
Tel: 934-515 550

O.N.C.E. (Spanish Association for the Blind)
Tel: 915-773 756
www.once.es

Eating Out

Andalucía offers a good range of eating experiences, from tapas in bars to Michelin-starred tasting menus and from game in mountain inns to fresh fish in seaside restaurants (*chiringuitos*). Lunch is generally eaten around 2pm and dinner after 9pm. In and around markets is a good place to look for cheap, traditional restaurants where the locals go. You'll find plenty of fast food and sandwich shops in the major cities and Costa del Sol resorts. Children are generally very welcome in restaurants. Vegetarians and vegans will find eating out a struggle in all but the major cities – check that the vegetable dishes don't contain any meat.

Electricity

The current in Spain is 225AC or 220V – the same as the UK and most of Europe but twice the mains voltage in the US. Americans bringing any 110V appliances must have a converter/transformer.

Spanish sockets take plugs with two large round pins, so bring a plug adaptor with any British appliances or buy one at the airport.

Embassies and Consulates

Spanish Embassy website: www.maec.es
Spanish Embassy in Australia
15 Arkana Street, Yarralumla ACT 2600, POB 9076 ACT Deakin
Tel: 6273 35 55
Spanish Embassy in Canada
74 Stanley Avenue, Ottawa (Ontario), K1M 1P4
Tel: 613-747 2252/7293
Spanish Embassy in Great Britain
39 Chesham Place, London, SW1X 8SB
Tel: 0207 235 5555
Spanish Embassy in Ireland
17A Merlyn Park, Ballsbridge, Dublin 4
Tel: 269 1640/2597, 283 8827/9900
Spanish Embassy in New Zealand
Level 11, 50 Manners Street, Wellington 6142
Tel: 4 802 5665
Spanish Embassy in South Africa
337 Brooklyn Road, Menlo Park, Pretoria 0102, POB 35353, Pretoria 0001
Tel: 012 460 01 23
Spanish Embassy in the US
2375 Pennsylvania Avenue NW, Washington DC
Tel: 202-452 01 00

Embassies in Spain

Australia
Torre Espacio, Paseo de la Castellana 259D – Level 24, 28046 Madrid
Tel: 913-536 600
www.spain.embassy.gov.au
Great Britain
Torre Espacio, Paseo de la Castellana 259D, 28046 Madrid
Tel: 917-146 300
www.gov.uk/government/world/spain
New Zealand
Pinar 7, 3rd Floor, Madrid
Tel: 915-230 226
www.nzembassy.com/spain
South Africa
Calle Claudio Coello 91, 6th Floor, 28006 Madrid
Tel: 914-363 780
www.dirco.gov.za/madrid/en
United States
Calle de Serano 75, 28006 Madrid
Tel: 915-872 200
https://es.usembassy.gov

Consulates in Andalucía

Canada
Plaza de la Malagueta, 2, Málaga
Tel: 952-223 346
www.canadainternational.gc.ca
Great Britain
Calle Mauricio Moro Pareto, 2, Edificio Eurocom, Málaga
Tel: 952-352 300
http://ukinspain.fco.gov.uk

Ireland

Fuengirola, Galerias Santa Monica,
Avenida Los Boliches, 15
Tel: 952 475 108

Seville

Avenida de Jerez, 21, Edificio Bayort
Tel: 954 690 689
www.irlanda.es

Emergencies

The nationwide emergency telephone number is 112. If you need an ambulance, call 061 (see emergency numbers below). If you get stopped for a traffic violation, fines are generally payable on the spot. If you are subject to theft, report it to the local police immediately.

In the event of you being arrested, Article 17 of the Spanish constitution states that you must be informed of your rights and the grounds of your arrest in a manner that is understandable to you. You will also be entitled to the assistance of a lawyer during police interrogation and any judicial investigation. Within 72 hours of arrest, you must be brought before a judge or released.

National Police: 091
Local Police: 092
Emergencies (health and security): 112
Ambulance: 061

Etiquette

It can come as a surprise to British travellers that Spanish people tend not to say 'please' and 'thank you' and their animated way of speaking can sometimes seem as if they are arguing with each other. However, it always makes a good impression for visitors to be polite. Even speaking a little Spanish will endear you to the locals and remember to use the formal 'usted' and not familiar 'tu' form when addressing someone.

Respectable dress, even it is T-shirts and long shorts, is recommended anywhere other than the beach, especially when going into religious buildings. Smart hotels and restaurants will require suitable attire.

Festivals

The following is a list of some of the more important or interesting festivals and events in the region. As dates vary each year, it is advisable to check with local tourist offices for exact details of each year's event.

Throughout Andalucía

January

New Year, greeted at midnight by eating 12 grapes, one for each chime of the clock. Fiesta de los Reyes (Three Kings parades), on the eve of the Epiphany (5 January), when men dressed as kings ride around towns, scattering sweets to children; 6 January is a holiday throughout Spain.

February

Carnival celebrations in most towns.

March/April

Semana Santa processions, from Palm Sunday to Easter Sunday.

June

Noche de San Juan, midsummer bonfires lit on the beaches at midnight (23 June).

July

Virgen del Carmen, the patroness of fishermen, honoured with seaborne processions in fishing communities along the coast, particularly Estepona (16 July).

November

Día de los Difuntos (Day of the Dead), Andalusians honour their ancestors (1 November).

December

Spaniards celebrate Nochebuena (the Good Night), on 24 December, Christmas Eve, with a family meal followed by the Misa del Gallo ("Mass of the Cockerel" – Midnight Mass); the Día de los Inocentes (Day of the Innocents) on 28 December is the Spanish equivalent of April Fools' Day.

Cádiz

February

The city hosts one of Spain's best-known carnivals.
Festival de Jerez. Prestigious annual flamenco festival.

March/April

Coinciding with Holy Week, running of bulls in Vejer de la Frontera and Arcos de la Frontera.

May

World Motorcycling Championship at Jerez race track.
Jerez Horse Fair. Display of horses and horsemanship.

August

Sanlucar de Barrameda. Horse races along the beach.
Sotogrande. International Polo Competition, with matches throughout the month.

September/October

Jerez. Fiesta de la Vendimia (Harvest Festival), including sherry harvest festival.

Córdoba

May

Córdoba. Festival of the Patios, floral competition with private courtyards opened to public (first week of month); Annual Fair (last week of month).

June

Romería de los Gitanos (Pilgrimage of the Gypsies) in Cabra.

July

International Guitar Festival at the Gran Teatro in Córdoba.

Granada

January

Día de la Toma (Day of the Conquest) commemorating the city's capture from the Moors (2 January).

May

Día de la Cruz festival in Granada.

May/June

Corpus Christi marks Granada's annual fair.

June/July

International Festival of Music and Dance. One of Spain's leading festivals offers a varied programme of music and dance by national and international companies, with concerts in the Auditorio Manuel de Falla and the Palacio Carlos V in the Alhambra, and dance in the Generalife.

August

Pilgrimage sets out from village of Trevélez and heads for the peak of La Veleta in the Sierra Nevada (5 August).

November

Granada International Jazz Festival (with emphasis on modern jazz).

Huelva

May

Romería del Rocío, Spain's biggest pilgrimage, to the shrine of the Virgin in El Rocio (Doñana), finishing the weekend before Pentecost Monday. A million pilgrims travel on horseback and in decorated wagons.

Málaga

July

International Music and Dance Festival in the Caves of Nerja.

August

Málaga fair, the second biggest in Andalucía. The village of Cómpeta celebrates in Noche del Vino (Night of Wine), on 15 August.

September

Goyesca Fair in Ronda, with carriage displays and bullfight.

October
Fuengirola. Fiesta del Rosario, the Costa del Sol's biggest annual fair.

December
Festival of Verdiales, celebrating mountain music (28 December).

Seville
April
Seville. Feria (Spring Fair), the biggest Andalusian festival and most magnificent. The city also hosts an antiques fair in April, with exhibitors from all over Spain.

May/June
Corpus Christi celebrations in the city, including performance of the medieval dance, Los Seises, in the cathedral.

July
Italica. International Festival of Theatre and Dance. Contemporary dance and classical ballet performances by prestigious international companies, held in the Roman amphitheatre.

September
Biennial Flamenco Festival (next one in 2018). Lasts throughout the month and represents the very best in flamenco dancing.

Health and Medical Care

Common sense is the best preventative medicine. Don't over-expose yourself to the sun, which can be surprisingly fierce, don't drink too many iced drinks, and beware of excessive alcohol consumption. The last can produce devastating effects on your stomach, especially when eating food fried in olive oil with liberal doses of garlic and peppers. Take it easy until your body has become accustomed to changes in climate and diet. You are particularly warned to partake sparingly of cheap wine, as this is almost certain to give you a headache or worse, and is foolish in a country where superb wines can be enjoyed for just a little more.

Bottled water is the best bet for visitors. Tap water is safe to drink, but it tends to taste strongly of chlorine. Local stomachs are used to it, but those of newcomers may revolt to begin with.

Over-the-counter remedies are available at any *farmacia* (chemist), recognisable by the large green crosses outside.

Buying medicines
Farmácias (chemists) are well stocked and over-the-counter remedies are available at any *farmacia* recognisable by the large green cross outside. They all display lists of the duty chemists at night and at weekends. Farmacia Amador de los Ríos (Calle Amador de los Ríos 31; tel: 954 421 153) in Seville is open 24 hours as is Farmacia Caffarena (Alameda Principal 2; tel: 952-212 858) in Málaga. Be sure to bring any regular medicines that you need plus a letter from your doctor explaining any medical conditions, including generic names of medicines if possible.

If you contract a stomach problem ask for *un antidiarreico*, the general term for antidiarrheal medicine. *Fortasec* is a well-known local brand.

Medical services
Private clinics offering a range of medical services – some open 24 hours a day – are located in most towns of any size. Emergency services are also provided by *ambulatorios*, national health clinics run by Spain's Seguridad Social (social security system).

Free medical attention is available if you are from EU countries, which have reciprocal arrangements with Spain. However, you must obtain a European Health Insurance Card (EHIC) in your home country prior to your departure. These are valid for five years and can be applied for online by logging onto www.ehic.org.uk. As Seguridad Social facilities are often over-stretched, visitors are also advised to take out private health insurance. Private health insurance is essential for non-EU visitors.

Dental treatment
Your EHIC does not cover private medical consultations or treatment, which includes virtually all dentists. If you need dental care urgently, check at the local *farmacia* or tourist office, or consult staff in your hotel, for advice on finding an English-speaking dentist. On the Costa del Sol, there are several, including the **English Dental Practice**, Edificio Don Marcelo, Avda Jesús Santos Rein 10, Fuengirola, tel: 952-466 056.

I

Insurance

The most comprehensive travel-insurance should cover trip cancellation, delay, medical expenses – naturally excluding any pre-existing medical condition – and loss of property (though you may want to check that loss of property isn't already

Semana Santa procession in Málaga.

covered by your household insurance). If EU visitors don't get medical insurance, which is strongly recommended, you must at least get the EHIC, which entitles EU members to reciprocal medical care (see Medical Services). Drivers must ensure they have at least third-party insurance.

Internet

Internet cafés do still exist but are fewer on the ground than they used to be thanks to the rise of smartphones and Wi-Fi; you'll find the latter in most tourist offices, public buildings, hotels, restaurants and cafés.

Among the online information about Andalucía and Spain, the following private sites are useful:
www.andalucia.com
http://almeria.angloinfo.com, http://costa delaluz.angloinfo.com, http://costadel sol.angloinfo.com – very useful websites containing local listings and classifieds.
www.azahar-sevilla.com – Seville tapas guide
www.cordoba24.info
www.exploreseville.com
www.infocordoba.com
www.granadainfo.com
www.malaga.com
www.piccavey.com – Granada guide
www.visitcostadelsol.com

Left Luggage

Most of the main bus and train stations have coin-operated lockers or left-luggage offices.

LGBTQ Travellers

Attitudes towards same sex relationships have relaxed considerably in recent years. In fact, gay marriage became legal in Spain in 2005. In 2017, Madrid hosted World Pride. All the major cities and resorts have lively gay scenes, especially Torremolinos, Málaga and Seville. The following websites include listings of gay bars, clubs, beaches and hotels and general information: www. travelgayeurope.com and www.patroc.com.

Lost Property

If you lose anything, report it immediately to the municipal police, who

The summer fair of Algeciras (Feria Real).

will issue a certificate for any insurance claim. Lost property offices *(Oficina de Objetos Perdidos)* are usually located in town halls *(ayuntamiento)* and railway stations *(estación de tren)*.

Lost passports should be reported to your nearest consulate (see page 229). If you lose or have credit cards or travellers' cheques stolen go to the nearest bank, or phone the relevant emergency number.

Maps

A useful touring map is found in the back of this book. Other good maps include **Michelin map 446**, on a scale of 1:400.000 (1 centimetre to 4 kilometres), which is the clearest road map of Andalucía. **Guía Repsol** includes maps, as well as details of sights, hotels and restaurants.

Hikers and horse-trekkers will find most useful the military maps, scale 1:50.000, produced by Spain's **Servicio Geográfico del Ejército**. Handy maps of the Sierra Nevada, 1:40.000 and the Alpujarras 1:25.000 are published by Cartografica del Sur (Calle Pedro Antonio de Alarcón, 21, Granada, tel: 958-204 901).

Free city maps are available at tourist offices, where you will also

usually find a selection of maps for sale, and free local transport maps are available from bus and train stations.

Media

Newspapers

National papers published in Madrid are available every morning. Dailies such as *El País*, *El Mundo* and *ABC* have special Andalusian editions printed in Seville. At least one local daily is published in each of Andalucía's provincial capitals. They can be very useful for finding out what events are scheduled locally and usually include emergency telephone numbers and transport information.

European newspapers are readily available on the Costa del Sol and in larger cities. Some UK dailies print editions in Spain and are distributed in the morning. Otherwise, foreign newspapers are available at midday or early afternoon.

A number of English-language publications serve the large number of expatriates living along the Mediterranean coast.

Several free newspapers come out weekly, with details of events in the expatriate community. They include *Sur in English* (www.surinenglish.com). The *Costa del Sol News* (www.costa-news.com) is a weekly newspaper sold on the newsstands.

Absolute Marbella and *Essential Marbella* (www.essentialmagazine.com) are glossy monthlies devoted to the lifestyle of the rich and famous.

Television and radio

Andalucía is served by the two national state-run television channels, as well as two independent national stations, two Andalusian channels, several private networks and local television in many towns and villages. Satellites allow the beaming in of foreign programmes in English, Italian and other languages.

Most communities have their own FM radio stations in Spanish. Several radio stations on the Costa del Sol broadcast in English. These include ACE FM (106.8 FM), Central FM (98.6 FM/103.8 FM), Talk Radio Europe (91.9/104.8 FM) and Spectrum FM (105.5 FM).

Money

The currency of Spain is the euro, which comes in coins valued 1 euro, 2 euros, plus 50, 20, 10, 5, 2 and 1 cents. Bills are worth 5, 10, 20, 50, 100, 200 and 500 euros.

Although most major credit cards are known, the most widely used and accepted are Mastercard and Visa. Smaller establishments may be unwilling to take your Diner's or Amex card.

ATMs

ATMs (Automated Teller Machines) are often the most convenient way of obtaining money. Most banks have a hole-in-the-wall ATM with instructions in several languages. For both credit and debit cards you will need a PIN number in order to withdraw money. Most banks charge for using your card abroad.

Travellers' cheques

Travellers' cheques remain one of the safest ways of transporting your cash. Travel agencies and hotels will change currency as well as banks but it is worth checking rates – and commissions charged. You may often find that the savings banks *(cajas de ahorros)* offer a better deal than the big commercial banks. To get the most favourable rate, avoid changing small amounts at a time.

Banks have varied hours. Normal opening times are: Mon–Fri

8.30am–2pm and Sat 9am–1pm. During summer trading (June–September) banks do not open on Saturday. Some banks now stay open until 4pm on one or more days a week.

Opening Hours

Shops usually open 9.30am or 10am–1.30pm, opening again from 5–7.30pm or 8pm. **Department stores** and supermarkets open 10am–9pm or 10pm. Shops close on Sunday, although newsagents are open on Sunday mornings. In tourist areas, some shops open on Sunday in summer.

Government offices are usually open to the public Mon–Fri 9am–1pm.

Banks open Mon–Fri 8.30am–2pm and 9am–1pm Sat.

Museums and other tourist sights are often closed on Monday. Some also close for up to three hours at lunchtime.

Restaurants rarely open before 8pm for dinner, and most stop serving at 11.30pm. Lunch is normally around 1.30pm.

Postal Services

Post Offices Usual opening times for the *Correos* (post office) are from 8.30am–8.30pm, Mon–Fri and 9am–1pm, Sat. More often than not, there are long queues at the stamp counters, but stamps can also be bought in *estancos* (they advertise themselves with a 'Tabacos' sign in yellow and brown). Within Europe all letters go by air. *Aerogramas* (special airmail letters) are also available at post offices. See www.correos.es for general information.

You can receive mail at post offices if it is addressed to *Lista de Correos* (equivalent to Poste Restante), followed by the place name. Remember that Spaniards usually have two surnames, that of their father first with their mother's tagged on after it. This can lead to confusion with foreign names. Thus, if a letter is addressed, for example, to James Robertson Justice, it will

probably be filed under "R" rather than "J".

Postboxes are bright yellow but you may also come across red postboxes; these are for express mail only.

Public Holidays

There are a lot of public holidays. Apart from national holidays, every region and every community has its own celebrations, which usually fall on the most inconvenient day for a visitor. Remember also that if a holiday falls, for example, on a Thursday, Spaniards like to make a *puente* (bridge), meaning that they also take Friday off to create a long weekend. Many factories and offices, some restaurants and shops close during August when most of Spain, including the government, is on holiday. It is a month to be avoided if you intend to do much more than lie on a beach.

National holidays

January 1 New Year's Day (Año Nuevo)

January 6 Twelfth Night *(Día de los Reyes)*

February 28 Andalucía Day *(Día de Andalucía)*

Holy Thursday *(Jueves Santo)*, moveable feast, March or April.

Good Friday *(Viernes Santo)*, moveable feast, March or April.

May 1 Labour Day *(Fiesta del Trabajo)*

August 15 Assumption of the Virgin *(Fiesta de la Asunción)*

October 12 Columbus Day *(Día de la Hispanidad)*

November 1 All Saints' Day *(Todos los Santos)*

December 6 Constitution Day *(Día de la Constitución)*

December 8 Immaculate Conception *(Inmaculada Concepción)*

December 25 Christmas Day *(Navidad)*

Local holidays

Each town has two extra fiesta days when all businesses are closed. It is also likely you will encounter half-day opening during Semana Santa (Easter week), particularly in Seville and Málaga, and during the major fiestas, especially those of Córdoba, Jerez, Seville and Málaga.

Almería 25 August, 26 December.

Cádiz Monday after Carnival week, 7 October.

Córdoba 8 September, 24 October

Estepona 15 May, 16 July

Fuengirola 16 July, 7 October

Granada 2 January, 1 February, Corpus Christi
Huelva 3 August, 8 September
Jaén 11 June, 18 October.
Málaga 19 August, 8 September
Marbella 11 June, 19 October.
Mijas 8 September, 15 October.
Nerja 15 May, 24 June
Torremolinos 16 July, 29 September
Seville 30 May, Corpus Christi

Religious Services

Spain is predominantly a Catholic country. In tourist areas, especially the Costa del Sol, there are many churches and synagogues serving resident and visiting non-Catholics. There are also several mosques.

Student Travellers

Under-26s can obtain reduced rates on rail travel with the InterRail pass, which is valid for travel throughout Europe. The system divides Europe into five zones, Spain and Portugal representing one of those zones. For students holding an **International Student Identity Card** (www.isic.org) discounts are available on bus and rail travel and selected Iberia flights, accommodation, as well as entrance

Málaga Cathedral service.

to museums, monuments and sports and cultural events.

Information can be obtained from **Inturjoven**, the Spanish youth hostel network tel: 955-181 181, www.inturjoven.com.

Telecommunications

Telephone boxes *(cabinas)* take coins or phone cards, available from *estancos* and many newsstands. You cannot make reverse charge calls, or receive calls, from a *cabina*.

All Spanish phone numbers have nine digits.

In tourist areas in season you will find glass Portacabin structures housing small exchanges *(locutorios)*. These are handy for long-distance calls as instead of fumbling with change you pay the operator afterwards and have the added advantage of being able to pay by credit card (they are no more expensive than phone boxes). Bars also have telephones but make a surcharge. Avoid calling from hotels if at all possible, as they often treble the charge.

Probably the cheapest way to make calls is via www.skype.com on a computer or smartphone.

Moblile phones

If you are going to make lots of calls within Spain it is worth buying a Spanish SIM card (or a new phone), which you can do from most mobile phone shops. Well-known networks are Movistar (www.movistar.es), Orange (www.orange.es) and Vodafone (www.vodafone.es). If you are using your usual phone and SIM, check with your network provider before you go that you have international roaming and find out if you can buy bundles of minutes to use abroad. In any case, it's cheaper to receive calls when abroad than to make them. Spanish mobile phones operate on GSM 900/1800 or 3G 2100.

International calls

Dial 00, then the international code for the country you require:
UK 00 44 + number (minus first zero)
Australia 00 61 + city code + local number
Canada 00 + 1 + city code + local number
Ireland 00 353 + number
New Zealand 00 64 + number

South Africa 00 27 + number
United States 00 1 + city code + local number

Time Zone

Spain is on European Standard Time, which is one hour ahead of Greenwich Mean Time (UK) and six hours ahead of Eastern Standard Time (New York). The clocks go back one hour on the last Sunday in October and forward on the last Sunday of March.

Toilets

Public toilets can be found in cities and resorts and are clearly sign-posted and well-maintained. It may be more convenient, however, to use the *servicios* at a bar, which is perfectly acceptable, even if you do not buy a drink. It's worth carrying some toilet paper with you, as many places don't provide it.

Tourist Information Offices

The official tourism site of the Junta de Andalucía is: www.andalucia.org.
For individual tourist offices see below.

Algeciras
Oficina de Turismo, Paseo del Río de la Miel, tel: 956-571 254

Almería
Regional Tourist Office, Parque Nicolás Salmerón, s/n, tel: 950-175 220, www.turismodealmeria.org
City Tourist Offices: Plaza de la Constitución, tel: 950-210 538, www.turismoalmeria.com

Antequera
Oficina de Turismo, Plaza de San Sebastián, 7, tel: 952-702 505, http://turismo.antequera.es

Benalmádena-Costa
Oficina de Turismo, Avenida Antonio Machado, 10, tel: 952-442 494; www.disfrutabenalmadena.com

Cádiz
Regional Tourist Office, Plaza de Madrid, Estadio Ramón de Carranza, tel: 956-807 061, www.cadizturismo.com
City Tourist Offices: Paseo de Canalejas, tel: 956-241 001; Avenida José León de Carranza, tel: 956-285 601; Playa de la Caleta; Módulo Central

de la Playa Victoria (May–Sept); www.turismo.cadiz.es

Córdoba

Regional Tourist Office, Calle Rey Heredia 22, tel: 957-201 774.
City Tourist Offices: in Plaza del Triunfo, Plaza de las Tendillas and at the train station, tel: 902-201 774 www.turismodecordoba.org

Estepona

Oficina de Turismo, Plaza de las Flores, tel: 952-802 002, www.estepona.es/turismo

Fuengirola

Oficina de Turismo, Paseo Jesús Santos Rein, 6 (near the train station), tel: 952-467 457; www.visitafuengirola.com

Granada

Regional Tourist Office, Cárcel Baja 3, tel: 958-247 128; www.turgranada.es.
City Tourist Office, Plaza del Carmen 5, tel: 958-248 280; www.granadatur.com

Huelva

Regional Tourist Office, Calle Jesús Nazareno 21, tel: 959-650 200, www.turismohuelva.org
Oficina de Turismo, Plaza de las Monjas, tel: 959-251 218.

Jaén

Oficina de Turismo, Calle Maestra 8, tel: 953-190 455, www.turjaen.org

Jerez de la Frontera

Oficinas de Turismo: Plaza del Arenal, Edificio Los Arcos, tel: 956-338 874 and at the airport; www.turismojerez.com.

Málaga

Oficinas de Turismo: Calle Granada 70 and Plaza de la Marina 11. There are also information points on Avenida Cervantes, at the Alcazaba, the train station and the airport; tel: 951-929 250, www.malagaturismo.com

Marbella

Oficinas de Turismo: Glorieta de la Fontanilla s/n, tel: 952-768 760; Plaza de los Naranjos 1, tel: 952-768 707; Plaza Antonio Banderas, Puerto Banús, tel: 952-768 749; www.turismo.marbella.es

Nerja

Oficina de Turismo, Calle del Carmen 1 (in the town hall), tel: 952-548 400; www.nerja.es

Ronda

Regional Tourist Office, Paseo de Blas Infante, tel: 952-169 311
City Tourist Office, Paseo de Blas Infante, tel: 952-187 119; www.turismoderonda.es

Seville

Regional Tourist Office, Plaza del Triunfo 1, tel: 954-210 005; www.turismosevilla.org.
City Tourist Offices: Paseo de las Delicas 9, Costurero de la Reina, tel: 954-234 465; also at the airport and at Santa Justa train station; www.visitasevilla.es

Torremolinos

Oficina de Turismo, Plaza de Andalucía, tel: 951-954 379, www.turismotorremolinos.es

Tour Operators and Travel Agents

Classic Collection, tel: 0800 047 1066, www.classic-collection.co.uk. Tailor-made hotel holidays to Andalucía.
Cresta, tel: 0844 800 7020, www.crestaholidays.co.uk. Short breaks to Seville.
CV Villas, tel: 0203 411 0609, www.cvvillas.com. Villa holidays in Andalucía.
First Choice, tel: 0844 871 1604, www.firstchoice.co.uk. All-inclusive holidays for families and couples on the Costa del Sol, Costa de la Luz and Costa de Almería.
Global Coach Tours, tel: UK 0800 612 8288, US 1-800-715-2860, www.globalcoachtours.com. Escorted coach tours of Andalucía.
Global Gate Vacations, tel: US 1-800-814-4283, www.globalgatevacations.com. Escorted tours of Andalucía.
Great Rail Journeys, tel: 01904 521 936, www.greatrail.com. Escorted rail tours to Andalucía.
James Villa Holidays, tel: 0800 074 0122, www.jamesvillas.co.uk. Villa holidays.
Kirker Holidays, tel: 0207 593 1899, www.kirkerholidays.com. Tailor-made luxury short breaks.
Leger, tel: 0844 846 8080, www.leger.co.uk. Escorted coach tours of Andalucía.
Responsible Travel, tel: 01273 823700, www.responsibletravel.com. Wide range of activity holidays in Andalucía.
Thomson, tel: 0871 231 4691, www.thomson.co.uk. A wide range of holidays for all tastes and budgets.
Totally Spain, tel: UK 0871 666 0214, US 1-561-828-0238, www.totallyspain.com. Spain-based company offering a wide variety of holidays and tours.

Travelsphere, tel: 01858 898730, www.travelsphere.co.uk. Hotel stays and escorted tours in Andalucía.

Visas and Passports

As requirements are subject to change, you should always check before leaving your home country. Visitors from **European Union** countries can enter and leave freely. However, they are still required to carry a passport or national identity card. If EU citizens stay six months or more in any calendar year, they are required to obtain a residence permit.

North Americans and Canadians can stay for three months without a visa, after which time they can request an extension of stay (see below).

Visitors from **Australia** and **New Zealand** need a visa if staying more than three months. Note that in all cases, the three-month period counts from the time you first arrive in any of the Schengen States; i.e. if you spent six weeks in France first, that time is deducted from your three months in Spain.

Many other nationalities need a visa to visit Spain. Stays cannot be extended beyond the length of the visas, which must be obtained before arriving in Spain.

Weights and Measures

Spain has followed the **metric system** since 1971. To convert kilometres into miles divide by 1.6093; to convert metres into feet divide by 0.3048; to convert kilograms into pounds divide by 0.4536; to convert hectares into acres divide by 0.4047. To convert from imperial to metric multiply by the factor shown.

Some traditional Spanish weights and measures are still in use. These include: *fanega* (6,460 sq. metres or 1.59 acres); *arroba* (11.5 kg/25 lb); *quintal* (4 *arrobas* or 46 kg/101 lb). Farmers sell wine and olive oil by the *arroba*, referring to a wine container with a capacity of 15 to 16 litres.

LANGUAGE

Spanish – like French, Italian, Portuguese – is a Romance language, derived from the Latin spoken by the Romans who conquered the Iberian peninsula more than 2,000 years ago. The Moors who settled in the peninsula centuries later contributed a great number of new words (see box). Following the discovery of America, Spaniards took their language with them far and beyond. Today, Spanish is spoken by 250 million people in north, south and central America and parts of Africa.

In addition to Spanish, which is spoken throughout the country, some regions have a second language. Catalan (spoken in Catalonia), Valenciano (Valencia), Mallorquín (the Balearics) and Gallego (Galicia) are all Romance languages, unlike Euskera, the language of the Basques, which is notoriously complex and difficult – it is unrelated to any other European tongue. It origins are unclear, but the most widely accepted theory is that this was an aboriginal Iberian language widely spoken on the Iberian Peninsula and best defended in the northern pocket of the Basque Country.

Unlike English, Spanish is a phonetic language: words are pronounced exactly as they are spelt, which is why it is somewhat harder for Spaniards to learn English than vice versa (although Spanish distinguishes between the two genders, masculine and feminine, and the subjunctive verb form is an endless source of headaches for students). The English language is one of Britain's biggest exports to Spain. Spaniards spend millions on learning aids, language academies and sending their children to study English in the UK or Ireland, and are eager to practise their linguistic skills with foreign visitors. Even so,

they will be flattered and delighted if you make the effort to communicate in Spanish. You should beware, however, of some misleading 'false friends' (see page 239).

THE ALPHABET

Learning the pronunciation of the Spanish alphabet is a good idea. In particular learn how to spell out your own name. Spanish has a letter that doesn't exist in English, the ñ (pronounced "ny" as in "onion").

a = *ah*
b = *bay*
c = *thay* (strong th as in "thought")
d = *day*
e = *ay*
f = *effay*
g = *hay*
h = *ah-chay*
i = *ee*
j = *hotah*
k = *kah*
l = *ellay*
m = *emmay*
n = *ennay*
ñ = *enyay*
o = *oh*
p = *pay*
q = *koo*
r = *erray*
s = *essay*
t = *tay*
u = *oo*
v = *oobay*
w = *oobay doe-blay*
x = *ek-kiss*
y = *ee gree-ay-gah*,
z = *thay-tah*

BASIC RULES

English is widely spoken in most tourist areas, but even if you speak no Spanish at all, it is worth trying to master a few simple words and phrases.

As a general rule, the accent falls on the second-to-last syllable, unless it is otherwise marked with an accent (´) or the word ends in D, L, R or Z.

Vowels in Spanish are always pronounced the same way. The double LL is pronounced like the y in "yes", the double RR is rolled, as in Scots. The H is silent in Spanish, whereas J (and G when it precedes an E or I) is pronounced like a guttural H (as if you were clearing your throat).

When addressing someone you are not familiar with, use the more formal *"usted"*. The informal *"tu"* is reserved for relatives and friends.

MOORISH CONNECTIONS

The Moors arrived in Spain in 711, and occupied parts of the peninsula for the next eight centuries. They left behind hundreds of Arabic words, many related to farming and crops, as well as place names including those of towns (often identified by the prefix Al-, meaning "the" or Ben-, meaning "son of") and rivers (the prefix Guad- means "river").

Some of these Arabic words passed on to other languages, including French, and from there into English. Among those present in both English and Spanish are sugar *(azúcar)*, coffee *(café)*, apricot *(albaricoque)*, saffron *(azafrán)*, lemon *(limón)*, cotton *(algodón)*, alcohol *(alcohol)*, karat *(kilate)*, cipher *(cifra)*, elixir *(elixir)*, almanac *(almanaque)*, zenith *(cenit)*, and zero *(cero)*.

USEFUL WORDS & PHRASES

Hello *Hola*
How are you? *¿Cómo está usted?*
How much is it? *¿Cuánto es?*
What is your name? *¿Cómo se llama usted?*

My name is... *Yo me llamo...*
Do you speak English? *¿Habla inglés?*
I am British/American *Yo soy británico/norteamericano*
I don't understand *No comprendo*
Please speak more slowly *Hable más despacio, por favor*
Can you help me? *¿Me puede ayudar?*
I am looking for... *Estoy buscando...*
Where is...? *¿Dónde está...?*
I'm sorry *Lo siento*
I don't know *No lo se*
No problem *No hay problema*
Have a good day *Que tenga un buen día*
That's it *Ese es*
Here it is *Aquí está*
There it is *Allí está*
Let's go *Vámonos*
See you tomorrow *Hasta mañana*
See you soon *Hasta pronto*
Show me the word in the book *Muéstreme la palabra en el libro*
At what time? *¿A qué hora?*
When? *¿Cuándo?*
What time is it? *¿Qué hora es?*
yes *sí*
no *no*
please *por favor*
thank you (very much) *(muchas) gracias*
you're welcome *de nada*
excuse me *perdóneme*
OK *bien*
goodbye *adiós*
good evening/night *buenas tardes/ noches*
here *aquí*
there *allí*
today *hoy*
yesterday *ayer*
tomorrow *mañana* (note: mañana also means "morning")
now *ahora*
later *después*
right away *ahora mismo*
this morning *esta mañana*
this afternoon *esta tarde*
this evening *esta tarde*
tonight *esta noche*

TRAVELLING

I want to get off at... *Quiero bajarme en...*
Is there a bus to the museum? *¿Hay un autobús al museo?*
What street is this? *¿Qué calle es ésta?*
Which line do I take for...? *¿Qué línea cojo para...?*
How far is...? *¿A qué distancia está...?*
airport *aeropuerto*
customs *aduana*

train station *estación de tren*
bus station *estación de autobuses*
metro station *estación de metro*
bus *autobús*
bus stop *parada de autobús*
platform *apeadero*
ticket *billete*
return ticket *billete de ida y vuelta*
hitch-hiking *auto-stop*
toilets *servicios*

AT THE HOTEL

This is the hotel address *Ésta es la dirección del hotel*
I'd like a (single/double) room *Quiero una habitación (sencilla/doble)*
... with shower *con ducha*
... with bath *con baño*
... with a view *con vista*
Does that include breakfast? *¿Incluye desayuno?*
May I see the room? *¿Puedo ver la habitación?*
washbasin *lavabo*
bed *cama*
key *llave*
lift *ascensor*
air conditioning *aire acondicionado*

ON THE ROAD

Where is the spare wheel? *¿Dónde está la rueda de repuesto?*
Where is the nearest garage? *¿Dónde está el taller más próximo?*
Our car has broken down *Nuestro coche se ha averiado*
I want to have my car repaired *Quiero que reparen mi coche*
It's not your right of way *Usted no tiene prioridad*
I think I must have put diesel in my car by mistake *Me parece que he puesto gasoil por error*
the road to... *la carretera a...*
left *izquierda*
right *derecha*
straight on *derecho*
far *lejos*
near *cerca*
opposite *frente a*
beside *al lado de*
car park *aparcamiento*
over there *allí*
at the end *al final*
on foot *a pie*
by car *en coche*
town map *mapa de la ciudad*
road map *mapa de carreteras*
street *calle*
square *plaza*
give way *ceda el paso*

exit *salida*
dead end *calle sin salida*
wrong way *dirección prohibida*
no parking *prohibido aparcar*
motorway *autovía*
toll highway *autopista*
toll *peaje*
speed limit *límite de velocidad*
petrol station *gasolinera*
petrol *gasolina*
unleaded *sin plomo*
diesel *gasoil*
water/oil *agua/aceite*
air *aire*
puncture *pinchazo*
bulb *bombilla*
wipers *limpia-parabrisas*

ON THE TELEPHONE

How do I make an outside call? *¿Cómo hago una llamada exterior?*
What is the area code? *¿Cuál es el prefijo?*
I want to make an international (local) call *Quiero hacer una llamada internacional (local)*
I'd like an alarm call for 8 tomorrow morning *Quiero que me despierten a las ocho de la mañana*
Hello? *¿Dígame?*
Who's calling? *¿Quién llama?*
Hold on, please *Un momento, por favor*
I can't hear you *No le oigo*
Can you hear me? *¿Me oye?*
He/she is not here *No está aquí*
The line is busy *La línea está ocupada*
I must have dialled the wrong number *Debo haber marcado un número equivocado*

SHOPPING

Where is the nearest bank? *¿Dónde está el banco más próximo?*
I'd like to buy *Quiero comprar*
How much is it *¿Cuánto es?*
Do you accept credit cards? *¿Aceptan tarjeta?*
I'm just looking *Sólo estoy mirando*
Have you got...? *¿Tiene...?*
I'll take it *Me lo llevo*
I'll take this one/that one *Me llevo éste/ese*
What size is it? *¿Que talla es?*
Anything else? *¿Otra cosa?*
size (clothes) *talla*
small *pequeño*
large *grande*
cheap *barato*
expensive *caro*
enough *suficiente*
too much *demasiado*

a piece *una pieza*
each *cada una/la pieza/la unidad (eg. melones, 100 ptas la unidad)*
bill *la factura* (shop), *la cuenta* (restaurant)
bank *banco*
bookshop *librería*
chemist *farmacia*
hairdressers *peluquería*
jewellers *joyería*
post office *correos*
shoe shop *zapatería*
department store *grandes alma-cenes*
fresh *fresco*
frozen *congelado*
organic *biológico*
flavour *sabor*
basket *cesta*
bag *bolsa*
bakery *panadería*
butcher's *carnicería*
cake shop *pastelería*
fishmonger's *pescadería*
grocery *verdulería*
tobacconist *estanco*
market *mercado*
supermarket *supermercado*
junk shop *tienda de segunda mano*

SIGHTSEEING

mountain *montaña*
hill *colina*
valley *valle*
river *río*
lake *lago*
lookout *mirador*
city *ciudad*
small town, village *pueblo*
old town *casco antiguo*
monastery *monasterio*
convent *convento*
cathedral *catedral*
church *glesia*
palace *palacio*
hospital *hospital*
town hall *ayuntamiento*
nave *nave*
statue *estátua*
fountain *fuente*
staircase *escalera*
tower *torre*
castle *castillo*
Iberian *ibérico*
Phoenician *fenicio*
Roman *romano*
Moorish *árabe*
Romanesque *románico*
Gothic *gótico*
museum *museo*
art gallery *galería de arte*
exhibition *exposición*
tourist information office *oficina de turismo*

free *gratis*
open *abierto*
closed *cerrado*
every day *diario/todos los días*
all year *todo el año*
all day *todo el día*
swimming pool *piscina*
to book *reservar*

EATING OUT

In Spanish, *el menú* is not the main menu, but a fixed menu offered each day at a lower price. The main menu is *la carta.*
breakfast *desayuno*
lunch *almuerzo/comida*
dinner *cena*
meal *comida*
first course *primer plato*
main course *plato principal*
made to order *por encargo*
drink included *incluida bebida/consumición*
wine list *carta de vinos*
the bill *la cuenta*
fork *tenedor*
knife *cuchillo*
spoon *cuchara*
plate *plato*
glass *vaso*
wine glass *copa*
napkin *servilleta*
ashtray *cenicero*
waiter, please! *camarero, por favour*

Table Talk

I am a vegetarian *Soy vegetariano/vegetariana*
I am on a diet *Estoy a régimen*
What do you recommend? *¿Qué recomienda?*
Do you have local specialities? *¿Hay especialidades locales?*
I'd like to order *Quiero pedir*
That is not what I ordered *Ésto no es lo que he pedido*
May I have more wine? *¿Más vino, por favor?*
Enjoy your meal *Buen provecho*

MENU DECODER

Snacks

pan bread
bollo bun/roll
mantequilla butter
mermelada jam
confitura jam
pimienta pepper

sal salt
azúcar sugar
huevos eggs
... *cocidos* boiled, cooked ...
... *con beicon* with bacon
... *con jamón* with ham
... *fritos* fried
... *revueltos* scrambled
yogúr yoghurt
tostada toast
sandwich sandwich in square slices of bread
bocadillo filled bread roll

Main Courses

Carne/Meat

buey beef
carne picada minced meat
cerdo pork
chivo kid
chorizo sausage seasoned with paprika
chuleta chop
cochinillo suckling pig
conejo rabbit
cordero lamb
costilla rib
entrecot beef rib steak
filete steak
jabalí wild boar
jamón ham
jamón cocido cooked ham
jamón serrano cured ham
lomo loin
morcilla black pudding
pierna leg
riñones kidneys
sesos brains
salchichón sausage
solomillo fillet steak
ternera veal or young beef
lengua tongue
a la brasa charcoal grilled
al horno roast
a la plancha grilled
asado roast
bien hecho well done
en salsa in sauce
en su punto medium
estofado stew
frito fried
parrillada mixed grill
pinchito skewer
poco hecho rare
relleno stuffed

Fowl

codorniz quail
faisán pheasant
pavo turkey
pato duck
perdiz partridge
pintada guinea fowl
pollo chicken

Pescado/Fish

almeja **clam**
anchoas **anchovies**
anguila **eel**
atún **tuna**
bacalao **cod**
besugo **red bream**
bogavante **lobster**
boquerones **fresh anchovies**
caballa **mackerel**
calamar **squid**
cangrejo **crab**
caracola **sea snail**
cazón **dogfish**
centollo **spider crab**
chopito **baby cuttlefish**
cigala **Dublin Bay prawn/scampi**
dorada **gilt head bream**
fritura **mixed fry**
gamba **shrimp/prawn**
jibia **cuttlefish**
langosta **spiny lobster**
langostino **large prawn**
lenguado **sole**
lubina **sea bass**
mariscada **mixed shellfish**
mariscos **shellfish**
mejillón **mussel**
merluza **hake**
mero **grouper**
ostión **Portuguese oyster**
ostra **oyster**
peregrina **scallop**
pescadilla **small hake**
pez espada **swordfish**
pijota **hake**
pulpo **octopus**
rape **monkfish**
rodaballo **turbot**
salmón **salmon**
salmonete **red mullet**
sardina **sardine**
trucha **trout**

Vegetables/Cereals/Salads

ajo **garlic**
alcachofa **artichoke**
apio **celery**
arroz **rice**
berenjena **aubergine/eggplant**
cebolla **onion**
champiñon **mushroom**
col **cabbage**
coliflor **cauliflower**
crudo **raw**
ensalada **salad**
espárrago **asparagus**
espinaca **spinach**
garbanzo **chick pea**
guisante **pea**
haba **broad bean**
habichuela **bean**
judía **green bean**
lechuga **lettuce**

lenteja **lentil**
maíz **corn/maize**
menestra **cooked mixed vegetables**
patata **potato**
pepino **cucumber**
pimiento **pepper**
puerro **leek**
rábano **radish**
seta **wild mushroom**
tomate **tomato**
verduras **vegetables**
zanahoria **carrot**

Fruit and Desserts

fruta **fruit**
aguacate **avocado**
albaricoque **apricot**
cereza **cherry**
ciruela **plum**
frambuesa **raspberry**
fresa **strawberry**
granada **pomegranate**
higo **fig**
limón **lemon**
mandarina **tangerine**
manzana **apple**
melocotón **peach**
melón **melon**
naranja **orange**
pasa **raisin**
pera **pear**
piña **pineapple**
plátano **banana**
pomelo **grapefruit**
sandía **watermelon**
postre **dessert**
tarta **cake**
pastel **pie**
helado **ice cream**
natilla **custard**
flan **caramel custard**
queso **cheese**

Liquid Refreshment

coffee *café*
... black *solo*
... with milk *con leche*
... decaffeinated *descafeinado*
sugar *azúcar*
tea *té*
milk *leche*
mineral water *agua mineral*
fizzy *con gas*
non-fizzy *sin gas*
juice (fresh) *zumo (natural)*
cold *fresco/frío*
hot *caliente*
beer *cerveza*
... bottled *en botella*
... on tap *de barril*
soft drink *refresco*
diet drink *bebida "light"*
with ice *con hielo*

wine *vino*
red wine *vino tinto*
white *blanco*
rosé *rosado*
dry *seco*
sweet *dulce*
house wine *vino de la casa*
sparkling wine *vino espumoso*
half litre *medio litro*
quarter litre *cuarto de litro*
cheers! *salud*

DAYS AND MONTHS

Days of the Week

Monday *lunes*
Tuesday *martes*
Wednesday *miércoles*
Thursday *jueves*
Friday *viernes*
Saturday *sábado*
Sunday *domingo*

Months of the Year

January *enero*
February *febrero*
March *marzo*
April *abril*
May *mayo*
June *junio*
July *julio*
August *agosto*
September *septiembre*
October *octubre*
November *noviembre*
December *diciembre*

Seasons

Spring *primavera*
Summer *verano*
Autumn *otoño*
Winter *invierno*

FALSE AMIGOS

'False friends' are words that look like English words but mean something different. Such as:

simpático **friendly**
tópico **a cliché**
actualmente **currently**
sensible **sensitive**
disgustado **angry**
embarazada **pregnant**
suplir **substitute**
informal **unreliable (to describe a person)**
rape **monkfish**
billón **a million million**

soportar **tolerate**
estar constipado **to have a cold**

Emergencies

Help! *¡Socorro!*
Stop! *¡Alto!*
Call a doctor *Llame a un médico*
Call an ambulance *Llame a una ambulancia*
Call the police *Llame a la policia*
Call the fire brigade *Llame a los bomberos*
Where's the nearest telephone? *¿Dónde hay un teléfono?*
Where's the nearest hospital? *¿Dónde está el hospital más próximo?*
Where's the nearest pharmacy? *Dónde está la farmacia más próxima?*
I am sick *Estoy enfermo*

I have lost my passport/purse *He perdido mi pasaporte/bolso*

Numbers

0 *cero*
1 *uno*
2 *dos*
3 *tres*
4 *cuatro*
5 *cinco*
6 *seis*
7 *siete*
8 *ocho*
9 *nueve*
10 *diez*
11 *once*
12 *doce*
13 *trece*
14 *catorce*
15 *quince*
16 *dieciseis*
17 *diecisiete*
18 *dieciocho*
19 *diecinueve*
20 *veinte*
21 *veintiuno*
30 *treinta*
40 *cuarenta*
50 *cincuenta*
60 *sesenta*
70 *setenta*
80 *ochenta*
90 *noventa*
100 *cien*
200 *doscientos*
500 *quinientos*
1,000 *mil*
10,000 *diez mil*
1,000,000 *un millón*

GENERAL BACKGROUND

A Rose for Winter, by Laurie Lee. The author returns to Andalucía in the 1950s.

A Handbook for Travellers in Spain, by Richard Ford. Classic 19th-century travel book about Spain.

Sunny Side Up, by David Baird. Old and new values collide in a traditional Andalusian village.

South From Granada, by Gerald Brenan. An account of the author's experiences living in an Andalusian village in the 1920s.

Tales of the Alhambra, by Washington Irving. The 19th-century American author's account of Moorish legends is still enjoyable.

The Face of Spain. Gerald Brenan's grim view of an impoverished post-war Spain.

The Road from Ronda, by Alastair Boyd. Vivid account of a horse-ride through the Serrania de Ronda.

Death in the Afternoon, by Ernest Hemingway. Hemingway's explanation of the bullfight, although much maligned by purists, is still informative and gripping.

Federico Garcia Lorca: A Life by Ian Gibson. Fascinating biography of the Granada-born writer.

Or I'll Dress You in Mourning, by Larry Collins and Dominique Lapierre. Brilliant insights into Spain's post-Civil War hardships which moulded the Andalusian matador El Cordobés.

Driving Over Lemons, by Chris Stewart. Amusing autobiographical account of an Englishman living the good life in the Alpujarras.

Duende: A Journey in Search of Flamenco by Jason Webster. An Anlgo-American's foray into the world of flamenco.

Ghosts of Spain: travels through a country's hidden past, by Giles Tremlett.

The Return by Victoria Hislop. Romantic but harrowing novel about love and loss in Granada during the Spanish Civil War.

The Factory of Light by Michael Jacobs. A British writer's account of the reality of life in an Andalucían village in the 21st century.

The Moor's Last Stand by Elizabeth Drayson. The story of Boabdil, the last Muslim king of Granada.

The Flavours of Andalucía by Elisabeth Luard. A good introduction to the region's cuisine with recipes from each of the provinces.

Spanish Wine Guide by David and Jennifer Raezer. An insightful overview of the region's wines and sherries.

Costa del Sol by Des Wilson. Thriller about shady shenanigans on the Costa del Crime.

OTHER INSIGHT GUIDES

Other **Insight Guides** to the Iberian peninsula include: Spain, Northern Spain and Portugal. There is also a **City Guide** to Barcelona.

Insight Explore guides are itinerary-based guides written by local hosts. They come complete with a pull-out map. Titles include Barcelona and, new in 2018, Madrid.

Insight Experience Guide to Barcelona is a compilation of around 100 authentic experiences, organised by area.

⊙ Send Us Your Thoughts

We do our best to ensure the information in our books is as accurate and up-to-date as possible. The books are updated on a regular basis using local contacts, who painstakingly add, amend and correct as required. However, some details (such as telephone numbers and opening times) are liable to change, and we are ultimately reliant on our readers to put us in the picture.

We welcome your feedback, especially your experience of using the book "on the road". Maybe you came across a great bar or new attraction we missed.

We will acknowledge all contributions, and we'll offer an Insight Guide to the best letters received.

Please write to us at:
Insight Guides
PO Box 7910
London SE1 1WE

Or email us at:
hello@insightguides.com

CREDITS

PHOTO CREDITS

Alamy 59ML, 99BR, 99TR, 137, 202BL
AWL Images 12/13, 16/17, 58/59T, 202/203T
Colección Carmen Thyssen-Bornemisza 9T
Corbis 31
Corrie Wingate/Apa Publications 7MR, 8T, 19T, 23, 27, 51, 52, 53, 56, 73T, 76, 77, 79, 81, 82, 83, 84B, 84T, 85, 86, 87, 88, 89, 92, 94/95, 110, 113, 130, 131, 133, 134T, 135, 136, 139, 141, 142, 143, 160, 161, 162, 163, 165B, 165T, 166B, 166T, 167, 168, 169, 186, 187, 189, 191, 192, 193B, 193T, 194B, 194T, 195, 196, 197, 198, 229, 236
Design Pics Inc/REX/Shutterstock 117
FLPA 60, 63, 64
Getty Images 1, 6ML, 7ML, 18, 20, 22,

24, 25, 26, 28/29, 32, 34, 35, 37, 40, 41, 43, 44, 45, 46, 47, 48/49, 50, 55, 58BR, 59BR, 62, 65, 66/67, 68/69, 70/71, 93, 98/99T, 99ML, 105, 107, 114/115, 116, 124B, 145, 146, 150, 152, 153, 171B, 174, 175, 177, 178, 180, 201, 204, 205, 208, 209, 213, 214/215, 216, 222
Gianni Dagli Orti/REX/Shutterstock 98BR
Granger/REX/Shutterstock 38, 39
iStock 6MR, 6BL, 6MR, 7TR, 7ML, 7BR, 7TL, 10B, 10T, 19B, 73B, 102/103, 121, 123, 125, 126/127, 129, 134B, 147, 149B, 151B, 151T, 155, 158, 200, 203BL, 221, 225, 226, 231, 232, 234, 241
Jose Pedrosa/Epa/REX/Shutterstock 99BL
Pat Jackson/REX/Shutterstock 144

PHAS/Universal Images Group/REX/Shutterstock 36
Public domain 42
REX/Shutterstock 179
Shutterstock 4, 8B, 9B, 11, 30, 54, 57, 58BL, 59BL, 59TR, 61, 80, 97T, 104, 106, 108, 111, 115, 118, 119, 124T, 128, 148, 149T, 156, 157B, 157T, 170, 171T, 172, 181, 183, 199, 202BR, 203ML, 203TR, 210/211, 211, 217, 218, 219, 224
Starwood Hotels & Resorts 91, 226/227
SuperStock 14/15, 21, 33, 72, 90, 96, 97B, 100, 101, 109, 120, 138, 154, 159, 173, 182/183, 184, 185, 203BR, 207, 212, 220
The Art Archive/REX/Shutterstock 98BL

COVER CREDITS

Front cover: Ronda *iStock*
Back cover: La Mezquita, Cordoba *iStock*
Front flap: (from top) Plaza de la

Encarnacion, Seville *Corrie Wingate/Apa Publications*; Alcazar, Seville *Corrie Wingate/Apa Publications*; Harveys Bodega, Jerez *Corrie Wingate/Apa

Publications*; Gazpacho *Corrie Wingate/Apa Publications*
Back flap: Plaza de Toros, Ronda *Corrie Wingate/Apa Publications*

INSIGHT GUIDE CREDITS

Distribution

UK, Ireland and Europe
Apa Publications (UK) Ltd;
sales@insightguides.com

United States and Canada
Ingram Publisher Services;
ips@ingramcontent.com

Australia and New Zealand
Woodslane; info@woodslane.com.au

Southeast Asia
Apa Publications (SN) Pte;
singaporeoffice@insightguides.com

Worldwide
Apa Publications (UK) Ltd;
sales@insightguides.com

Special Sales, Content Licensing and CoPublishing
Insight Guides can be purchased in bulk quantities at discounted prices. We can create special editions, personalised jackets and corporate imprints tailored to your needs. sales@insightguides.com
www.insightguides.biz

Printed in China by CTPS

First Edition 1990
Fifth Edition 2018

Every effort has been made to provide accurate information in this publication, but changes are inevitable. The publisher cannot be responsible for any resulting loss, inconvenience or injury. We would appreciate it if readers would call our attention to any errors or outdated information. We also welcome your suggestions; please contact us at:
hello@insightguides.com

www.insightguides.com

Editor: Carine Tracanelli
Author: Victoria Trott
Head of Production: Rebeka Davies
Update Production: Apa Digital
Picture Editor: Tom Smyth
Cartography: original cartography Dave Priestley, updated by Carte

CONTRIBUTORS

This new edition of *Insight Guide: Southern Spain* was commissioned by **Carine Tracanelli** and thoroughly updated by **Victoria Trott**, a freelance travel writer who specialises in France and Spain. A graduate in French and Spanish from Leeds University, she contributes to a wide variety of publications and has also updated *Insight Guide Spain*.

This edition is based on an earlier version by **Clara Villanueva** and **Nicholas Inman**, travel writers and editors who divide their time between France and Spain. Past contributors also include: **Norman Renouf**, **MichelleTaylor**, **Josephine Quintero**, **David Baird**, **Thomas Hinde**, **Alastair Boyd**, **Jane Mendel**, **Nigel Bowden**, **Vicky Hayward** and **Philip Sweeney**.

This edition was proofread and indexed by **Penny Phenix**.

ABOUT INSIGHT GUIDES

Insight Guides have more than 45 years' experience of publishing high-quality, visual travel guides. We produce 400 full-colour titles, in both print and digital form, covering more than 200 destinations across the globe, in a variety of formats to meet your different needs.

Insight Guides are written by local authors, whose expertise is evident in the extensive historical and cultural background features. Each destination is carefully researched by regional experts to ensure our guides provide the very latest information. All the reviews in **Insight Guides** are independent; we strive to maintain an impartial view. Our reviews are carefully selected to guide you to the best places to eat, go out and shop, so you can be confident that when we say a place is special, we really mean it.

Legend

City maps

	Freeway/Highway/Motorway
	Divided Highway
	Main Roads
	Minor Roads
	Pedestrian Roads
	Steps
	Footpath
	Railway
	Funicular Railway
	Cable Car
	Tunnel
	City Wall
	Important Building
	Built Up Area
	Other Land
	Transport Hub
	Park
	Pedestrian Area
	Bus Station
	Tourist Information
	Main Post Office
	Cathedral/Church
	Mosque
	Synagogue
	Statue/Monument
	Beach
	Airport

Regional maps

	Freeway/Highway/Motorway (with junction)
	Freeway/Highway/Motorway (under construction)
	Divided Highway
	Main Road
	Secondary Road
	Minor Road
	Track
	Footpath
	International Boundary
	State/Province Boundary
	National Park/Reserve
	Marine Park
	Ferry Route
	Marshland/Swamp
	Glacier	Salt Lake
	Airport/Airfield
	Ancient Site
	Border Control
	Cable Car
	Castle/Castle Ruins
	Cave
	Chateau/Stately Home
	Church/Church Ruins
	Crater
	Lighthouse
	Mountain Peak
	Place of Interest
	Viewpoint

INDEX

MAIN REFERENCES ARE IN BOLD TYPE

INSIGHT ⊙ GUIDES

OFF THE SHELF

Since 1970, **INSIGHT GUIDES** has provided a unique perspective on the world's best travel destinations by using specially commissioned photography and illuminating text written by local authors.

Whether you're planning a city break, a walking tour or the journey of a lifetime, our superb range of guidebooks and phrasebooks will inspire you to discover more about your chosen destination.

INSIGHT GUIDES

offer a unique combination of stunning photos, absorbing narrative and detailed maps, providing all the inspiration and information you need.

PHRASEBOOKS & DICTIONARIES

help users to feel at home, when away. Pocket-sized with a free app to download, they go where you do.

CITY GUIDES

pack hundreds of great photos into a smaller format with detailed practical information, so you can navigate the world's top cities with confidence.

EXPLORE GUIDES

feature easy-to-follow walks and itineraries in the world's most exciting destinations, with our choice of the best places to eat and drink along the way.

POCKET GUIDES

combine concise information on where to go and what to do in a handy compact format, ideal on the ground. Includes a full-colour, fold-out map.

EXPERIENCE GUIDES

feature offbeat perspectives and secret gems for experienced travellers, with a collection of over 100 ideas for a memorable stay in a city.

www.insightguides.com

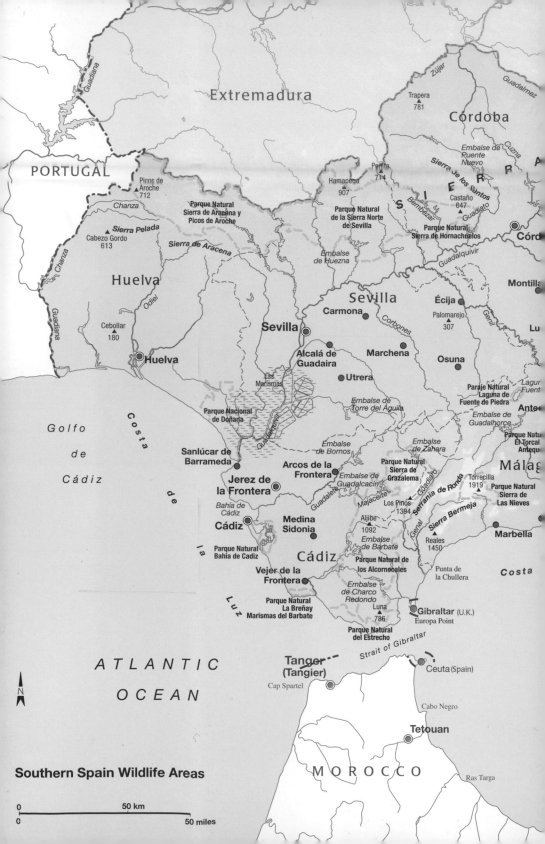

Southern Spain Wildlife Areas